BLOOM'S

HOW TO WRITE ABOUT

William Shakespeare

PAUL GLEED

BLOOM'S
LITERARY CRITICISM
An imprint of Infobase Publishing

Bloom's How to Write about William Shakespeare

Chelsea House
An imprint of Infobase Publishing
132 West 31st Street
New York NY 10001

Gleed, Paul.
  Bloom's how to write about William Shakespeare/Paul Gleed; introduction by Harold Bloom.
    p. cm.
  Includes bibliographical (p.) references and index.
  ISBN-13: 978-0-7910-9484-6 (hc: alk paper) 1. Shakespeare, William, 1564–1616—Criticism and interpretation. 2. Criticism—Authorship. 3. Report writing. I. Bloom, Harold. II. Title. III. Title: How to Write about William Shakespeare.

  PR2976.G54 2007
  822.3'3—dc22

Chelsea House books are available at special discounts when purchased in bulk quantities for businesses, associations, institutions, or sales promotions. Please call our Special Sales Department in New York at (212) 967-8800 or (800) 322-8755.

You can find Chelsea House on the World Wide Web at http://www.chelseahouse.com

Text design by Annie O'Donnell
Cover design by Ben Peterson

Printed in the United States of America
Bang MSRF 10 9 8 7 6 5 4 3 2 1

This book is printed on acid-free paper.

CONTENTS

SERIES INTRODUCTION

BLOOM'S How to Write about Literature series is designed to inspire students to write fine essays on great writers and their works. Each volume in the series begins with an introduction by Harold Bloom, meditating on the challenges and rewards of writing about the volume's subject author. The first chapter then provides detailed instructions on how to write a good essay, including how to find a thesis; how to develop an outline; how to write a good introduction, body text, and conclusions; how to cite sources; and more. The second chapter provides a brief overview of the issues involved in writing about the subject author and then a number of suggestions for paper topics, with accompanying strategies for addressing each topic. Succeeding chapters cover the author's major works.

The paper topics suggested within this book are open-ended, and the brief strategies provided are designed to give students a push forward on the writing process rather than a roadmap to success. The aim of the book is to pose questions, not answer them. Many different kinds of papers could result from each topic. As always, the success of each paper will depend completely on the writer's skill and imagination.

HOW TO WRITE
ABOUT SHAKESPEARE
INTRODUCTION

THE BEST advice at this time is how *not* to write about Shakespeare. Mere fashion now dictates Marxist, feminist, New Historicist (Foucault), deconstructive (Derrida), semiotic, and stage performance—oriented approaches. Reading any of these, I come away with a handful of dust.

Shakespeare's differences from all other writers include the original power of his thinking, his extraordinary control over the largest vocabulary ever employed by any author, his enduring wisdom, and his creation of more than 100 major characters and 1,000 minor characters, almost all of whom speak with individual voices and appear to have minds of their own. Some of them, according to A. C. Bradley, prove inexhaustible to meditation: Falstaff, Hamlet, Iago, Cleopatra. I myself would add Shylock, Rosalind, Malvolio, Macbeth, Prospero, and the extraordinary fourfold from *King Lear*: Lear himself, his Fool, and the enemy half brothers Edmund and Edgar.

I subtitled my longest book on Shakespeare *The Invention of the Human*. A decade later, journalists keep scolding me because their notion of invention is Edison giving us the electric light bulb and Singer the sewing machine. Dr. Samuel Johnson remarked that "The essence of poetry is invention," meaning by that an uncovering more than a discovering. Much in us that always was there would still be unknown to us had we never *read* Shakespeare.

I italicize "read" because Shakespeare wrote to be read forever as well as played upon a stage. His plays are *not* scripts comparable to even the best of Hollywood screenplays. Shakespeare *knew* his own genius: How could it have been otherwise? Read *The Tempest* side-by-side with Marlowe's *Doctor Faustus, Antony and Cleopatra* in juxtaposition with Ben Jonson's *Sijanus: His Fall.* Case closed.

As for current Resentments, societal and academic, naming themselves as criticism Marxist, feminist, New Historical, and so forth: Already these dwindle into rubbish and will end in the dustbins with Harry Potter, Stephen King, and similar phenomena. One of the few advantages of going on 77 is that a longer perspective becomes open to me, after a lifetime of reading, teaching, writing, and thinking. There are Shakespeare's two dozen or so strongest plays, and their eminence is unique. They *contain* all of us, including every new approach we think *we* have devised. Shakespeare is always there ahead of you, genially waiting for you to catch up. You never will catch up to him, but if you read and reread him, closely and deeply, and without ideologies, you will find yourself more truly and more strange. He is a humane education in himself, and no other writer—not even Homer, Plato, Dante, Chaucer, Cervantes, Milton, Goethe, Tolstoy, Whitman, Joyce, Proust—can do that much for you.

The question of how to write about Shakespeare, therefore, is akin to how to live your life. I am not a guru and can tell no one how to do that, myself alas included, though by my age life is set, and I shall live as I must, not necessarily as I might want to do. Much of my life now seeks finally to come to terms with Shakespeare. He *is* the living labyrinth of literature and so illuminates life's labyrinth. We need to understand Shakespeare's influence upon himself, as he progressed from early farces and histories into tragedies and equivocal later comedies on to the tragi-comedies we wrongly call "romances." And then came the three-year silence of the final return to Stratford. Virgil, Dante, Chaucer, Cervantes, Molière, Montaigne all wrote down to the end, as did the great writers who came after Shakespeare: Milton, Blake, Goethe, Pushkin, Tolstoy, Chekhov, Flaubert, Balzac, Whitman, Dickens on to Kafka, Freud, Yeats, Joyce, Henry James, Proust, Thomas Mann, and our own contemporaries. Shakespeare, whose inwardness remains a mystery, simply stopped, and we never will know why. I read incessantly what might prove of value about Shakespeare, but nobody helps me understand that cessation.

Since we have God's plenty—at least 38 plays, of which some two dozen are masterpieces—perhaps we should not mind that Shakespeare, like his Hamlet, finally told us "The rest is silence," but I think he was passing a judgment—whether upon himself, the theater, or life I cannot surmise. It is not possible that he burnt out, because he incarnated that creative furnace W. B. Yeats termed the Condition of Fire.

How do you begin writing about Shakespeare? If you are free to do so, let one of his plays *find* you. Then read it and read it again, preferably out loud, whether to yourselves and to others as well (should they consent). Shakespeare's unmatched art of characterization is founded on self-overhearing. I do not mean that Hamlet or Iago listens in to himself but that their will or identities are started by what they overhear. Plato hated flux and change: No writer loved metamorphosis more than Shakespeare, who never ceased loving and learning from Ovid.

To study the self-transformations of Shakespeare's characters shows you why he, more even than Cervantes, accomplished the transition from the primacy of the epic and the prevalence of the picaresque romance to the novel. Stendhal and Victor Hugo, Dostoevsky and Turgenev, Dickens and George Eliot, Melville and Hawthorne are all Shakespearean novelists, as are Proust, Joyce, Thomas Mann, and our best ongoing artist of fiction, Philip Roth. One way, not yet fully explored, to write about Shakespeare is to ask: "What is novelistic about Falstaff, Shylock, and Hamlet and about the greatest of all villains: Iago, Edmund in *King Lear*, Macbeth?"

I have barely touched upon Shakespeare's vast literary wealth, but that is not my function here. "Read him and read him, for everything is in him," said his friends and fellow-actors Hemings and Condell when they edited the First Folio, in 1623, seven years after Shakespeare's death. That is also the best advice I can offer in 2007, to those who will continue to write about Shakespeare.

HOW TO WRITE
A GOOD ESSAY

WHILE THERE are many ways to write about literature, most assignments for high school and college English classes call for analytical papers. In these assignments, you are presenting your interpretation of a text to your reader. Your objective is to interpret the text's meaning in order to enhance your reader's understanding and enjoyment of the work. Without exception, strong papers about the meaning of a literary work are built upon a careful, close reading of the text or texts. Careful, analytical reading should always be the first step in your writing process. This volume provides models of such close, analytical reading, and these should help you develop your own skills as a reader and as a writer.

As the examples throughout this book demonstrate, attentive reading entails thinking about and evaluating the formal (textual) aspects of the author's works: theme, character, form, and language. In addition, when writing about a work, many readers choose to move beyond the text itself to consider the work's cultural context. In these instances, writers might explore the historical circumstances of the time period in which the work was written. Alternatively, they might examine the philosophies and ideas that a work addresses. Even in cases where writers explore a work's cultural context, though, papers must still address the more formal aspects of the work itself. A good interpretative essay that evaluates Charles Dickens's use of the philosophy of utilitarianism in his novel *Hard Times*, for example, cannot adequately address the author's treatment of the philosophy without firmly grounding this discussion in the book itself. In other words, any analytical paper about a text, even one that seeks to evaluate the work's cultural context, must also have a

1

firm handle on the work's themes, characters, and language. You must look for and evaluate these aspects of a work, then, as you read a text and as you prepare to write about it.

WRITING ABOUT THEMES

Literary themes are more than just topics or subjects treated in a work; they are attitudes or points about these topics that often structure other elements in a work. Writing about theme therefore requires that you not just identify a topic that a literary work addresses but also discuss what that work says about that topic. For example, if you were writing about the culture of the American South in William Faulkner's famous story "A Rose for Emily," you would need to discuss what Faulkner says, argues, or implies about that culture and its passing.

When you prepare to write about thematic concerns in a work of literature, you will probably discover that, like most works of literature, your text touches upon other themes in addition to its central theme. These secondary themes also provide rich ground for paper topics. A thematic paper on "A Rose for Emily" might consider gender or race in the story. While neither of these could be said to be the central theme of the story, they are clearly related to the passing of the "old South" and could provide plenty of good material for papers.

As you prepare to write about themes in literature, you might find a number of strategies helpful. After you identify a theme or themes in the story, you should begin by evaluating how other elements of the story—such as character, point of view, imagery, and symbolism—help develop the theme. You might ask yourself what your own responses are to the author's treatment of the subject matter. Do not neglect the obvious, either: What expectations does the title set up? How does the title help develop thematic concerns? Clearly, the title "A Rose for Emily" says something about the narrator's attitude toward the title character, Emily Grierson, and all she represents.

WRITING ABOUT CHARACTER

Generally, characters are essential components of fiction and drama. (This is not always the case, though; Ray Bradbury's "August 2026: There

Will Come Soft Rains" is technically a story without characters, at least any human characters.) Often, you can discuss character in poetry, as in T. S. Eliot's "The Love Song of J. Alfred Prufrock" or Robert Browning's "My Last Duchess." Many writers find that analyzing character is one of the most interesting and engaging ways to work with a piece of literature and to shape a paper. After all, characters generally are human, and we all know something about being human and living in the world. While it is always important to remember that these figures are not real people but creations of the writer's imagination, it can be fruitful to begin evaluating them as you might evaluate a real person. Often you can start with your own response to a character. Did you like or dislike the character? Did you sympathize with the character? Why or why not?

Keep in mind, though, that emotional responses like these are just starting places. To truly explore and evaluate literary characters, you need to return to the formal aspects of the text and evaluate how the author has drawn these characters. The 20th-century writer E. M. Forster coined the terms *flat* characters and *round* characters. Flat characters are static, one-dimensional characters who frequently represent a particular concept or idea. In contrast, *round* characters are fully drawn and much more realistic characters who frequently change and develop over the course of a work. Are the characters you are studying flat or round? What elements of the characters lead you to this conclusion? Why might the author have drawn characters like this? How does their development affect the meaning of the work? Similarly, you should explore the techniques the author uses to develop characters. Do we hear a character's own words, or do we hear only other characters' assessments of him or her? Or, does the author use an omniscient or limited omniscient narrator to allow us access to the workings of the character's minds? If so, how does that help develop the characterization? Often you can even evaluate the narrator as a character. How trustworthy are the opinions and assessments of the narrator? You should also think about characters' names. Do they mean anything? If you encounter a hero named Sophia or Sophie, you should probably think about her wisdom (or lack thereof), since *sophia* means "wisdom" in Greek. Similarly, since the name *Sylvia,* is derived from the word *sylvan,* meaning "of the wood," you might want to evaluate that character's relationship with nature. Once again, you might look to the title of the work. Does Herman Melville's "Bartleby, the Scrivener" signal anything about Bartleby himself? Is Bartleby adequately defined by his job as scrivener? Is this part of Melville's point? Pursuing questions like these can help you develop thorough papers about characters from psychological, sociological, or more formalistic perspectives.

WRITING ABOUT FORM AND GENRE

Genre, a word derived from French, means "type" or "class." Literary genres are distinctive classes or categories of literary composition. On the most general level, literary works can be divided into the genres of drama, poetry, fiction, and essays, yet within those genres there are classifications that are also referred to as genres. Tragedy and comedy, for example, are genres of drama. Epic, lyric, and pastoral are genres of poetry. *Form,* on the other hand, generally refers to the shape or structure of a work. There are many clearly defined forms of poetry that follow specific patterns of meter, rhyme, and stanza. Sonnets, for example, are poems that follow a fixed form of 14 lines. Sonnets generally follow one of two basic sonnet forms, each with its own distinct rhyme scheme. Haiku is another example of poetic form, traditionally consisting of three unrhymed lines of five, seven, and five syllables.

While you might think that writing about form or genre might leave little room for argument, many of these forms and genres are very fluid. Remember that literature is evolving and ever changing, and so are its forms. As you study poetry, you may find that poets, especially more modern poets, play with traditional poetic forms, bringing about new effects. Similarly, dramatic tragedy was once quite narrowly defined, but over the centuries playwrights have broadened and challenged traditional definitions, changing the shape of tragedy. When Arthur Miller wrote *Death of a Salesman,* many critics challenged the idea that tragic drama could encompass a common man like Willy Loman.

Evaluating how a work of literature fits into or challenges the boundaries of its form or genre can provide you with fruitful avenues of investigation. Once again, you might find it helpful to ask why the work does or does not fit into traditional categories. Why might Miller have thought it fitting to write a tragedy of the common man? Similarly, you might compare the content or theme of a work with its form. How well do they work together? Many of Emily Dickinson's poems, for instance, follow the meter of traditional hymns. While some of her poems seem to express traditional religious doctrines, many seem to challenge or strain against traditional conceptions of God and theology. What is the effect, then, of her use of traditional hymn meter?

WRITING ABOUT LANGUAGE, SYMBOLS, AND IMAGERY

No matter what the genre, writers use words as their most basic tool. Language is the most fundamental building block of literature. It is essential that you pay careful attention to the author's language and word choice as you read, reread, and analyze a text. Imagery is language that appeals to the senses. Most commonly, imagery appeals to our sense of vision, creating a mental picture, but authors also use language that appeals to our other senses. Images can be literal or figurative. Literal images use sensory language to describe an actual thing. In the broadest terms, figurative language uses one thing to speak about something else. For example, if I call my boss a snake, I am not saying that he is literally a reptile. Instead, I am using figurative language to communicate my opinions about him. Since we think of snakes as sneaky, slimy, and sinister, I am using the concrete image of a snake to communicate these abstract opinions and impressions.

The two most common figures of speech are similes and metaphors. Both are comparisons between two apparently dissimilar things. Similes are explicit comparisons using the words *like* or *as,* and metaphors are implicit comparisons. To return to the previous example, if I say, "My boss, Bob, was waiting for me when I showed up to work five minutes late today—the snake!" I have constructed a metaphor. Writing about his experiences fighting in World War I, Wilfred Owen begins his poem "Dulce et decorum est" with a string of similes: "Bent double, like old beggars under sacks, / Knock-kneed, coughing like hags, we cursed through sludge." Owen's goal was to undercut clichéd notions that war and dying in battle were glorious. Certainly, comparing soldiers to coughing hags and to beggars underscores his point.

"Fog," a short poem by Carl Sandburg, provides a clear example of a metaphor. Sandburg's poem reads:

The fog comes
on little cat feet.

It sits looking
over harbor and city
on silent haunches
and then moves on.

Notice how effectively Sandburg conveys surprising impressions of the fog by comparing two seemingly disparate things—the fog and a cat.

Symbols, by contrast, are things that stand for, or represent, other things. Often they represent something intangible, such as concepts or ideas. In everyday life we use and understand symbols easily. Babies at christenings and brides at weddings wear white to represent purity. Think, too, of a dollar bill. The paper itself has no value in and of itself. Instead, that paper bill is a symbol of something else, the precious metal in a nation's coffers. Symbols in literature work similarly. Authors use symbols to evoke more than a simple, straightforward, literal meaning. Characters, objects, and places can all function as symbols. Famous literary examples of symbols include Moby-Dick, the white whale of Herman Melville's novel, and the scarlet *A* of Nathaniel Hawthorne's *The Scarlet Letter.* As both of these symbols suggest, a literary symbol cannot be adequately defined or explained by any one meaning. Hester Prynne's Puritan community clearly intends her scarlet *A* as a symbol of her adultery, but as the novel progresses, even her own community reads the letter as representing not just *adultery,* but *able, angel,* and a host of other meanings.

Writing about imagery and symbols requires close attention to the author's language. To prepare a paper on symbolism or imagery in a work, identify and trace the images and symbols and then try to draw some conclusions about how they function. Ask yourself how any symbols or images help contribute to the themes or meanings of the work. What connotations do they carry? How do they affect your reception of the work? Do they shed light on characters or settings? A strong paper on imagery or symbolism will thoroughly consider the use of figures in the text and will try to reach some conclusions about how or why the author uses them.

WRITING ABOUT HISTORY AND CONTEXT

As noted above, it is possible to write an analytical paper that also considers the work's context. After all, the text was not created in a vacuum. The author lived and wrote in a specific time period and in a specific cultural context and, like all of us, was shaped by that environment. Learning more about the historical and cultural circumstances that surround the author and the work can help illuminate a text and provide you with productive material for a paper. Remember, though, that when you write analytical papers, you should use the context to illuminate the text. Do not lose sight of your goal—to interpret the meaning of the literary work. Use historical or philosophical research as a tool to develop your textual evaluation.

Thoughtful readers often consider how history and culture affected the author's choice and treatment of his or her subject matter. Investigations into the history and context of a work could examine the work's relation to specific historical events, such as the Salem witch trials in 17th-century Massachusetts or the restoration of Charles to the British throne in 1660. Bear in mind that historical context is not limited to politics and world events. While knowing about the Vietnam War is certainly helpful in interpreting much of Tim O'Brien's fiction, and some knowledge of the French Revolution clearly illuminates the dynamics of Charles Dickens's *A Tale of Two Cities,* historical context also entails the fabric of daily life. Examining a text in light of gender roles, race relations, class boundaries, or working conditions can give rise to thoughtful and compelling papers. Exploring the conditions of the working class in 19th-century England, for example, can provide a particularly effective avenue for writing about Dickens's *Hard Times.*

You can begin thinking about these issues by asking broad questions at first. What do you know about the time period and about the author? What does the editorial apparatus in your text tell you? These might be starting places. Similarly, when specific historical events or dynamics are particularly important to understanding a work but might be somewhat obscure to modern readers, textbooks usually provide notes to explain historical background. These are a good place to start. With this information, ask yourself how these historical facts and circumstances might have affected the author, the presentation of theme, and the presentation of character. How does knowing more about the work's specific historical context illuminate the work? To take a well-known example, understanding the complex attitudes toward slavery during the time Mark Twain wrote *Adventures of Huckleberry Finn* should help you begin to examine issues of race in the text. Additionally, you might compare these attitudes to those of the time in which the novel was set. How might this comparison affect your interpretation of a work written after the abolition of slavery but set before the Civil War?

WRITING ABOUT PHILOSOPHY AND IDEAS

Philosophical concerns are closely related to both historical context and thematic issues. Like historical investigation, philosophical research can provide a useful tool as you analyze a text. For example, an investigation into the working class in Dickens's England might lead you to a topic on the philosophical doctrine of utilitarianism in *Hard Times.* Many other works explore philosophies and ideas quite explicitly. Mary Shelley's famous novel *Frankenstein,* for example, explores John Locke's tabula rasa theory of human knowledge as she portrays the intellectual and emotional development of Victor Frankenstein's creature. As this example indicates, philosophical issues are somewhat more abstract than investigations of theme or historical context. Some other examples of philosophical issues include human free will, the formation of human identity, the nature of sin, or questions of ethics.

Writing about philosophy and ideas might require some outside research, but usually the notes or other material in your text will provide you with basic information and often footnotes and bibliographies suggest places you can go to read further about the subject. If you have identified a philosophical theme that runs through a text, you might ask yourself how the author develops this theme. Look at character development and the interactions of characters, for example. Similarly, you might examine whether the narrative voice in a work of fiction addresses the philosophical concerns of the text.

WRITING COMPARE AND CONTRAST ESSAYS

Finally, you might find that comparing and contrasting the works or techniques of an author provides a useful tool for literary analysis. A comparison and contrast essay might compare two characters or themes in a single work, or it might compare the author's treatment of a theme in two works. It might also contrast methods of character development or analyze an author's differing treatment of a philosophical concern in two works. Writing comparison and contrast essays, though, requires some special consideration. While they generally provide you with plenty of material to use, they also come with a built-in trap: the laundry list. These papers often become mere lists of connections between the works. As this chapter will discuss, a strong thesis must make an assertion that you want to prove or validate. A strong comparison/contrast thesis, then, needs to comment on the significance of the similarities and differences you observe. It is not enough merely to assert that the works contain similarities and differences. You might, for example, assert why the similarities and differences are important and explain how they illuminate the works' treatment of theme. Remember, too, that a thesis should not be a statement of the obvious. A comparison/contrast paper that focuses only on very obvious similarities or differences does little to illuminate the connections between the works. Often, an effective method of shaping a strong thesis and argument is to begin your paper by noting the similarities between the works but then to develop a thesis that asserts how these apparently similar elements are different. If, for example, you observe that Emily Dickinson wrote a number of poems about spiders, you might analyze how she uses spider imagery differently in two poems. Similarly, many scholars have noted that Hawthorne created many "mad scientist" characters, men who are so devoted to their science or their art that they lose perspective on all else. A good thesis comparing two of these characters—Aylmer of "The Birthmark" and Dr. Rappaccini of "Rappaccini's Daughter," for example—might initially identify both characters as examples of Hawthorne's mad scientist type but then argue that their motivations for scientific experimentation differ. If you strive to analyze the similarities or differences, discuss significances, and move beyond the obvious, your paper should move beyond the laundry list trap.

PREPARING TO WRITE

Armed with a clear sense of your task—illuminating the text—and with an understanding of theme, character, language, history, and philosophy, you are ready to approach the writing process. Remember that good writing is grounded in good reading and that close reading takes time, attention, and more than one reading of your text. Read for comprehension first. As you go back and review the work, mark the text to chart the details of the work as well as your reactions. Highlight important passages, repeated words, and image patterns. "Converse" with the text through marginal notes. Mark turns in the plot, ask questions, and make observations about characters, themes, and language. If you are reading from a book that does not belong to you, keep a record of your reactions in a journal or notebook. If you have read a work of literature carefully, paying attention to both the text and the context of the work, you have a leg up on the writing process. Admittedly, at this point, your ideas are probably very broad and undefined, but you have taken an important first step toward writing a strong paper.

Your next step is to focus, to take a broad, perhaps fuzzy, topic and define it more clearly. Even a topic provided by your instructor will need to be focused appropriately. Remember that good writers make the topic their own. There are a number of strategies—often called "invention"—that you can use to develop your own focus. In one such strategy, *freewriting,* you spend 10 minutes or so just writing about your topic without referring back to the text or your notes. Write whatever comes to mind; the important thing is that you just keep writing. Often this process allows you to develop fresh ideas or approaches to your subject matter. You could also try *brainstorming.* Write down your topic and then list all the related points or ideas you can think of. Include questions, comments, words, important passages or events, and anything else that comes to mind. Let one idea lead to another. In the related technique of *clustering,* or *mapping,* write your topic on a sheet of paper and write related ideas around it. Then list related sub points under each of these main ideas. Many people then draw arrows to show connections between points. This technique helps you narrow your topic and can also help you organize your ideas. Similarly, asking journalistic questions—Who? What? Where? When? Why? and How?—can develop ideas for topic development.

Thesis Statements

Once you have developed a focused topic, you can begin to think about your thesis statement, the main point or purpose of your paper. It is imperative that you craft a strong thesis; otherwise, your paper will likely be little more than random, disorganized observations about the text. Think of your thesis statement as a kind of road map for your paper. It tells your reader where you are going and how you are going to get there.

To craft a good thesis, you must keep a number of things in mind. First, as the title of this subsection indicates, your paper's thesis should be a statement, an assertion about the text that you want to prove or validate. Beginning writers often formulate a question that they attempt to use as a thesis. For example, a writer exploring the character Shylock in *The Merchant of Venice* might ask, Although the Venetian Christians tell us that Shylock is a villain, does Shakespeare himself appear to agree? While a question like this is a good strategy to use in the invention process to help narrow your topic and find your thesis, it cannot serve as the thesis statement because it does not tell your reader what you want to assert about Shylock. You might shape this question into a thesis by instead proposing an answer to that question: Although the Venetian Christians tell us that Shylock is a villain, there is enough evidence in the play to suggest that Shakespeare has a much more complex, even sympathetic view of his character. We can see this not only in Shylock's statements of vulnerability and weakness but also in the dubious, hypocritical conduct of the play's Christians. Notice that this thesis provides an initial plan or structure for the rest of the paper—I will establish how the Venetian community perceives Shylock, then move into a discussion of scenes where Shylock's words reveal him to be a victim in his own right, and then finally discuss the portrait of the apparently "good" Christians of Venice who are really no better than Shylock. Notice, too, that the thesis statement does not necessarily have to fit into one sentence.

Second, remember that a good thesis makes an assertion that you need to support. In other words, a good thesis does not state the obvious. If you tried to formulate a thesis about *Macbeth* by simply saying, *Macbeth is a play in part about witchcraft,* you have done nothing but state the obvious. This example gives the reader merely a theme, and a thesis is much more than a theme or subject: It is what you have to say about your theme. In other words, while your essay certainly can be about witchcraft in *Macbeth,* it must make a precise point about witchcraft. And the theme of witchcraft in *Macbeth* is a very rich one, one that might stimulate many good thesis statements. For example: The witches in *Macbeth* are part of a series of female threats to Macbeth's masculine authority. Indeed, Shakespeare emphasizes symbolic connections between the weird sisters and Lady Macbeth, banding them together to form a vision of unnaturally powerful women.

As the comparison with the road map also suggests, your thesis should appear near the beginning of the paper. In relatively short papers (three to six pages) the thesis almost always appears in the first paragraph. Some writers fall into the trap of saving their thesis for the end, trying to provide a surprise or a big moment of revelation, as if to say, "TA-DA! I've just proved that Lady Macbeth is a witch, and you didn't even see it coming!" While surprise endings may be thrilling in a murder mystery novel, they are utterly self-destructive in an academic essay. Placing a thesis at the end of an essay can seriously mar the paper's effectiveness. If you fail to define your essay's point and purpose clearly at the beginning, your reader will find it difficult to assess the clarity of your argument and understand the points you are making. When your argument comes as a surprise at the end, you force your reader to reread your essay in order to assess its logic and effectiveness.

Finally, you should avoid using the first person ("I") as you present your thesis. Though it is not strictly wrong to write in the first person, it is difficult to do so gracefully. While writing in the first person, beginning writers often fall into the trap of writing self-reflexive prose (writing *about* their paper *in* their paper). Often this leads to the most dreaded of opening lines: "In this paper I am going to discuss. . . ." Not only does this self-reflexive voice make for very awkward prose, it frequently allows writers to boldly announce a topic while completely avoiding a thesis statement.

Outlines

As are most tasks in life, essay writing is made easier by some advance planning. Many students avoid making plans because they feel it wastes time or that "it's just not my style." While there certainly is something to be said for spontaneity, making a plan will not prevent you from having "eureka" moments as you write. Nor will making an outline mean that you spend an extra hour or so in the company of an essay you would so dearly love to finish. In fact, it is almost certain that making an outline will allow you and your essay to bid each other good night significantly sooner than you otherwise might have. Think of it this way. If somebody asked you to get in a car and drive from Binghamton, New York, to Washington, D.C., you would want a map and detailed directions. You would certainly get to Washington quicker—and with far less stress—than if all you knew was that you wanted to get to the capital. Think of all the wrong turns you would make without your map and directions. Writing an essay is exactly the same. Making an outline means not only that you will get to your desired destination sooner but also that you will probably steer clear of the single-lane, standstill traffic jam known as writer's block.

However, not all outlines are created equal. While some planning is better than none, when it comes to essay writing, better planning is best. Here is a method I have found very useful over the years. Imagine that you will be writing an essay on Caliban in Shakespeare's *The Tempest.* All you have right now is a general topic. Take a sheet of paper and brainstorm on Caliban, not editing or ordering your thoughts in any way. This should take a while, and ideally you should do it with *The Tempest* in hand, thumbing through the pages and looking at your margin notes and underlining. Write down everything that might go into an essay on Caliban. The result should be a page of brief notes, lots of points, details, and thoughts. Study the list carefully, thinking about possible arguments that could be developed from your material. After some reflection, you decide on the following thesis: *The Tempest* encourages us to view Caliban as a tragic figure, a victim of Prospero's colonial project. Here is what your brainstormed notes may look like:

```
Caliban tried to rape Miranda

Prospero's famous line about Caliban: "This thing of
darkness I / Acknowledge mine." But what does this
line mean?

Caliban's mother ruled the island before Prospero's
arrival

At first Caliban and Prospero got along

Prospero and Miranda need Caliban

Caliban is repeatedly referred to as "slave"

Prospero keeps Caliban in line by hurting and pun-
ishing him
```

Caliban knows the island and seems to be in tune with it

Caliban is actually very eloquent and makes several strong arguments against Prospero's Rule—*act 1, scene 2 and act 4, scene 1 especially.*

Prospero seems really shocked and angry (*are these the right words*?) by Caliban's attempt to kill him, even though Prospero is so much more powerful and not really in any danger. *I wonder why this is*?

Count up the number of points you have and then take a clean piece of paper. Write down numbers for each of your points, plus two more. For example, there are 10 points above, so you would write 12 numbers on my second piece of paper. If you had 30 points, you would write 32 numbers, and so on. For the example above, your paper would look like this.

1.

2.

3.

4.

5.

6.

7.

8.

9.

10.

11.

12.

The next step is the really important—and most difficult—one. Alongside number one, write something like "Introduction / clear statement of thesis"; next to the final number, write "conclusion." In this case, your argument is *The Tempest* encourages us to view Caliban as a tragic figure, a victim of Prospero's colonial project. You need to pick a strong first point now to follow this thesis statement. What is your most compelling piece of evidence that Caliban is anything but the monstrous savage that the Europeans take him for? This will be subjective; different writers might pick different starting points. The important thing is to believe that the chosen point is your strongest piece of evidence and to be confident in it. Let us say that you picked the point about Caliban's eloquence and the powerful speeches he makes against his mistreatment. You would scratch this out from your notes and write it alongside number two on your second sheet. After this you are no longer concerned about the strength of the points but rather about how they tie in or connect with my point about Caliban's eloquence. What you are aiming for is to produce a list of points that moves from idea to idea logically and seamlessly. Think of it as a bit of a puzzle. Here is one solution that works:

1. Introduction and thesis: *The Tempest* encourages us to view Caliban as a tragic figure, a victim of Prospero's colonial project

2. Caliban's eloquent appeals against his treatment (1.2 and 4.1, in particular)

3. Caliban is repeatedly referred to as "slave"

4. Prospero keeps Caliban in line by hurting and punishing him

5. Caliban's mother ruled the island before Prospero's arrival

6. Caliban knows the island and seems to be in tune with it

7. At first Caliban and Prospero got along

8. Caliban tried to rape Miranda

9. Prospero and Miranda *need* Caliban

10. Prospero's shock and anger at Caliban's betrayal

11. "This thing of darkness . . . "

12. Conclusion

You now know exactly where you are going in this essay, and exactly how you are going to get there. Each point moves logically to the next. Here, for example, points two, three, and four all address Prospero's abuses of Caliban and his intelligent response to them. It is easy to make a transition from here into points five through nine, all of which describe the emergence of the colonial relationship, charting the move from encounter to conflict. These points, then, suggest the foundation of the relationship between Prospero and Caliban, while points 10 and 11 build on this to show how complex and tragic, how harmful to all parties, the relationship between these two antagonists has become. This essay will certainly provide ample support and exploration of the thesis claim about the tragic quality of Caliban. Keep in mind that each point does not necessarily represent a paragraph or any other fixed amount of page space. For example, you could spend several pages on point two, assessing Caliban's intellectual resistance through a close reading of some of his speeches, while only dedicating a few lines to point number six.

Some students may wish to develop an outline even more, attaching to it more detail and specificity. For example, I like to know which quotes I will be using and when, so I make sure my outline includes a list of act, scene, and line numbers to refer to as I write. A more elaborate version of an outline for the same essay could look something like this:

1. Introduction and thesis
   - Prospero often seen as the central tragic figure in *The Tempest*
   - The tragedy of the play is also traditionally viewed as being one of "time"
   - However, Caliban is in fact a figure of the same tragic power as Prospero, because they are both victims of the colonial system

2. Caliban's sophistication
   - Introduce the idea of a sympathetic Caliban
   - Is modern interest in Caliban simply a result of a contemporary distrust of colonialism?
   - On the contrary, Shakespeare seems to have worked hard to make Caliban a sympathetic and complex figure
   - Caliban claims that his right to the island is superior to Prospero's (1.2.334)
   - Caliban is able to recognize that he has not benefited from the supposed "civilizing" process of colonialism (1.2.364–65)

3. The mistreatment of Caliban
   - Introduce the idea that sympathy for Caliban comes not only from his intelligence but from his mistreatment
   - Instances of Caliban being treated as a "slave"
   - Prospero's justification for the ill treatment of Caliban does not hold up to scrutiny (4.1.188–89)

4. A reconsideration of the relationship between Prospero and Caliban

- Caliban seems essentially "good" (1.2.335)
- If Caliban's "nature" is not flawed, it must be the "nurture" provided by Prospero
- Eventually, Prospero recognizes that he and Caliban are victims of the same political power system
- This thing of darkness . . . (5.1.277). A close reading of this line and its implications. For example, is Prospero claiming "responsibility" for the moral failures of Caliban?
- A better reading might be that Prospero recognizes not responsibility but rather equality; they are both victims

5. Conclusion
   - Recap the concept of a "shared" tragedy for both Prospero and Caliban
   - Their tragedy is rooted in the political/social bonds of colonialism that enslave *both* to the mutually destructive logic of that system

At the end of this chapter is a sample essay based on this outline, so you can see one version of how this paper might look. The most important thing for now is to know that this road map will save you time and produce a better essay, one that flows well and builds its argument logically and carefully.

Body Paragraphs

Once your outline is complete, you can begin drafting your paper. Paragraphs, units of related sentences, are the building blocks of a good paper, and as you draft you should keep in mind both the function and the qualities of good paragraphs. Paragraphs help you chart and control the shape and content of your essay, and they help the reader see your organization and your logic. You should begin a new paragraph whenever you move from one major point to another. In longer, more complex essays you might use a group of related paragraphs to support major points. Remember that in addition to being adequately developed, a good paragraph is both unified and coherent.

Unified Paragraphs

Each paragraph must be centralized around one idea or point, and a unified paragraph carefully focuses on and develops this central idea without including extraneous ideas or tangents. For beginning writers, the best way to ensure that you are constructing unified paragraphs is to include a topic sentence in each paragraph. This topic sentence should convey the main point of the paragraph, and every sentence in the paragraph should relate to that topic sentence. Any sentence that strays from the central topic does not belong in the paragraph and needs to be revised or deleted. Consider the following paragraph about ethnicity and *Othello:*

> At the heart of *Othello* is the theme of race. Indeed, it is possible to say that the play's tragedy is built on a careful, multifaceted analysis of the implications of Othello's blackness in white Venice. Certainly the play opens by foregrounding the theme of race through Iago's crude slurs and innuendos against Othello. We learn in these opening scenes that Iago is a character driven by hate, though we may not apprehend the origins of that hate. It may be that we can do no better than Samuel Coleridge's declaration of Iago's "motiveless" evil. However, it is vital that we attempt to find some meaning behind Iago's actions in order to better understand the play's vision of hate and evil.

Although the paragraph begins solidly and the second sentence provides the central theme, the author soon goes on a tangent. Apparently carried away by his train of thought, the author's mention of Iago triggers a divergent set of musings that distract the reader from the projected topic of race. While Iago certainly does belong in an essay about race—he works hard to make Othello insecure about his ethnicity—the material in the second half of this paragraph fractures from the first half by talking broadly about Iago and the theme of hate. Just as whole essays need structure and strong transition to provide continuity, so too do individual paragraphs.

Coherent Paragraphs

In addition to shaping unified paragraphs, you must also craft coherent paragraphs, paragraphs that develop their points logically with sentences that flow smoothly into one another. Coherence depends on the order of your sentences, but it is not strictly the order of the sentences that is important to paragraph coherence. You also need to craft your prose to help the reader see the relationship among the sentences. Let us imagine that a writer revised the paragraph above to create a unified passage, but the text he settled on now highlights a different problem:

> Othello is a play about race. The problems that befall Othello do so not because of any tragic flaws but because of racism. This includes his own feelings of difference and inadequacy. The white Venetians appear to accept Othello by and large because of what he offers them. What does Desdemona see in Othello? Even where racism seems absent, it is playing a vital role. He believes she loves him because of his differences. Iago is able to make Othello feel deeply insecure about the position of a black man married to a white women in Venice at that time.

This paragraph demonstrates that unity alone does not guarantee paragraph effectiveness. The argument is hard to follow because the author fails both to show connections between the sentences and to indicate how they work to support the overall point.

A number of techniques are available to aid paragraph coherence. Careful use of transitional words and phrases is essential. You can use transitional flags to introduce an example or an illustration (*for example, for instance*), to amplify a point or add another phase of the same idea (*additionally, furthermore, next, similarly, finally, then*), to indicate a conclusion or result (*therefore, as a result, thus, in other words*), to signal a contrast or a qualification (*on the other hand, nevertheless, despite this, on the contrary, still, however, conversely*), to signal a comparison (*likewise, in comparison, similarly*), and to indicate a movement in time (*afterward, earlier, eventually, finally, later, subsequently, until*).

In addition to transitional flags, careful use of pronouns aids coherence and flow. If you were writing about *The Wizard of Oz*, you would not want to keep repeating the phrase *the witch* or the name *Dorothy*. Careful substitution of the pronoun *she* in these instances can aid coherence. A word of warning, though: When you substitute pronouns for proper names, always be sure that your pronoun reference is clear. In a paragraph that discusses both Dorothy and the witch, substituting *she* could lead to confusion. Make sure that it is clear to whom the pronoun refers. Generally, the pronoun refers to the last proper noun you have used.

While repeating the same name over and over again can lead to awkward, boring prose, it is possible to use repetition to help your paragraph's coherence. Careful repetition of important words or phrases can lend coherence to your paragraph by reminding readers of your key points. Admittedly, it takes some practice to use this technique effectively. You may find that reading your prose aloud can help you develop an ear for effective use of repetition.

To see how helpful transitional aids are, compare the paragraph below to the preceding paragraph about race in *Othello*. Notice how the author works with the same ideas but shapes them into a much more coherent paragraph whose point is clearer and easier to follow. The result is a paragraph that is both unified and coherent.

```
At the heart of Othello is the theme of race. Indeed,
it is possible to say that the play's tragedy is
built on a careful, multifaceted analysis of the
implications of Othello's blackness in white Venice.
Particularly important here is the irony of Othello's
own heightened sense of difference and inadequacy.
While the white Venetians broadly appear to accept
Othello, he has internalized his sense of "other-
ness" in a way that leads to paranoia. For example,
he frequently asks what Desdemona could possibly see
in him. Indeed, he appears to believe that she was
drawn to him precisely because he is racially dif-
ferent or exotic. Moreover, Iago is able to increase
```

Othello's sense of inferiority by consistently and craftily causing him to reflect on the racial dynamics of his marriage. In other words, Othello becomes the principle mouthpiece of the latent racism that surrounds him in Venice.

Introductions

Introductions present particular challenges for writers. Generally, your introduction should do two things: capture your reader's attention and explain the main point of your essay. In other words, while your introduction should contain your thesis, it needs to do a bit more work than that. You are likely to find that the first paragraph is one of the most difficult parts of the paper. It is hard to face that blank page or screen, and as a result, many beginning writers, in desperation to start somewhere, start with overly broad, general statements. For example, the mere sight of an opening line like Throughout history Shakespeare's plays have been considered the greatest ever written will likely create in the experienced reader a feeling of exasperation. Not only will he or she have seen this type of opening in scores and scores of essays before (perhaps even several times in the current pile of essays), the phrase, frankly, just does not make sense. Very few things have applied throughout history or throughout time; there was a time when Shakespeare was utterly unheard of because he had not been born. While some instructors do encourage students to start broadly and proceed to a more narrow focus—and this can work well—it is a risky strategy. Potentially, it creates a funnel effect: a wide chunk of writing at the start of an essay that narrows into the desired focus of the paper somewhere below. But why not just get right to the point? There is a great rule of thumb to remember: If you have a sentence, paragraph, or page of writing that could be erased entirely from the paper without anyone noticing it is missing, that sentence, paragraph, or page probably should not be there in the first place. Academic writing is a very economical genre of writing, and, generally speaking, every line and paragraph should play a part in supporting your thesis and developing your arguments—moving forward. So it makes sense to hit the ground running in an introduction, starting with a powerful quotation from your text, precise questions that will moments later allow you to arrive at your thesis statement by answering them, or even the thesis itself. Each of these methods will draw readers into a paper, enveloping them immediately in the issues and problems at hand. In whatever way you feel is best, get right to the principal text or texts of your essay. See how not a moment is wasted in the following introduction. After initially establishing the key topic—components of two Shakespeare texts that are separate from the main body of action in each play—the introduction quickly poses questions and follows up with an answer that functions as the essay's thesis statement:

> The "Induction" scene from *The Taming of the Shrew* and the play within the play in *A Midsummer Night's Dream* are both departures from the dramas they are part of. However, while the humiliation of Christopher Sly by an aristocratic hunting party brings forth many of the themes that will be central to the play, its relationship to the text as a whole is more questionable than Bottom's play in *Dream*. What effect does the "disappearance" of Sly from the play have on the action in Padua? What are the metaphysical implications of a framing device that does not frame? In a comparison of the Sly episodes with the play within a play from *Dream,* two distinct "types" of metatheatrical devices become clearly visible. While Bottom's play offers an alternative ending and threatens to darken the outcome of Shakespeare's play, the Sly action fundamentally calls into question the "reality" of the play it introduces.

Conclusions

If many writers struggle with introductions, the act of starting a paper, they frequently also struggle with conclusions, the appropriate wrapping up of the work. Both introductions and conclusions should receive special attention from the writer because they mark important moments of engagement with the reader. Just as the introduction is your opportunity to make a good first impression on the reader, to give an early sense of the paper's quality—and teachers marking large stacks of papers, unfortunately but almost inevitably, have learned to form early opinions about the essays they read—the conclusion is an opportunity to leave your reader with a pleasant aftertaste. If an instructor is juggling between a B+ and an A–, for example, a rousing and skillful conclusion might be just enough to nudge him toward the higher grade (while, conversely, a poor conclusion could deflate his enthusiasm just enough for him to award the lower grade). There are two main reasons that writers struggle with conclusions. First, by the time the writer gets to a conclusion, he or she is exhausted and often desperate to be done. The conclusion is like the last guest at a dinner party who cannot take a hint and leave. It is late, you want to go to bed, the rest of the essay has gone safely home to the word processor, but the conclusion is still hanging around demanding your attention. Second, conclusions are very difficult to write. Sometimes students simply give up and come to a sudden stop. It is as if they feel that they have said all they wanted to say, so any further writing would just be a waste of time. This tends to be one hallmark of an extremely weak paper.

A safe but rather boring and mechanical solution to the conclusion problem is what I call the "sports highlights" approach. While a soccer match might have lasted 90 minutes, for example, the "highlights" package on the evening news may be just a few seconds. It will show the score and probably the goals. It may also show a near miss or two. A basic, competent conclusion does something similar. It restates the thesis (the score) and recalls the key pieces of evidence that helped support that argument (the most memorable action). More creative conclusions might also suggest related problems outside the essay's scope but potentially of interest to your reader (see the last few sentences of the example below). Braver souls might also see the conclusion as an opportunity to get a little lyrical or poetic in the final lines (again, see the example below), the verbal equivalent of fireworks at the end.

What a good conclusion will not do is any of the three following things. First, it will not begin with the phrase In conclusion. . . . The fact that it is the last one or two paragraphs of your essay should be enough to clue most readers into the fact that you are now concluding your essay. Second, it will not introduce big new ideas—it is too late. If a good idea does arrive very late in the essay, revise the paper and put the idea where it fits best in the work. (Sometimes you might even find that you have an idea good enough to become a new thesis statement. This is great, but you must tweak the body of the essay so that it appears that this argument was what you had in mind all along.) Finally, it should not end with a moral. Students often channel memories of childhood stories by ending an essay along the lines of Thus, we see Othello is the victim of racism, but also the perpetrator of it against himself. This, then, is one of the tragedies of racism as it makes people not only hate others but hate themselves too. We should seek a world without bigotry, one in which black and white coexist in harmony. While the final sentiments of this conclusion are noble, they have taken the essay away from *Othello* and into the ethical world of the author's life and hopes. This "moral swing" has been noted by a number of commentators on student work, and writers should guard against it.

Here, then, is a conclusion that serves its purpose quite well. The thesis for this essay is Although *As You Like It* appears to be a wholehearted comedy, ending in not one but four marriages, the play is nonetheless busy questioning, even undermining the commonplaces of the comic genre.

As we have seen, then, *As You Like It* is a play that creates strong tensions between form and content. While it is finally a comedy, it is comedy in part about the very limits of comedy. It is clear that all four of the final pairings, to varying degrees, are faulty and, despite the nuptial ceremonies, do not necessarily promise "happy ever after." Moreover, the impossibility of Frederick's conversion, along with the exaggerated convenience of Rosalind's resolution of the play's otherwise intractable problems of romance, further add to the sense of Shakespeare writing a play that asks its audience to question not only the structure of the play but also their own theatrical expectations and desires. The play, of course, represents just one stage in Shakespeare's examination of comedy. What is certainly evident here, however, is that Shakespeare was drawn to the idea of providing what the audience anticipated, while at the same time offering them plays that tested the very boundaries of theatrical form.

Citations and Formatting

Using Primary Sources

As the examples included in this chapter indicate, strong papers on literary texts incorporate quotations from the text in order to support their points. It is not enough for you to assert your interpretation without providing support or evidence from the text. Without well-chosen quotations to support your argument you are, in effect, saying to the reader, "Take my word for it." It is important to use quotations thoughtfully and selectively. Remember that the paper presents *your* argument, so choose quotations that support *your* assertions. Do not let the author's voice overwhelm your own. With that caution in mind, there are some guidelines you should follow to ensure that you use quotations clearly and effectively.

Integrate Quotations:

Quotations should always be integrated into your own prose. Do not just drop them into your paper without introduction or comment. Otherwise, it is unlikely that your reader will see their function. You can integrate textual support easily and clearly with identifying tags, short phrases that identify the speaker. For example:

```
According to Antonio, "In nature there's no blemish
but the mind."
```

While this tag appears before the quotation, you can also use tags after or in the middle of the quoted text, as the following examples demonstrate:

```
"In nature there's no blemish but the mind," suggests
Antonio.
```

You can also use a colon to formally introduce a quotation:

```
It is at this point that Antonio gives us one of the
most concise visions of tolerance found anywhere in
Shakespeare's work: "In nature there's no blemish but
the mind."
```

When you quote brief sections of poems (three lines or fewer), use slash marks to indicate the line breaks in the poem:

> Antonio's frustration at what he believes to be Sebastian's betrayal is the catalyst for a powerful outburst against superficial beauty that masks moral weakness: "But, O, how vile an idol proves this god! / Thou hast, Sebastian, done good feature shame. / In nature there's no blemish but the mind.

Note that not all of Shakespeare's dialogue is written in poetry. Sometimes his characters speak in prose too. Often the distinction is an important one, loaded with implications. For example, lower-class characters are more likely to speak in prose rather than verse, or the use of prose may suggest a moment of intimacy when a character feels he or she can shed the niceties of poetic speech and just talk. Whatever the reason, prose is easily identified by the fact that each line does not begin with a capital letter. When quoting prose lines from Shakespeare's plays, there is no need for the slash marks. So, for example, a few lines after Antonio's moving outburst in *Twelfth Night,* Sir Toby (an aristocrat, but a drunk and waster, too—hence the prose) speaks the following line:

> "Come hither, Knight. Come hither, Fabian. We'll whisper o'er a couplet or two of most sage saws."

Longer quotations (more than four lines of prose or three lines of poetry) should be set off from the rest of your paper in a block quotation. Double-space before you begin the passage, indent it 10 spaces from your left-hand margin, and double-space the passage itself. Because the indentation signals the inclusion of a quotation, do not use quotation marks around the cited passage. Use a colon to introduce the passage:

> Antonio's frustration at what he believes to be Sebastian's betrayal is the catalyst for a powerful outburst against superficial beauty that masks moral weakness:

```
But,  O,  how  vile  an  idol  proves  this  god!
Thou  hast,  Sebastian,  done  good  feature  shame.
In  nature  there's  no  blemish  but  the  mind.
None  can  be  called  deformed  but  the  unkind.
Virtue  is  beauty,  but  the  beauteous  evil
Are  empty  trunks  o'er-flourished  by  the  devil.

For  Antonio,  it  is  fidelity  and  honesty  that  are
the  true  markers  of  beauty,  not  the  "empty"  features
of  a  handsome  face.
```

It is also important to interpret quotations after you introduce them and explain how they help advance your point. You cannot assume that your reader will interpret the quotations the same way that you do. My line that begins "For Antonio . . ." is an attempt to start this process.

Quote Accurately:

Always quote accurately. Anything within quotations marks must be the author's exact words. There are, however, some rules to follow if you need to modify the quotation to fit into your prose.

1. Use brackets to indicate any material that might have been added to the author's exact wording. For example, if you need to add any words to the quotation or alter it grammatically to allow it to fit into your prose, indicate your changes in brackets:

   ```
   Viola confesses that "As [he] is a man, [his]
   state is desperate for [his] Master's love."
   ```

2. Conversely, if you choose to omit any words from the quotation, use an ellipsis (three spaced periods) to indicate missing words or phrases:

   ```
   Orsino  announces  that  "When  that  is
   known  .  .  .  /  A  solemn  combination  shall  be
   made  /  Of  our  dear  souls."
   ```

3. If you delete a sentence or more, use an ellipsis after a period:

> It is at this point that Antonio gives us one of the most concise visions of tolerance found anywhere in Shakespeare's work: "In nature there's no blemish but the mind. . . . Virtue is beauty, but the beauteous evil / Are empty trunks o'er-flourished by the devil."

Punctuate Properly:

Punctuation of quotations often causes more trouble than it should. Once again, you just need to keep these simple rules in mind.

1. Periods and commas should be placed inside quotation marks, even if they are not part of the original quotation:

> Shakespeare, in Kevin Webster's pithy phrase, was "rooted in his moment, not born of the eternal."

The only exception to this rule is when the quotation is followed by a parenthetical reference. In this case, the period or comma goes after the citation (more on these later in this chapter):

> Shakespeare, in Kevin Webster's pithy phrase, was "rooted in his moment, not born of the eternal" (135).

2. Other marks of punctuation—colons, semicolons, question marks, and exclamation points—go outside the quotation marks unless they are part of the original quotation:

> What does Webster mean when he writes that Shakespeare was "rooted in his moment, not born of the eternal"?

```
The fastidious Webster asks, "Are you certain
you have cited me properly?"
```

Documenting Primary Sources

Unless you are instructed otherwise, you should provide sufficient information for your reader to locate material you quote. Generally, literature papers follow the rules set forth by the Modern Language Association (MLA). These can be found in the *MLA Handbook for Writers of Research Papers* (sixth edition). You should be able to find this book in the reference section of your library. Additionally, its rules for citing both primary and secondary sources are widely available from reputable online sources. One of these is the Online Writing Lab (OWL) at Purdue University. OWL's guide to MLA style is available at http://owl.english.purdue.edu/owl/resource/557/01/. The Modern Language Association also offers answers to frequently asked questions about MLA style on this helpful Web page: http://www.mla.org/style_faq. Generally, when you are citing from literary works in papers, you should keep a few guidelines in mind.

Parenthetical Citations:

MLA asks for parenthetical references in your text after quotations. When you are working with prose (short stories, novels, or essays) include page numbers in the parentheses:

```
Shakespeare, in Kevin Webster's pithy phrase, was
"rooted in his moment, not born of the eternal"
(135).
```

When you are quoting poetry, include line numbers:

```
Shakespeare's Sonnet 18 has developed the reputation
of a classic love poem. Many readers, then, are sur-
prised to learn that the following oft-quoted lines
are addressed to a man: "Shall I compare thee to a
summer's day? / Thou art more lovely and more temper-
ate" (1-2).
```

Shakespeare's plays—and early modern drama more generally—also have a specific format for citations. Included in the parenthetical reference, in this order, are the act, scene, and line numbers. The first of the two line numbers indicates where the quote begins, while the second tells the reader the number of the last line you quoted. It should look like this:

> The entire meaning of *The Taming of the Shrew* can be changed by an ironic reading of Kate's last speech. Does she really mean it, for example, when she states that "Thy husband is thy lord, thy life, thy keeper, / Thy head, thy sovereign . . ." (5.2.150–51)?

Works Cited Page:

These parenthetical citations are linked to a separate works cited page at the end of the paper. The works cited page lists works alphabetically by the authors' last name.

> Shakespeare, William. *The Taming of the Shrew*. *The Norton Shakespeare*. Ed. Stephen Greenblatt, et al. New York: Norton, 1997: 133–203.

The *MLA Handbook* includes a full listing of sample entries, as do many of the online explanations of MLA style.

Documenting Secondary Sources

To ensure that your paper is built entirely upon your own ideas and analysis, instructors often ask that you write interpretative papers without any outside research. If, on the other hand, your paper requires research, you must document any secondary sources you use. You need to document direct quotations, summaries, or paraphrases of others' ideas and factual information that is not common knowledge. Follow the guidelines above for quoting primary sources when you use direct quotations from secondary sources. Keep in mind that MLA style also includes specific guidelines for citing electronic sources. OWL's Web site provides a good summary: http://owl.english.purdue.edu/owl/resource/557/09/.

Parenthetical Citations:

As with the documentation of primary sources, described above, MLA guidelines require in-text parenthetical references to your secondary sources. Unlike the research papers you might write for a history class, literary research papers following MLA style do not use footnotes as a means of documenting sources. Instead, after a quotation, you should cite the author's last name and the page number:

> According to one recent biography of Shakespeare, "the dramatist borrowed heavily from a variety of sources, but the originality of each and every play is still without doubt" (Kazinski 216).

If you include the name of the author in your prose, then you would include only the page number in your citation. For example:

> As Robert Kazinski observes of Shakespeare, "the dramatist borrowed heavily from a variety of sources, but the originality of each and every play is still without doubt" (216).

If you are including more than one work by the same author, the parenthetical citation should include a shortened yet identifiable version of the title in order to indicate which of the author's works you cite. For example:

> As Mary Rudolph puts it, "the final notes of A Midsummer Night's Dream, with Puck's evocation of dead men and ominous owls, mar the comic resolution of the play and encourage us to reconsider the preceding events from the play in this new, dark light—the dream becomes a faintly awkward and uncomfortable nightmare" (Midnight 134).

Similarly, and just as important, if you summarize or paraphrase the particular ideas of your source, you must provide documentation:

> It has been observed that Puck's somber speech at the close of the play is potent enough to challenge the comic character of the play (Rudolph 134).

Ordering the Bibliography or Works Cited Page

Like the primary sources discussed above, the parenthetical references to secondary sources are keyed to a separate works cited page at the end of the paper. Here is an example of a works cited page that uses the examples cited above. Note that when two or more works by the same author are listed, you should use three hyphens followed by a period in the subsequent entries. You can find a complete list of sample entries in the *MLA Handbook* or from a reputable online summary of MLA style.

WORKS CITED

Kazinski, Robert. *Shakespeare from Afar.* New York: NY Press, 2006.

Rudolph, Mary. *Another Book about Shakespeare.* London: Cockney Press, 1993.

——. *Shakespeare at Midnight.* New York: NY Press, 2005.

Plagiarism

Failure to document carefully and thoroughly can leave you open to charges of stealing the ideas of others, which is known as plagiarism, and this is a very serious matter. Remember that it is important to use quotation marks when you use language used by your source, even if you use just one or two words. If you had read the above quotation from Mary Rudolph, it would be plagiarism if you wrote the following: Because of Puck's dark, ominous speech at the play's close, the comic ending of the play is marred, and the dream of the play becomes an uncomfortable nightmare. See how the words and ideas of Rudolph plainly make up the core of this sentence. Instead, you should write in such a way as to acknowledge the source of the thoughts and language in your writing. Something like the following would be fine: Critics have observed that Puck's lines about shadowy night creatures might even make the play something other than a comedy. But what does it become? Is there enough in the play, perhaps, to transform it so far as to become "a faintly awkward and uncomfortable nightmare" (Rudolph 134)?

Some cases of plagiarism are the result of students simply not understanding how to quote from secondary sources. This can be avoided simply by having a nonnegotiable bottom line: If the words are not yours, put them in quotation marks and tell the reader who wrote them. Paraphrasing the arguments of others is fine, but again you must acknowledge the source: Mary Rudolph has written convincingly about the distorting effect of Puck's speech about lions, corpses, and owls, suggesting that the play at this point is transformed from dream to nightmare.

Closely related to all of this is the question of how to use secondary sources. Accidental plagiarism is often the result of students wanting to use outside opinions and ideas but not knowing what to do with them. The two most effective ways of using outside sources—both of which have built-in guards against accidental plagiarism—are either as evidence to support your argument or as a challenge to your ideas that you must defeat. In the first case, you are basically saying, here is someone who thinks the same as I do: Mary Rudolph makes a fine point when she argues that *A Midsummer Night's Dream* finally may be seen as more nightmare than dream (134). In the second, you challenge the author: While Mary Rudolph has suggested that the play is more nightmare than dream (134), this seems like an exaggeration. The first strategy can become a little static if used too often, but the second can generate energy in your paper.

However, to be blunt, many cases of plagiarism are simply the result of dishonesty and laziness. Be aware that plagiarism can haunt a student years after the event, perhaps even preventing him or her from getting into certain schools or programs down the road. While it has become all too easy to plagiarize using the Internet, Web-based methods for catching plagiarists are developing quickly as well. Perhaps the greatest weapon instructors have against plagiarism, however, is a well-trained eye; many instructors will have read hundreds if not thousands of student essays and will have become adept at noticing the telltale signs of plagiarism. It is certainly possible that you may know people who have plagiarized and gotten away with it, but their luck is sure to run out sooner rather than later.

Finally, while it is not necessary to document well-known facts, often referred to as "common knowledge," any ideas or language that you take from someone else must be properly documented. Common knowledge generally includes the birth and death dates of authors or other well-documented facts of their lives. An often-cited guideline is that if you can find the information in three sources, it is common knowledge. Despite this guideline, it is, admittedly, often difficult to know if the facts you uncover are common knowledge or not. When in doubt, document your source.

Sample Essay

Richard Kline
Eng 210
Professor Gleed

"THIS MISSHAPEN KNAVE": THE TRAGEDY OF CALIBAN
IN SHAKESPEARE'S *THE TEMPEST*

At the close of *The Tempest,* Prospero says that, despite his complete victory over his enemies, "Every third thought shall be my grave" (5.1.314). Indeed, Prospero is a profoundly melancholy figure at the close of the play, bereft of his books, magic, and those many long years passed away in banishment. Because we are used to associating Prospero with his author Shakespeare, understanding the great speeches of the former to be the latter's farewell to the stage, it is all too easy to understand the play simply as a tragedy of time, of growing old, and of things changing. While this is clearly a powerful current in *The Tempest,* the text's sadness, its tragedy, is wider still. Indeed, the play roots its tragedy not only in the fact that men must grow old but also in the power struggles and relationships that characterize human society. The key figure here is Caliban, Prospero's island slave and would-be revolutionary. For all its charm and magic, for all the traditional association of Prospero with Shakespeare, the play encourages us to see Caliban as no less a tragic figure than Prospero. Moreover, because Caliban is a victim of Prospero's colonial project, his tragedy becomes intimately twinned with Prospero's, suggesting that a clear understanding of each figure can only be achieved through a reading of their relationship. Caliban, no less than Prospero, is at the heart of the play's wistful tragic qualities.

It would be possible for critics to argue that foregrounding of Caliban in this way, however, is simply the product of a 21st-century sensibility, one accustomed to noticing the undesirable consequences of colonialism in all its forms. However, while it is unquestionably true that the present generation of critics is keenly drawn to the theme of colonialism in *The Tempest* for contemporary reasons, Shakespeare writes into his treatment of Caliban a tragic depth that cannot simply be the product of hindsight on our part. The figure of Caliban could certainly have been a mere brute, a murderous beast that threatened Prospero's plotting. This would have been enough from a narrative point of view. But for Shakespeare's thematic purposes, for his tragic ambitions in this romance, much more was required. We see powerful evidence of this investment, for example, in Caliban's eloquent insights into the nature of his plight.

First, Caliban argues that Prospero's rule over the island and its inhabitants is illegitimate. Instead, he posits an alternative line of descent, one in which he is the natural heir to power. "This island's mine," he tells Prospero, "by Sycorax my mother, / Which thou tak'st from me" (1.2.334). Perhaps more perceptive and persuasive still, Caliban argues that Prospero's influence has been corruptive and that the process of "civilizing" Caliban has finally been destructive rather than beneficial: "You taught me language, and my profit on't / Is I know how to curse" (1.2.364–65). Language becomes a metaphor for civilization, and Caliban's argument suggests not only that he resents Prospero's power but that he has compelling moral and ideological reasons for doing so.

Of course, Caliban also has more immediately painful reasons to resent the new order. Shakespeare makes it clear that Caliban exists in forced servitude (the word *slave* appears frequently throughout the text), and also that Prospero is a harsh, punitive taskmaster. Naturally, we cannot assume that the language of slavery stimulated the same responses in Renaissance audiences as it does in 21st-century audiences and readers (in fact, it certainly did not), but the way Shakespeare vividly represents both the cruel, animal-like treatment of Caliban and his refined, intellectual resistance to that treatment does establish a social and psychological paradox that makes Caliban a clearly tragic figure.

Indeed, it is even more tragic because the relationship between Caliban and Prospero has not always been this way. The encounter between Prospero and Caliban follows a familiar pattern of infatuation and fascination, followed by conflict and violence; such was the pattern of a great many encounters between European explorers and indigenous natives. Moreover, despite Prospero's claim that Caliban is "a born devil, on whose nature / Nurture can never stick . . . " (4.1.188–89), there is ample evidence that Caliban welcomed his new neighbors at first with kindness. As Caliban recalls:

> . . .   When   thou   cam'st   first,
> Thou strok'st me and made much of me, woulds't give me
> Water with berries in't, and teach me how
> To name the bigger light, and how the less,
> That burn by day and night; and then I loved thee,
> And showed thee all the qualities o'th'
> isle. . . . (1.2.335–40)

The relationship is a reciprocal one, built on mutual fascination and profit. In exchange for Caliban's local knowledge, Prospero shares his knowledge of science and letters. Caliban's "nature" appears to be benign, even affectionate; it can only, therefore, be Prospero's "nurture" that turns Caliban into a drunken monster who tries to rape Miranda. Or, to be more precise, it is the nature of the relationship between them, established within the dynamics of a colonial encounter, that corrupts both of them. Indeed, perhaps the greatest proof of this inextricable bond of tragedy between Prospero and Caliban can be found in Prospero's faint, ambiguous half-recognition of their shared fate.

We see Prospero's awareness of his profound tie with Caliban develop from a purely emotional gut instinct, fired by anger and rage, into a firmer but still opaque understanding. Prospero's awareness of Caliban seems to reach a new level when the magician interrupts his own show, staged for the benefit of Ferdinand and Miranda, because he recalls Caliban's plot against him. The anger he shows does not reflect the amount of danger he is in; rather, it signals the emotional depth of his bond with Caliban. This raw, uncertain sense of Caliban reaches its apex with Prospero's famous declaration: "This thing of darkness I / Acknowledge mine" (5.1.277–78). Critics have interpreted this statement various ways. For example, one point of view is that the line is Prospero's recognition of his responsibility for Caliban's crimes. In other words, Prospero has arrived at an understanding of the relationship that mirrors Caliban's assessment in the first act. This is very possible, but Prospero's comment may be less about guilt and responsibility than it is about a broader kinship or interconnectivity. To read the line as Prospero taking responsibility nonetheless still puts Prospero above Caliban, Prospero in the position of authority, and puts Caliban in a position of subservience. A better model might be to see in Prospero's acknowledgment not a paternal, grudging claim of responsibility but rather recognition of himself in Caliban. After all, Prospero had sought initially to take revenge on his enemies as Caliban has sought revenge on Prospero. Francis Barker and Peter Hulme argue that Prospero takes from Caliban's failed mutiny a "final and irrevocable confirmation of the natural treachery of savages" (42). However, it is also possible to argue that what Prospero finally sees in Caliban is his frailty, a tragic frailty born of Caliban's humanity. The colonial project of Prospero is the immediate connection between the pair, but behind it is a bond of common weakness reaching into their shared natures.

What we can see by assessing the relationship between Caliban and Prospero is that Prospero's tragedy is Caliban's tragedy, and Caliban's is Prospero's. Clifford Leech is only half right when he argues that the close of *The Tempest* witnesses "a kind of death for Prospero" (102). We can also read the fifth act as a powerful and emboldening epiphany, one that makes Prospero more aware of his own mortality but also significantly more alive to the life and humanity of others. Through moments of eloquence and insight, both characters attempt to unravel the complex chains that connect them.

What they discover is that the tragedy of power relations, here in the colonial context, rests on the fact that both those on the top and those on the bottom are divided and joined by the same forces: the nature of power itself and the frailties and weakness of human beings. Caliban, then, as a component of Prospero himself, is far from a brute or monster; instead he is a figure whose tragic flaw is nothing more or less than the colonial system in which he exists.

WORKS CITED

Barker, Francis, and Peter Hulme. "Discursive Con-Texts of *The Tempest*." *New Casebooks: The Tempest*. Ed. R. S. White. New York: St. Martin's Press, 1999: 32–49.

Leech, Clifford. "View Point on *The Tempest.*" *Twentieth Century Interpretations of* The Tempest. Ed. Hallett Smith. New Jersey: Prentice Hall, 1969: 100–02.

Shakespeare, William. *The Tempest. The Norton Shakespeare.* Ed. Stephen Greenblatt et al. New York: W. W. Norton, 1997: 133–203.

READING
SHAKESPEARE:
AN OVERVIEW

SHAKESPEARE'S LANGUAGE

As I wrote this book, I asked my students to share with me their thoughts on writing about Shakespeare. With few exceptions, the students reported that the greatest obstacle to writing about Shakespeare, indeed, to doing anything with Shakespeare at all, was the process of reading Shakespeare. One student who said that she found the plays "boring and confusing" in high school was perhaps more candid than others, but the sentiment was widespread nonetheless. The root of the problem for many, not surprisingly, is Shakespeare's language.

Shakespeare is difficult to read. There is no getting around that, at least at first. However, like everything else, practice, patience, and a little effort will help. But in the meantime, there are some things you can do that will make Shakespeare much more accessible to you. First, do not overestimate the role Shakespeare's language should play in your encounter with his work. For many dedicated readers of Shakespeare, it is precisely the language, its poetic power and verbal creativity, that separates Shakespeare from the ordinary. But this is not something that needs to come immediately. Rather, at the core of the plays are themes, questions, and ideas that buzz and pulse with the energy of humanity, and these are open and accessible to all. Do not let the language get in the way or convince you that Shakespeare is a lost cause. Read to understand the play, not to understand the line. If you allow yourself to get bogged down in every word, every line, the task of reading Shakespeare will become painful. Here are some things to bear in mind:

1. **Before you read, know the plot:** Shakespeare's language causes most problems for those who do not already know the play's plot. If you do not know what is going on in the narrative, you will feel lost and confused—and no one likes that feeling (the opening scenes in particular will seem overwhelming in this case). Conversely, if you have a sense of the plot, of roughly what will be happening at each point in the play, it is easy to push through unfamiliar language and still broadly understand what you read. Plot summaries of the plays are widely available on the Web and in print. Ask your instructor too if he or she would not mind giving an overview of the whole plot for you before you read.

2. **Watch a movie:** As most people will not have the opportunity to see a Shakespeare play performed on stage at exactly the moment they begin reading it in class, a film adaptation can be an excellent second-best option. There is an important caution to be offered here, though. All film versions of Shakespeare's plays will change the text in some way. Whether it is a faithful adaptation that merely chops off a few minor scenes or offers interesting and original interpretations of a character or scene, or a film that radically overhauls its Shakespearean source, a movie should never, ever be used as a substitute for the play. Good film versions of a play, however, allow students to see a version of the play acted out, to hear the language spoken, and to experience the passion and drama of the text made real. You will find the subsequent reading of the play easier and smoother if you watch the movie. (Be careful to keep play and film separate in your thinking, as there will be differences. Also, do not accept the film's interpretation of the play as the only one available.)

   Shakespeare on film is a large and active area of study for contemporary scholars. There are many versions of the major plays (*Hamlet, Othello, Macbeth,* etc.), and these vary in quality and purpose. Watch as many as you can find of your play before reading. Often, unless the movie is quite new or has attained classic status, Shakespeare films can be difficult to track down, however. An internet DVD rental membership, Netflix or something similar, with its access to a huge catalog of titles, is probably the best way to find many of the films. You can sometimes find used copies on Internet auction sites too.

Perhaps the best Shakespeare adaptations for understanding the bare bones of the text are, unfortunately, also the least entertaining. During the early 1980s, the BBC set about filming the bulk of Shakespeare's canon, shooting most of the text scene for scene and adding very little in the way of radical interpretation. Indeed, having watched many of the films in the BBC series (released in the United States under the banner of Time/Life distribution), I have come to the conclusion that they aimed to interpret the plays as closely to the Renaissance mentality as possible. The result can often be embarrassing or worse (the *Othello* film, for example, has a howling, grunting, spluttering Anthony Hopkins killing Desdemona in a way that supports the interpretation of Othello the Moor collapsing from European humanity into a Moorish animal). While the series looks especially dated today (in part because of its made-for-television budget) and offers some performances that induce chuckles in the back row of almost any class, the films do give an accurate account of the text, thereby making excellent tools for reading support. Unfortunately, at the time of writing, the DVDs are only available in box sets that package together the comedies and the tragedies, but a careful search can uncover them individually for rent or sale.

3. **Use glosses, but not obsessively:** Good editions of Shakespeare's plays come with glosses printed on the page. Glosses are used when the editor of the play believes a word will be particularly unfamiliar to modern audiences, so a "translation" is provided either in the margins of the text or at the bottom of the page. Of course, glosses are very helpful, and even accomplished readers use them frequently. However, do not check every word; do not look at every gloss. Checking the glosses too frequently drastically slows your reading pace and is simply unnecessary. If you read a speech and it makes no

sense whatsoever, then check glossed words to see if this will help. If you have a sense of the speech overall, it might just be better to keep on reading and become absorbed in the text.

4. **Use secondary sources as reading tools:** This will be a controversial point perhaps, but a number of students have suggested to me that reference sources helped them with Shakespeare in high school. Such sources tend to be looked down on by teachers, no doubt because they have encountered too many students who read only the reference notes for *Julius Caesar* when asked to read *Julius Caesar.* In my opinion, however, as long as you use such tools just as one part of your engagement with the play, there should be no great problem. These texts can provide good summaries of the plot that facilitate reading, and they introduce important themes that are best considered before or as you read the text rather than after it. This way you can be thinking about, say, anti-Semitism in *The Merchant of Venice* as you read, examining the text with the theme in mind.

5. **Talk to teachers and participate in discussions:** Perhaps the greatest resource you have will be your instructor. If you have questions about any aspect of the play, ask. Become involved too in class discussions about the plays—just as Shakespeare's language is clearest when spoken, so are his themes most accessible when debated. Indeed, class discussion is often the best place for an important aspect of studying Shakespeare's drama: finding contemporary relevance. It is often said that despite 400 years' distance, Shakespeare is still contemporary. This is sometimes true, but it is also undeniable that much—sometimes for better, sometimes for worse—has changed too. While some instructors might not encourage it as a paper topic, a fascinating discussion could be started, for example, by asking what life might be like for Othello and Desdemona today. What has changed over the centuries for interracial couples? Starting or playing a part in these conversations can make Shakespeare seem alive and real even to the most disconnected of students. If no such opportunities arise in class, try to chat about it elsewhere with friends from class. It is fascinating to reflect on how

much we are like and how much we are different from those who lived long before us.

SHAKESPEARE'S WORLD

While Shakespeare's language is the most visible "relic" of his lost world, as many students see it, this is simply the tip of the iceberg. For a large number of first-time readers, the battle with Elizabethan language is part of a larger war. Students report that the plays are filled with countless contemporary references that are entirely meaningless to them. It seems to some, indeed, that the plays comprise a long sequence of jokes, observations, references, slang, and concepts that require years of study to decode. Here again, the teacher often appears to hold the keys. This can be demoralizing, as it potentially alienates first-time readers and makes them feel as though Shakespeare is the domain of the specialist, beyond their reach in another time and place.

Certainly, Shakespeare—like all artists—is of his moment and wrote for his contemporaries about his own world. But equally, as we have seen, Shakespeare's contemporaries were not as far removed from us, from our troubles and fears, our hopes and joys, as the archaic language and footnote-laden lines of a Shakespeare volume suggest. I have no doubt that 400 years from now, if human beings care to study our artists' work, they, too, will need the help of a future equivalent of glosses.

All cultures, however, are based on a system of shared knowledge, assumptions, and beliefs that distinguish them from others. Then, also, there are the more superficial codes such as manners and fashion. It can all be quite overwhelming. What many students experience, then, when reading Shakespeare, is nothing less than culture shock. But culture shock can also be thrilling and exciting. Think of taking a trip to Paris or Tuscany, Kenya or Thailand. What makes such journeys remarkable for us is the encounter with differences: the food, fashions, manners, and "mentality" of the place is stimulatingly different. Even a trip to the supermarket in a foreign country can be a wonderfully bewildering experience. Just as a foreign country offers some uncertainties but a great many more thrills, so too does a journey to Shakespeare's England. It is a remarkable journey, rewarding us with many unfamiliar sights and sounds. We may not understand it because, simply put, we are not of that place; we do not and cannot ever belong there. We are merely visitors.

That said, what follows is a traveler's guide to Shakespeare's England for those who wish to read about the place before they visit. Some knowledge of important historical movements and backdrops will provide the writer with a valuable reservoir to draw from in virtually any essay on Shakespeare's drama. In the chapters on individual plays, I point out specific historical contexts and suggest how research into those contexts could provide the backbone of an excellent essay. But while a specific knowledge of events or trends will help depending on the play, essays generally become more authoritative and impressive when they demonstrate sensitivity to the broad strokes of Shakespeare's world. Here are some of the important movements, followed by a list of further reading to help take students beyond the nuggets offered here.

The Elizabethan and Jacobean Stage

Some understanding of Shakespeare's stage, its standing and its conventions, will assuredly help you as you assess texts written first and foremost to be performed there. However, though the stage was unquestionably important to English Renaissance culture, it meant different things to different people. Critics today, like Shakespeare's contemporaries, hold a variety of opinions about exactly how the theater worked, who controlled it, and what effect it had on the wider society. For example, modern critics are divided on the important issue of whether the Renaissance stage supported state authority or challenged it. In other words, was the theater a radical or a conservative institution? (The answer probably varies from play to play, author to author, of course.) Certainly it was heavily policed and censored by the authorities and frequently defended by the government (which suggests the latter of the two scenarios), but a great many things still found their way onto the stage that implicitly called into question the role and function of the English state. As you work, you can also usefully consider this question of ideology, especially if the Shakespeare play in question is an overtly political one—and many of the tragedies and all of the histories are explicitly political.

The main opponents of the stage, however, tended not to be government officials but rather religious radicals who saw the theater as a devilish hotbed of sin and deception. These critics objected to such things as the practice of boy actors playing women's roles, suggesting that such conventions toyed with moral and physical abomination. Shakespeare, however, seems to have found this aspect of stagecraft great fun. In many of his plays, Shakespeare playfully explores the implications of a boy playing a woman, who often further disguises "herself" as a man. It has to be said, though, that the locations of the playhouses did little to discourage the notion of theater as a seedy business. The stages were largely located south of the River Thames, away from the city and nestled among brothels, taverns, and the many other haunts of London's least fortunate. Indeed, many of the stages doubled as arenas for bloodthirsty entertainments such as cockfighting or bearbaiting (in which a chained bear fought off the attacks of savage dogs for the pleasure of a paying audience). It should come as no surprise, then, that actors, writers, and other stage people were by no means the thespians of our time but had the reputation of vagabonds and masterless men who were loosely protected and supported by royal or aristocratic patronage. They were seen largely as wasters and borderline criminals, and many of them at one point or another came to violent blows.

What might the reader and essay writer take from this? Broadly, it should be clear that the Elizabethan and Jacobean stage was a contested area, one whose politics and influence was as uncertain to contemporaries as it is to modern scholars. These plays were often much more than entertainment and, consciously or not, exerted a powerful force on English political and social life. Your task as a writer, then, is to judge the direction of any given play's "social energy," whether it be in matters of sexuality or statehood, and begin to unravel the complex and potentially explosive mix of intention and consequence.

The New World and the Ancient World

Only a small number of Shakespeare's plays explicitly treat the discovery of the Americas or life beyond the borders of Europe (see the chapters on *Othello* and *The Tempest* in this volume), but it is impossible to overestimate the effect of the New World on Renaissance consciousnesses. As a reader, you should be aware that exploration of the New World forced Europeans to reflect on their own identities as well as the identities of the indigenous people they newly encountered. Certainly, the tragic tale of European expansion into the Americas is well known, and most students will be familiar with the enormous suffering that resulted from the encounters. Less familiar, perhaps, are the philosophical debates that circulated in Europe, thousands of miles away from the front lines of colonialism and exploitation. At the loftiest level, the "discovery" of a New

World forced thoughtful people to ask what separated European civilization from the perceived wildness and disorder of indigenous life. Most entered into this debate, however, from the starting point of European superiority, unwilling to consider that there might be something to learn about human existence from these hitherto unknown cousins. Indeed, invariably the encounter merely confirmed and cemented the righteousness of a European, Christian model of life. A few sympathetic souls, however, most notably the Frenchman Michel de Montaigne, rejected the preconception of European superiority. De Montaigne argued that the savagery of Europeans in the New World meant that the colonizers had little right to consider themselves more civilized than the natives they butchered and abused.

On a more pragmatic level, much of the intellectual energy invested in the New World took the form of economic calculation. Shakespeare's England, along with Spain, led the way in trying to establish profitable and powerful outposts in the New World. As a result of the New World encounter, the economies of the Old World expanded, and an age of consumerism and mercantilism was rapidly accelerated (see the chapter on *The Merchant of Venice* for more on the explosion of capitalism). So the energy of the New World infused many aspects of life in Shakespeare's world, and the drama of the colonial encounter became an engine for powerful forces of social transformation.

Again, how does this help you as a writer? Well, unless you are dealing with a play such as *The Tempest*, the New World may not play a prominent role in an essay. However, what you should always keep in mind is the broad and far-reaching nature of change during the Renaissance, an important part of which was stimulated by the encounters with the New World. At this point, again with your essays in mind, it might be helpful to touch upon some recent changes in the way scholars talk and think about the Renaissance. Historians, in fact, now tend to prefer the term *early modern* to describe the century or so before and after Shakespeare's death. In part, this change of terminology comes out of a gathering consensus that the term *Renaissance,* or rather the image of wholesale rebirth and reinvention it conjures up, is misleading. These historians caution that not everyone experienced a *Renaissance,* and that the medieval world did not disappear instantly in a brilliant burst of collective genius. The truth is much more muddled. It is a fact that there was an enormous outpouring of artistic, scientific, and intellectual innovation and that elites across Europe (especially in Italy) sought to reconnect with the great achievements and spirit of the ancient world. It is also true, however, that this creativity had significant geographic and class-based limitations. For many people, life continued as it had done for centuries, rooted in the earth, the cyclical seasons, and the mysteries of the supernatural. The term *early modern* captures this duality nicely; the trick is in the *early.* The term *Renaissance* encourages us to see the period in which Shakespeare lived as the birth of our contemporary world, a time when humans grew up and become more or less us. *Early modern* is more judicious, however, pointing out that while it was in many ways the period that generated so many of the systems and ideas we continue to use, it was merely a stage of development rather than a "big bang" of civilization.

This duality is important to remember as you write on any aspect of the period, particularly the plays of Shakespeare, which so beautifully crystallize this coexistence of change and continuity. Shakespeare himself, a country-born man who found success in the exploding metropolis of London, might even serve as a metaphor for his age. As you read and write, think about this twofold nature and look for ways in which Shakespeare—who clearly knew the court and the latest ideas very well—represents the forces of change (in a play like *The Merchant of Venice*) but also remembers his simpler, country origins in plays that reflect on the old ways (such as *A Midsummer Night's Dream*). Like his world, though, all Shakespeare's plays retain traces of continuing, long-established ways of life alongside glimpses of and insight into new ways of thinking and behaving. You will do well to look for the harmonies and tensions between these two modes of life as you examine the themes, characters, and ideas in each play.

Elizabeth and James

Arguably, no dynasty of English monarchs left a greater mark on Britain than the Tudors. Beginning with the crowning of Henry VII in 1485 and ending with the death of Elizabeth I in 1603, the Tudor monarchs reigned over a period of epochal change for the English nation. Shakespeare lived during the final, tense years of Tudor England and continued his career into the reign of the first Stuart king, James I. Elizabeth and James, then, must be understood as key figures at the center of Shakespeare's world. However, while Shakespeare certainly sought to earn the approval of his monarch through writing, he also used his stage to participate in conversations about the nature of monarchical power and the latest affairs at court. Remember that the theater was not merely an art form that responded to events from a distance but a part of the Tudor and Stuart political system.

It is not really clear that we have an equivalent today. Perhaps film and television come closest, but the parallel is not a particularly strong one. These media (especially film) can be political, and they can mount powerful critiques of government and policies, though this is rare given the enormous budgets involved and the need for broad audience support. The key difference, perhaps, is the closeness of early modern theater to the seat of power. If the film industry today were based in Washington D.C., if those involved in the production of movies were themselves watchful hangers-on around powerful people, and if the government meddled directly and openly with the content of film, then the parallel might be a good one. But as it is, early modern theater differs markedly from anything in our time. The theater was policed by the government, but the theater, in delicate and subtle ways, in turn policed the government by offering a lively forum for veiled but serious political debate as well as tittle-tattle and in-jokes. The most powerful Elizabethans and Jacobeans may have watched the theater, but the theater also watched them and frequently, though always discretely, mindful of the terrible consequences of speaking too plainly or boldly, made those same individuals the subject of its drama. Most powerful of all, the monarch was a magnetic subject for many playwrights, not least Shakespeare.

Indeed, Shakespeare and Elizabeth are bound together in our historical imagination, twin symbols of the mythological greatness of their age. In his film *Shakespeare in Love,* Tom Stoppard depicts the sovereign as a powerful devotee of the playwright, even playing a hand in orchestrating his love life. This is a fantasy, no doubt, but the stage did link the two figures tightly; Elizabeth would have enjoyed Shakespeare's plays at private performances, and Shakespeare's livelihood was boosted by the continuance of that pleasure. But in the final years of Elizabeth's reign, there is evidence that Shakespeare's plays were significant components of an increasingly vexed conversation about the aging, fading queen.

Elizabeth had come to power in less than ideal circumstances. Although she was daughter of Henry VIII, still a much-loved king a decade after his death, her mother was Henry's disgraced and executed second wife, Anne

Boleyn. Moreover, Elizabeth inherited a weakened state, one destabilized by two brief and unsuccessful reigns. The boy king, Edward VI, Henry's sickly son, had ruled between 1547 and 1553, during which time his handlers enacted a vigorously Protestant agenda. After his death, Henry's first daughter, Mary, began her short and destructive time in power. She married a Spaniard, King Philip, and in the process annoyed a great many Englishmen; Mary's subjects balked at the prospect of their country's great enemy inheriting the reins of power. But more harmful still, Mary aggressively reversed the Protestant policies of Edward and set about a bloody and murderous defense of Catholicism against heretics. She put large numbers of Protestant reformers to the fire, and those executed became martyrs to the cause of the English Reformation.

We can only imagine what effect this theological back-and-forth had on the ordinary folk of England, but Elizabeth learned a great deal from it. One of her great triumphs as monarch was to nimbly walk the tightrope of religious difference in England, never adopting the extremes of her predecessors. Elizabeth was a Protestant queen, but her reign is characterized by a mood of relative religious tolerance, even while some around her pushed hard for a more hawkish model of reform. Still, for all her effective ambiguity in religious matters, the Catholic Church saw her as an enemy, and the Pope made loud noises to encourage Catholic assassins against England's Protestant queen. Such attempts were, of course, never successful, though they became increasingly frequent in the final years of her reign.

Indeed, those final years were generally unstable and fraught with danger and intrigue. Elizabeth's decision to never marry had been contested vigorously by England's political elites, but Elizabeth never wavered on this vital matter. During her childbearing years there was no shortage of suitors, foreign and domestic, suitable and undesirable. She encouraged some but accepted none; her rhetoric was as powerful as it was consistent: I am married to my people and have no need of a husband. Speculations never ceased, of course, and it does appear that Elizabeth, never a wife, was several times a woman in love. But by old age, these strategies that once strengthened Elizabeth's position were working against her. A general unease appears to have infused English life at the close of the 16th century: Who would rule when Elizabeth died?

The answer to that question—as a result of furtive negotiations carried on behind Elizabeth's back—was Scotland's King James VI, who became James I of England upon the queen's death. James does not cut as recognizable a figure as Elizabeth for us today, but for Shakespeare's fellow English, James, as a male monarch with an existing heir, was a welcome presence indeed. The nagging problems of succession had been resolved without great pain, and James's monarchy, though not necessarily as remarkable as Elizabeth's, was stable enough. James was an intellectual who wrote on numerous subjects, but he was particularly interested in political philosophy and theories of monarchy. His reign, however, was stained by a number of sexual and moral scandals, all of which, historians tend to agree, circumscribed the effectiveness of his rule. And if the Tudors appear now to have been the most successful of English dynasties, the Stuarts, James's heirs, arguably suffered the greatest ill luck and misery in English royal history. Nonetheless, James was the last king Shakespeare knew.

Whether it is in passing allusions to Elizabeth (such as we find in *A Midsummer Night's Dream*), engagements with James's intellectual interests (the use of witchcraft in *Macbeth*, for example), or displaced and buried consideration of contemporary royal politics (as many have found, say, in *Julius Caesar*), Shakespeare's plays are infused more with the presence of the monarchs of his lifetime, about which he could not openly write, than with that of English kings of history. The essay writer can find in the narratives of *Richard II* or *Henry IV*, for example, a great deal of conversation about Elizabeth I. Indeed, Elizabeth, late in life, identified herself with the embattled and deposed Richard II of Shakespeare's stage. The most important thing to take from this, however, is the sense that the plays are alive with an energy drawn from the political, cultural, and social life of his time. While so much of this is lost to us and can appear hopelessly arcane and inaccessible to many readers of Shakespeare, it is useful simply to be aware of Shakespeare's role as a chronicler of his time. Your task as a writer is not so much to reconstruct Shakespeare's world through your essays but to respect and conduct into your work the energy with which he wrote and observed the life around him.

Shakespeare and Anonymity

We have spoken a good deal about Shakespeare's times, his world, but not much about the man himself. Why not talk more about his beliefs, his opinions, his dreams, fears, personality, and so forth? Indeed, such information could help you greatly; however, surprisingly, given Shakespeare's near monolithic status in our culture, we actually know very little about the man behind the plays. This fact is made yet more difficult to believe by the countless biographies of Shakespeare committed to paper over the years, but it has undoubtedly added to the awe and power of Shakespeare's work, existing, as it seems to, independent of a human author. Shakespeare's dialogic method, staging in his plays philosophical conversations that are not satisfactorily resolved by a single answer, means that Shakespeare himself "disappears" into his plays, and so little is known of the man that it is impossible to recover him intact. The bare facts, mostly collected from mundane legal documents, are few. Shakespeare was born into a middle class family in the country town of Stratford-upon-Avon. As a young man, he married a somewhat older woman who, as a cross-checking of parish records reveals, was already pregnant. Shakespeare left his family in Stratford to seek—successfully—his fortune in London, first as an actor, then as a writer, then as a shareholder in a theatrical company. It is not known how often he returned to his wife and children while he was in London, nor very much of how he lived when in the city. By the time he retired, Shakespeare was wealthy enough to purchase one of the finest houses in his hometown of Stratford, where, coming full circle, he spent the final years of his life. As you can see, there is little in this silhouette of a man's life to illuminate the great works of literature he produced. It is ironic, poetically so, that we know his work so intimately but essentially know no more of his life than we could discover of any one of his countless, forgotten contemporaries. This speaks to the transience of human life and the longevity of art; it is a reminder, too, that literature has a life of its own, independent of the author's intentions. Essay writers, therefore, may fare better in the playwright's absence, for there is no one answer to uncover, but rather endless possibilities.

It may sound clichéd, but each reader and writer invents his or her own Shakespeare. As you do so, of course, you invent (and then reinvent) yourself as a Shakespeare scholar. The chapters that follow offer a variety of approaches to the plays, some of which are quite traditional, some quite modern. For example, Shakespeare scholarship over the last few decades has been largely dominated by the desire to historicize the plays, to explore them in the historical context in which they were written. In many of the chapters, I suggest historical approaches to a play, encouraging you to explore the interaction between Shakespeare's work and the material world that surrounded him. During the middle of the

20th century, however, criticism tended to be formalist in nature, examining the texts as self-contained worlds. Students, more or less free from the vagaries and fashions of the academy that often restrict their teachers, can enjoy this approach greatly, exploring the psyches, motivations, and personalities of Shakespeare's carefully crafted characters. You can engage in the seemingly academic matters of form and genre or make use of your 21st-century sensibilities and think about issues such as postcolonialism or homosexuality in Shakespeare's works. So much has been said and written about the plays already, but rest assured that you will see, think, or say something that is fresh and original as you encounter Shakespeare. The aim of this book is to help you put those ideas where they belong: on paper for someone to read and enjoy.

Bibliography

Bloom, Harold. *Shakespeare and the Invention of the Human.* New York: Penguin, 1999.

Fernie, Ewan, ed. *Reconceiving the Renaissance: A Critical Reader.* New York: Oxford UP, 2005.

Greenblatt, Stephen. *Will in the World: How Shakespeare Became Shakespeare.* New York: W. W. Norton, 2004.

Guy, John. *The Tudors: A Very Short Introduction.* New York: Oxford UP, 2000.

Hadfield, Andrew. *The English Renaissance: 1500–1620.* New York: Blackwell, 2001.

Hale, John. *The Civilization of Europe in the Renaissance.* New York: Simon and Schuster, 1993.

McDonald, Russ. *Shakespeare: An Anthology of Criticism and Theory, 1945–2000.* New York: Blackwell, 2004.

Morrill, John. *Stuart Britain: A Very Short Introduction.* New York: Oxford UP, 2000.

Shapiro, James. *A Year in the Life of William Shakespeare: 1599.* New York: HarperCollins, 2006.

HOW TO WRITE ABOUT SHAKESPEARE

WRITING ABOUT SHAKESPEARE: AN OVERVIEW

THE ACT of writing about one of Shakespeare's plays is more or less like writing about any other piece of literature. The strategies found in this volume's first chapter on essay writing apply as much, say, to an essay on Nathaniel Hawthorne as to one on William Shakespeare. At the heart of a good literary analysis essay is a strong central argument and perceptive use of evidence from the text in order to support that argument. In almost all cases, moreover, much of the work needed to write an essay has already been done with a careful, thoughtful reading of the text.

However, there is at least one unique aspect to consider when writing about Shakespeare: the remarkable thematic density of his plays coupled with the invisibility of the author himself. Shakespeare's approach to playwriting involved the construction of multifaceted philosophical discussions within his drama. While many authors have communicated their beliefs and ideas boldly through their work, hoping to convince the reader of some particular insight or worldview, Shakespeare appears to have shunned this archetypal ambition in favor of presenting, side-by-side, competing ideas about a theme or issue without claiming the author's right to favor one over the other. In part, as scholars have noted, this profound equivocation has its roots in Elizabethan censorship; on some issues, such as overthrowing a monarch, for example, Shakespeare and other playwrights would have had to—on pain of death, quite literally—hide potentially treasonous opinions deep within the text. Nonetheless, more than merely political issues receive this kind of treatment at Shakespeare's hands, and we are left to assume that Shakespeare was simply one of those people who can perceive and even make a case for opposing sides of many arguments. The result is that Shakespeare as the author, as the omnipotent puppeteer, is infinitely fragmented within his texts, lost and irrecoverable. It is as if, like a great clock maker, he created mechanisms and wound them up, the cogs and hands of which continue to turn so long after without their creator.

The implications of this for you are huge: Shakespeare's plays are open to a virtually limitless process of interpretation and reevaluation. They embrace essay writers and give them a remarkable degree of freedom. Consider your task as a writer to be one of uncovering, to pursue the elusive and impossible goal of finding Shakespeare and his intentions in the plays: Did Shakespeare write in *The Taming of the Shrew* a raucous celebration of male domination over women, or did he write a comedy that undercut and challenged the cruel treatment of Kate? Or is it something in the middle, perhaps? In *The Merchant of Venice*, did Shakespeare write a play that bears the hallmarks of medieval anti-Semitism, or did he urge his audience to reflect on and even question that tradition? And so on. Ironically, one typical complaint students make is that they feel they have nothing original to say. More precisely, many of my students report that they feel that writing about Shakespeare is simply a matter of putting into words what teachers tell them about the play. In some sense, teachers do hold the key to the works—that is their job, and it takes considerable effort and passion to do it well. But once a teacher has helped a student see the themes contained within the play, that student has a number of avenues available that lead to fresh and meaningful writing. Because Shakespeare writes his plays in layers, with much beneath the surface that demands interpretation and consideration, a student might have room to disagree carefully with a teacher's reading of the play (though, of course, use good judgment—there is a small number of instructors who resent this sort of freethinking) or develop it by finding more evidence in the play to support it or take it in a slightly different direction. The point is that once you are in the play, there is ample room to move freely in more or less whatever direction you like. The plays invite you to take part in the big conversations at their core.

While the chemists, biologists, and physicists of the world search for tangible things, reach out a hand into a physical universe that slowly gives up its secrets, scholars of Shakespeare's plays—and you become one the moment you write that first line—search a make-believe universe for an elusive truth that will never be found. As you search, however, and write, you develop and strengthen the parts of yourself that help you think beyond your moment of time, beyond your material space in the world. This chapter considers Shakespeare's career broadly as a subject for the writer.

TOPICS AND STRATEGIES

Every essay requires a focus; you cannot write about everything at once. In the chapter on how to write an essay, I show you a number of ways to turn a focus into a thesis, observations into arguments. However, the starting point is nearly always finding an initial focus, making first observations. What follows is a discussion of general topics about Shakespeare's work geared toward helping you make the most of your budding ideas. By no means should you feel limited to these topics, however.

Themes

It is difficult to think of a theme available to Shakespeare that he did not treat in some way. However, like all writers, Shakespeare had his favorite themes and preoccupations. When you consider thematic approaches to an essay on Shakespeare, remember the advice given above: Recognize that the playwright typically wants to pull the audience member or reader into a debate, one often furnished with strong cases on all sides. Let us consider a few of Shakespeare's most utilized themes.

1. **Love:** Is Shakespeare a romantic or a cynic when it comes to love?

   There are, of course, many different types of love, but many of Shakespeare's plays—especially his comedies—address the complexities of the timeless and profoundly human theme of romantic love. Plays that are especially valuable here include *Romeo and Juliet, A Midsummer Night's Dream, As You Like It, Twelfth Night, All's Well That Ends Well,* and *Othello.* Shakespeare's sonnets are also important nondramatic texts here. A question that seems to be of considerable interest to Shakespeare is, How constant and true is love? Look for examples of fickle and mercurial lovers who seem to suggest that romantic love is no more permanent than a happy or sad mood, something to be shaken off with the merest change of circumstance. Look for episodes of unrequited love, moments where one character's love for another is not returned, and, more important, how such impasses are resolved (and ask always how genuinely effective the resolution is, even if, as in *All's Well That Ends Well,* the play ends with marriage).

2. **Politics:** Is Shakespeare a progressive or a conservative?

In many ways this is an anachronistic question, but it is guaranteed to stimulate essay material. Today's labels of *liberal* and *conservative* (too rigidly defined and dangerously divisive as they are) are, of course, only of limited use when applied to a 16th-century writer. However, it might be an important point of connection for some readers and writers, even if a little artificial. Some feel that Shakespeare is liberal on social issues (such as cross-dressing, for example, a commonplace target of Puritan thinkers and diatribes, or witness his powerfully sympathetic portrait of the "homosexual" figure of Antonio in *Twelfth Night*) but—more arguably—something of a conservative when it comes to the rights and responsibilities of those who govern. For the latter, notice the sympathetic treatment of the deposed Richard II or the powerful and remarkable portrait of the Machiavellian Prince Hal. However, when Shakespeare talks politics, he equivocates. Richard II may earn our pity at the end of his play, but he has done little to earn our respect at any point before that. As a writer, you will always find Shakespeare's political plays set up as point/counterpoint debates, but it may be worth going out on a limb and identifying a dominant tone or opinion if you can (always acknowledging the convincing alternatives offered by the play). Plays that invite this approach might include all three parts of the *Henry VI* trilogy, *Richard II, 1 Henry 4* and *2 Henry 4,* and *Julius Caesar.*

Character

Arguably, Shakespeare's characters, rounded and unmistakably human in their contradictions and weaknesses, are the playwright's greatest achievement. A night sky's worth of ink has been devoted to understanding and explaining such figures as Hamlet, Lear, or Macbeth. However, while the greatest interest may lie in studying individual characters—for Shakespeare creates individuals and rarely just "types"—there are certain groupings that could provide a sweeping approach to the plays.

1. **Villains:** In what ways does Shakespeare complicate his villains?

> In uninspiring literature and film, the villain is a flat caricature of human depravity. In such work, it seems to not much matter why villains act the way they do; they simply do. Without the actions of the villain there would be no plot, no obstacles for the lovers to overcome, and no enemy for the hero to vanquish. That is what the villain is good for. Even in some of the most interesting creative traditions, the villain is little more than a walking, talking sin. For example, until not long before Shakespeare and his contemporaries were writing, the villains of English morality plays were one-dimensional vice figures, sins to be resisted and defeated by archetypal representatives of mankind; a character called Greed or Jealousy might try to corrupt a character called Every Man. Taking his cue from fellow playwright Christopher Marlowe, Shakespeare created villains who are well developed, ambiguous, even sometimes perversely attractive (Richard III might be an example of the last of these). Some of Shakespeare's villains seem to resemble the morality play tradition of the vice, but these apparently thin sketches of evil offer surprisingly complex psyches and symbolic power. For example, Edmund in *Lear* and Iago in *Othello* invite the writer to reflect on the darkest elements of human nature; these creatures of relentless and single-minded evil are anything but simplistic; they speak to the parts of humanity that made possible the Holocaust, the Rwandan genocide in the 1990s, or the unthinkable events of September

11, 2001. Sometimes, by contrast, Shakespeare invests his villains with an unexpected sympathetic value. Look for such figures, for example, in *The Merchant of Venice* or *The Tempest*. Can Shylock and Caliban even be called villains, though this is their function in each of their respective plays? Finally, look for figures in whom the gap between villain and hero arguably collapses. Hamlet and Prince Hal are heroes who nevertheless contain more than a trace of villainy. In *Julius Caesar,* moreover, the nature of villainy and the villain is complicated to the degree that it is not even clear who the hero and who the villain of the piece is. Arguably, the play's hero at first glance is Antony, but a second and more careful reading of the play might convince you that Antony is actually the ugliest and most morally distasteful character in the play.

2. **Women:** Is Shakespeare a "feminist"?

Again, this is an anachronistic question, but it is all but inevitable and well worth asking nonetheless. Perhaps the slightly less catchy (but a little more precise) version might be, Using his plays as evidence, can we make any general claims about Shakespeare's views on women? As you might guess, many of Shakespeare's plays could effectively be used in answering this question, but some particularly relevant texts include *The Taming of the Shrew, A Midsummer Night's Dream, As You Like It, Hamlet,* and *Macbeth.* In all honesty, though, each of these plays might encourage you to reach a radically different conclusion, and most of them are open to quite different interpretations on this matter. For example, Hamlet is famously appalled and disgusted by women, but does *Hamlet* the play expect us to go along with its protagonist's statements or question and challenge them? Even more drastically, as has been noted already, *The Taming of the Shrew* has been played both as a drama of incredible cruelty and violence toward women, one whose "comic" conclusion rests on the torture and breaking of an independent women, and also as a piece of protofeminist literature that subtly portrays its heroine's victory over her husband, winking away her final claims of subservience. The latter may be a wishful invention of latter-day directors and actresses, but the text does allow for it, though only just. So, as with nearly all subjects in Shakespeare, you will need to use your interpretive powers to shed light on this compelling but ambiguous area of study. You could even use the relative lack of women in many of Shakespeare's dramas and the peripheral nature of most of those who appear to arrive at some conclusions.

But perhaps the safest path to steer is one that acknowledges the variety of Shakespeare's women, the complexity of his dramatic use of female characters. After all, it is a hard task indeed to reconcile the author of Rosalind in *As You Like It*, quite possibly the most attractive woman ever conceived by the imagination of a male writer, and the dramatist responsible for *Macbeth*, a play that makes a strong connection between women and monstrosity, especially any woman who exerts a powerful influence over a man. One trick that essay writers can employ, however, is to use one play to "crack" an apparently intractable problem existing in another. For example, if you wanted to suggest that *The Taming of the Shrew* sides with Kate, not Petruccio, that it sympathizes with her rather than victimizes her, you might use *A Midsummer Night's Dream* to show another example of women being abused and controlled by men in a relatively early play. In this second text, the drama seems more openly troubled by the harsh treatment of Hippolyta by Theseus and, especially, Titania by Oberon. Perhaps the latter play can be used as evidence for an argument about the first—that if Shakespeare's sympathies tend this way in one play they are likely to follow the same path in another. However, the only thing that is clear—and really all that needs to be clear for an essay writer to begin work—is that Shakespeare's use of women is complex.

Philosophy and Ideas

Shakespeare's plays were financially successful and appealed to many types of people. However, on top of this enormous popular success, his work was always cerebral and reflective. Rarely do today's movies combine mass appeal and box office success with intense meditation on the world, but this is exactly what Shakespeare was able to do. Indeed, philosophy is built in to Shakespeare's dramatic style in the way he structures the plays as debates, as conversations that have not ended 400 years after the plays were first performed. Shakespeare seems to have more or less shunned the sensational and lurid aspects of Renaissance drama in favor of contemplative works based on characterization and intellectual dexterity (this must have been a conscious and perhaps risky move, as early modern audiences do seem to have relished bloody spectacle and excess). For example, *Hamlet,* as part of the revenge drama tradition and a play closely related to Thomas Kyd's savage *The Spanish Tragedy,* should be devoted to satiating the audience's blood-lust, but it tries hard not to be that kind of play; instead, the drama resembles the intellectual Hamlet far more than the impulsive and hot-headed Laertes. As a result of this impulse in Shakespeare's work, it is impossible for essay writers not to engage in philosophical speculation of one kind or another as they consider the plays. Moreover, writers should be aware that Shakespeare is broadly interested in the idea of things not being as they appear, and the notion of mutability and change, of fluidity rather than concreteness dominating the universe. Look for ways in which things that appear stable and fixed actually become movable and unsteady in Shakespeare's drama, regardless of the play or genre. Likewise, read for moments where "truth" fails, where knowledge fails, collapsing in the face of uncertainty and multiplicity. Pay close attention to the idea—it appears in so many ways—that something apparently natural, like gender, love, or even the identity of any given individual, is actually constructed and created, open to numerous interpretations and possibilities. Shakespeare asks us not to make assumptions, not to trust our senses or even our reason at times, not to simply pass through life without questioning what we see, feel, and know. Essays that specifically aim to treat Shakespeare's philosophical drive might do well to seek out this destabilizing sensibility, but—in this very spirit—be open to alternative possibilities. You may not agree at all that this is the core of Shakespeare's worldview, or you might uncover important exceptions. For example, a play like *Macbeth* seems positively frightened of mutability and disorder, of uncertainty, demonizing the androgynous witches and the "unsexed" Lady Macbeth, as well as the man who allows women to control him. Perhaps this very idea of Shakespeare's possessing—or at least voicing—numerous and utterly contradictory worldviews in his lifetime's work would have pleased and contented him enormously.

1. **Gender:** How does Shakespeare's work undermine a unified idea of gender or sexuality?

No element of our character seems more fixed and irresistible than that of our sex. And while we exist in the age of the sex-change operation, for the overwhelming majority of human beings, so much about their lives is defined by their sex and by the gender roles that accompany the biological imperatives of male and female. Shakespeare is fascinated, however, by the prospect of challenging this certainty, suggesting that even biology, gender roles, and sexual desire are open to a considerable degree of negotiation and shifting. Cross-dressing and disguise provide Shakespeare with his most common conceit for exploring this instability, but the theme appears in other ways too. Primary texts here include *The Two Gentlemen of Verona, The Merchant of Venice, As You Like It, Twelfth Night,* and the *sonnets.* Look for the multiple layers of gender confusion in a play like *As You Like It,* but always try to identify what emerges from the confusion; often there is a corrected or improved order (as, for example, we see in the education of Orlando, his progression from a hackneyed purveyor of love poetry to a realist capable of genuine love). Sometimes, however, the confusion leaves victims out in the cold (such as Antonio in *Twelfth Night*) or lingering and destabilizing uncertainties about the "rules" that order sexual attraction. For example, Orsino seems strangely unhurried at the close of *Twelfth Night,* apparently quite content for his love Viola to stay dressed in her disguise as a man for a while longer. Remember that while all of this cross-dressing comedy is funny and metatheatrical—milking the stage convention of having boy actors play female roles—it also forms a serious examination of how fluid human identities are, even at their most apparently fixed and determined points.

2. **Existentialism:** Does Shakespeare appear to perceive any sense of order to the universe, or any clear direction or purpose in existence?

Scholars and thoughtful readers of every kind perpetually examine Shakespeare's works for evidence of a belief in God, a belief in fate and destiny, or a reliance on some other kind of existential philosophy. We lack any definitive knowledge of Shakespeare's beliefs uttered in his own voice, and the plays refuse to offer easy answers. The tragedies are filled with dismal and sometimes even horrific visions of meaninglessness and human insignificance (*Hamlet, Macbeth*), but this worldview is set alongside possibilities of fate and destiny (*Julius Caesar, Macbeth*)—even though humans appear singularly incapable of foreseeing their own destinies—and the possibility that mankind, even against the relentless barrage of time and decay, distinguishes itself through forgiveness and love (*The Tempest, The Winter's Tale*). Arguably, the history plays tell of the enormous power of unintended consequences, illuminating how the passage of the decades and the centuries wastes not only individuals but their greatest triumphs and victories as well. For example, as Henry V celebrates his routing of the French, the audience already knows that the jubilee is to be short-lived. Henry's son, Henry VI, would be a weak and immature leader whose times were beset by war and tragedy (an irony emphasized by the fact that Shakespeare dramatized the turbulent times of Henry VI before he wrote of the glory of Henry V).

Shakespeare and his contemporaries were fond of saying, we are all but actors on the stage, playing our parts. But what forces author the "scripts" of human beings? Try to perceive what power appears to move the action of the play forward, not always trusting characters who believe they know. For example, Macbeth claims that life is a tale told by an idiot that signifies nothing, yet few of Shakespeare's plays contain such a relentless sense of destiny and predetermination as *Macbeth*. Look to see if the choices made by characters actually seem to matter or whether the play appears to be skeptical about human agency. Another important factor to consider is the origins of a character's hardships and misfortunes: Are they born of their own character or the evil of another? Does a play appear to make a skeptical comment on human nature or human institutions, suggesting perhaps that the tragic drive is hardwired into who we are and how we choose to live? Finally, even in the midst of the darkest tragedy, look for redemption, signs of goodness in operation. Especially at the close of a play, ask if there is hope beyond the immediate tragedy.

Form and Genre

Most of Shakespeare's works are plays, and Shakespeare does not appear to have been particularly interested in publishing them. This fact is often used by teachers to reinforce the need to hear rather than merely read Shakespeare's language, but it also shows how invested and committed the playwright was to the theater and to the development of the English stage. Because Shakespeare was such a devotee of stagecraft, it is fitting for writers to contemplate not simply the results of Shakespeare's drama but the skill and technique behind them as well. For example, one fascinating angle on virtually any Shakespeare play is a comparison of the text with its source material. Shakespeare's age did not value originality as highly as we do, instead placing great importance on the successful practice of imitation. Almost none of Shakespeare's plays are original in the sense that Shakespeare invented everything about them. Many of his stories are "borrowed" from history books, novels, or even a pamphlet in the case of *The Tempest*. Often the sources are short enough to read quickly, and a dedicated writer might reveal much about Shakespeare's thinking, his goals and aspirations for a particular work, by comparing the play with the source texts. What has been changed? Why? Focus on significant changes rather than cataloging minute ones; for example, if a character is added or augmented, made more sympathetic or loathsome, these changes signal a very precise purpose and intention behind Shakespeare's craftsmanship of the play.

Another approach to Shakespeare's artistry is through the study of genre. His plays can be categorized into three or four genres, none of which are mutually exclusive. In the 1623 First Folio (the first collection of Shakespeare's work, or canon, assembled by several friends of Shakespeare shortly after his death), the plays are divided into tragedies, comedies, and histories. Modern critics have added a fourth genre, that of the romances, to account for the sad, wistful comedies of the final years of Shakespeare's career. What is so notable about Shakespeare's work, however, is that he appears to question consciously the usefulness of genre and test the limits of generic expectations and conventions. Essays can grow out of the overlap between comedy and tragedy in many of Shakespeare's plays, papers that try to follow and understand the playwright's formal inventiveness.

1. **Comedy:** Does Shakespeare ever write "true" comedy?

> In everyday language, we tend to use the word *comedy* to mean "funny," but generically speaking comedy means something more like a happy ending. Typically a comedy is the coming together of lovers in marriage or the community in feasting after overcoming obstacles on the path to that reconciliation. A true comedy, then, might be a genuinely and uncomplicated happy ending. If you are studying one of Shakespeare's comedies, one strategy might be to look for problems that mar or darken the ending, finding the taint of tragedy in the festive resolution. Ask always if there are characters not included in the feast or reconciliation at the end, or if there are loose ends or lingering problems that leave you with an uneasy sense of incompleteness. By the second part of his career, Shakespeare was writing what we today call the "problem comedies" (plays that, despite their formulaic comic conclusion, deliberately undercut the comic movement), but it seems that all of Shakespeare's comedies contain elements that threaten or undermine the feast. Exploring the tragic tones, highlighting them for the reader, can be a useful, against-the-grain approach for an essay. Particularly strong candidates for this approach are *A Midsummer Night's Dream, The Merchant of Venice, As You Like It,* and *Twelfth Night.*
>
> Alternatively, students might work with Shakespeare's tragedies, perhaps looking for generic ambiguities or identifying similarities and differences among the tragic visions. In the first case, *Romeo and Juliet* and *Hamlet* are two tragedies that have strong comic veins running through them. Just as a writer might identify how a comic vision is tarnished by the stain of tragedy, so an essay might assess the presence of comic plots

or of laughter in tragedy. However, many of Shakespeare's trag-edies appear unrelenting in their pursuit of a tragic vision, of a picture of the world that resonates with pity and fear. If you are working with one or more tragedy, identify similarities or differences in the nature of each tragedy, of what each tragic ending says about humanity or the universe.

2. **Metadrama:** How does Shakespeare often make drama the subject of his drama?

Many Renaissance playwrights were drawn to what modern critics call "metadrama" or "metatheatricality." In such works, dramatists make theater visible on the stage, forcing the audi-ence to be aware of the stage and their role as audience. This can be done with a passing joke (such as when the conspirators who kill Caesar imagine that their actions will one day be the subject of a play) or through the creation of a dramatic space and performance within the play, often known as a play within a play. Shakespeare uses this device most memorably in *The Taming of the Shrew, A Midsummer Night's Dream,* and *Ham-let.* However, look for subtle appearances of metatheatricality in many more plays. For example, Rosalind arguably becomes the personification or embodiment of the playwright at the end of *As You Like It,* orchestrating the unlikely events of the comic resolution with wit and skill. Whenever theater becomes the subject of the play, philosophical questions about the nature of artifice and reality, as well as free will and human agency, can-not be far behind. When a play is performed on stage, assess the relationship between the play within a play and the main play. How do the themes of the main play appear in the play within a play? Does it parallel the action of the main play or transform it somehow, offering an alternative narrative?

Compare and Contrast Essays

All of Shakespeare's plays invite single-work compare and contrast essays, papers that address the relationships between characters and/or themes within one play. However, considering that he wrote more than 30 plays, the more you read of Shakespeare the more you will be able to appreciate the dramatic and intellectual fabric that connects all of his work. Look for reoccurring themes, issues, or character types, but always remember the golden rule of compare and contrast writing: If the items being discussed (characters, plays, approaches to a theme, etc.) are more alike than different, you should stress the differences you have uncovered. Similarly, if the items are quite obviously different, the achievement of the essay will lie in highlighting complex and unexpected similarities. Moreover, as you begin to think comparatively about Shakespeare's plays rather than simply about the one immediately assigned to you, a sense of the broad movements and trends of Shakespeare's career will crystallize into a narrative of sorts. With this in mind, start noticing dates of composition as you encounter new plays, or at least try to place a work roughly in the sequence of Shakespeare's writing.

1. **Contrasting Shakespeare's early career with his later career:** Does Shakespeare's work change or even improve as his career progresses?

   Shakespeare's career can be roughly divided into two periods: 1590–1600 and 1600–1610. Even more roughly still, the first 10-year period is dominated by comedies and histories, while the second 10-year period is characterized by the so-called turn to tragedy. It is possible to approach this kind of essay by simply arguing that Shakespeare gets better or, less controversially, matures, but such statements seem a bit limited and not as interesting as other ways of comparing the two periods. Given that so many critics have embraced—with reservations, of course—this division of the two decades, perhaps the most promising approach lies in finding a common ground between plays from the first decade and works from the second. For example, Shakespeare's problem comedies (the plays in which he experiments with and undercuts the comic genre) were written well into the second decade. This seems to support the generalization that Shakespeare's career darkens, turns tragic in the second half. However, a pretty large wrench can be thrown in the works of this argument by a comparison of the problem plays (such as *All's Well* and *Measure for Measure*) with *The Merchant of Venice,* a comedy from the first period.

Arguably, the earlier play is as dark and problematic as the later plays. Likewise, a comparison of the history plays from the first decade of Shakespeare's production with the tragedies from the second might find much common ground. There are, of course, some narratives of progress to be found, though. For example, Shakespeare's treatment of women, his ability to create fuller and more complicated women, as some critics have long since observed, does seem to develop as his career moves forward. If you hear such claims, however, spot the potential for a contrary essay in it. *The Merchant of Venice*'s Portia—though quite unlikable in many ways—could perhaps be offered as an early, independent, and complex female character. What should be clear by now is that when the entirety of Shakespeare's career is taken into account, it is impossible to make sweeping statements and generalizations. This can be used against the writer when a reader challenges the generalization, but you can also use it as a writer as you try to reveal unanticipated similarities or underappreciated differences across the two decades of Shakespeare's work.

2. **Comparing Shakespeare's drama to the work of other Renaissance playwrights:** What connects and distinguishes Shakespeare's work from the output of his contemporaries?

Shakespeare was not the only person writing for the stage in his lifetime, nor was he widely regarded as head and shoulders above the others. Yet the judgment of time has secured his place as the jewel in the crown of English Renaissance drama, and, indeed, of English literature itself. It can be fascinating to read the work of other Renaissance playwrights and compare it to Shakespeare's drama; often the result is that the gap between his legend and their relative obscurity diminishes, and a sense of the competition, the overlap, the shared interests and tricks, even of Shakespeare's indebtedness emerges. For example, Shakespeare's *Hamlet* could never have existed without Thomas Kyd's *The Spanish Tragedy* (and Kyd probably even wrote a version of the Hamlet story, now lost, before Shakespeare wrote his). As many critics concur, Shakespeare's great villains would probably not have haunted the stage for centuries were it not for the groundbreaking examples of Christopher Marlowe's overreaching and bombastic creations. Marlowe's Doctor Faustus, Tamburlaine, and Barabas are the immediate forefathers of Iago, Richard III, and Macbeth. The point of this is not to diminish Shakespeare's greatness, but rather to suggest that he was part of a vibrant, remarkable, and creative community of artists.

As you read works by other Renaissance dramatists and write about them alongside Shakespeare, do not necessarily assume Shakespeare's superiority; in fact, try as much as possible not to make any qualitative judgments. This will be made harder by the fact that almost all students find Shakespeare's contemporaries much more difficult to read than Shakespeare because they are unfamiliar with the plots and find far fewer resources and tools available to help. Most good libraries, however, will have or be able to get hold of ample, good materials to help you study playwrights like Marlowe or Ben Jonson.

Look to see how similar themes, issues important to the age, are handled alike or differently by individual writers. Sometimes, in some ways, Shakespeare's work may come off looking better. For example, some might argue that Marlowe's Barabas (in *The Jew of Malta*) is a stock Jew, greedy and murderous, and looks like a product of the Middle Ages compared to Shakespeare's more sympathetic handling of Shylock in *The Merchant of Venice.* But Shakespeare's portrayal of the witches in Macbeth is also a stock portrait imported directly from medieval tracts on witch hunting. By comparison, Thomas Dekker, John Ford, and William Rowley's *The Witch of Edmonton* offers a sympathetic picture of a woman driven to witchcraft by the abuse she suffers from her community. So again, humanizing Shakespeare, seeing him as a man of his time, one man among so many others, is a valuable process. For those who write about Shakespeare, the impulse to contextualize and historicize the playwright, to remember and illuminate his connection not only to other dramatists but to the events, fashions, and ideas of his age, can open up rich and exciting essays that rise above ordinary treatments of this extraordinary subject matter.

ROMEO AND JULIET

READING TO WRITE

PERHAPS ONLY *Hamlet* can match *Romeo and Juliet* for familiarity; the star-crossed lovers and their passage from balcony to sepulchre are instantly recognizable to many millions of people around the world. And for many, too, that familiarity is based on more than just cultural background information. The play is still widely read, a staple of high school English classes from Chattanooga to Calcutta. Why? The play's continued success may be best explained, among several factors, by its accessible and compelling storyline. Indeed, more than most Shakespeare plays, *Romeo and Juliet* appears to be driven by plot rather than thematic and intellectual concerns. It is not that the play is not intellectual but rather that the narrative is strong and the story demands the reader's attention. In light of this, *Romeo and Juliet* can be difficult to write about precisely because it seems so simple. A student who knows that good essays require much more than plot summary can sometimes be left wondering what exactly to write about in the wake of this tragic tale. The problem, in a sense, is exactly opposite to that of writing about a play like *Hamlet*, so intimidating because of its cerebral breadth and depth. The purpose of this chapter, then, is to show that *Romeo and Juliet* is far more than just a well-known story and that writers will find no shortage of material to work with.

The trick is to explore the play slowly, not to get swept up by the riptide plot. For example, in act 1, scene 4, we as readers are hot-footing it to the Capulet ball in act 1, scene 5. We want to see Romeo and Juliet meet for the first time, but if we read like this—for plot alone—we might well miss the following odd and unsettling speech by Mercutio on Queen

Mab. Responding to Romeo's love-struck talk of dreams, the skeptical Mercutio brings to his friend's attention the legend of Mab:

> She is the fairies' midwife, and she comes
> In shape no bigger than an agate stone
> On the forefinger of an alderman,
> Drawn with a team of little atomi
> Athwart men's noses as they sleep.
> . . .
> And in this state she gallops night by night
> Through lovers brains, and then they dream of love;
> O'er courtier's knees, that dream on curtsies straight;
> O'er ladies lips, who straight on kisses dream,
> Which oft the angry Mab with blisters plagues
> Because their breaths with sweetmeats tainted are.
> Sometime she gallops o'er a lawyer's lip,
> And then dreams he of smelling out a suit;
> . . .
> Sometimes she driveth o'er a soldier's neck,
> And then dreams he of cutting foreign throats,
> Of breaches, ambuscados, Spanish blades,
> Of healths five fathom deep; and then anon
> Drums in his ear, at which he starts and wakes,
> And being thus frightened, swears a prayer or two,
> And sleeps again. This is that very Mab
> That plaits the manes of horses in the night,
> And bakes the elf-locks in foul sluttish hairs,
> Which once untangled much misfortune bodes.
> This is the hag, when maids lie on their backs,
> That presses them and learns them first to bear,
> Making them women of good carriage.
> This is she—(1.4.55–94)

This passage acts as a perfect symbol of the play it is taken from. As Mercutio begins to speak, it looks as though the content and tone of the passage will be simple, even whimsical. However, by the end of the passage it is clear that something much more complex, much more unsettling has been expressed. Like *Romeo and Juliet,* then, this passage at first promises simplicity and an entertaining story but finally delivers something troubling and difficult to comprehend.

Immediately after introducing the figure of Mab, Mercutio continues to create a light and benign mood. Mab at first appears to be a positive force, the carrier of romantic dreams to lovers. But the mood is quickly tainted when we hear of Mab blistering the lips of ladies, apparently because their breath is sweet and fair. Fairies, of course, in popular folklore were often ambiguous entities, far from the good, wand-waving sprites we imagine today. But nonetheless, this image still marks a striking and unexpected turn in the passage, undermining the benign characteristics of the preceding lines.

This process of undermining romance continues, however, as Mercutio's narrative of Mab grows ever darker. If the image of blistered lips instead of kisses is disturbing, Mab's generation of a soldier's bloody and murderous dreams forces the play's tragic association of love and death; the soldier's bloodlust here has the same root and origin as a lover's dream of desire. By now the thematic relevance of this passage to the whole of *Romeo and Juliet* should be clear: The play presents more than one version of love, and the writer must be aware of this multiplicity. As you approach the romantic elements of this play, do not be seduced by custom into believing that *Romeo and Juliet* offers a unified, unqualified vision of love as bright and good. The "Themes" section below will explore in more detail these various interpretations of love.

Of additional interest in Mercutio's speech are issues of gender. Critics have been interested in uncovering and scrutinizing the play's gender dynamics, considering elements such as patriarchy and the oppression of women or the "homoerotic" connections between male characters, including Mercutio's relationship with Romeo (see the "History and Context" section of the *Merchant of Venice* chapter for more on the complex issue of male friendship and love in the Renaissance). Mercutio's speech, functioning as part of an ongoing attempt to challenge Romeo's heterosexual passions, may play a part in such a debate. The antifeminine tones of the passage's last lines, moreover, and in particular the anxiety surrounding female sexuality, have also been noted by critics. While the writer would do well to pursue some of these gender concerns, the main point here is that the relationships in *Romeo and Juliet* are open to interrogation and interpretation and that it is chiefly in these relationships that the "simplicity" of the plot is checked and infinitely complicated.

TOPICS AND STRATEGIES

Every essay requires a focus; you cannot write about everything in the play at once. The section on how to write an essay showed you a number of ways to turn a focus into a thesis, observations into arguments. However, the starting point is nearly always finding an initial focus and making first observations. What follows is a discussion of *Romeo and Juliet* geared toward helping you make the most of the budding ideas you will have as you read the play. By no means should you feel limited to these topics, however.

Themes

As with all texts, some of *Romeo and Juliet*'s themes are visible at the surface, while others must be uncovered and interpreted. As an example of the former, one plot element that has received attention over the years is the theme of vendetta. In writing about any surface-level theme—a theme that essentially functions as a plot device—there is the danger of plot summary. After all, to explain vendetta in the play, you might simply restate part of the plot. It is obviously not enough to have a thesis arguing that vendetta is an important part of the play; this much is clear to anyone who has read *Romeo and Juliet*. To turn theme into thesis, look for function: What does vendetta do in the play? One answer—and therefore one potential thesis—is that vendetta acts as a destabilizing force and is strongly condemned by the play. To support this claim, you might look at the figure of Prince Escalus, for example, who struggles to exert control over his state in the face of unrelenting gang warfare. But, of course, more pressingly, the fatal consequences of vendetta tear friend from friend and lover from lover. Arguably, in a play that is not driven by tragic flaws (such as Macbeth's susceptibility to dreams of power or Othello's naive jealousy), vendetta, the business of habitual hating, is the primary catalyst of tragedy. You could also take such an essay down the historical path, situating the clan feuds of Shakespeare's Verona within the real-life practices of Renaissance vendetta and revenge. Edward Muir's *Mad Blood Stirring: Vendetta in Renaissance Italy* is a good (but dense) text on this subject; it even takes its title from a line in *Romeo and Juliet*.

Of the second type of theme, the kind buried deep within the muscle of the play, time is an important example in the play. As you read a text, look for repeated patterns, words, or actions. Such a reading would reveal that there is much talk of time throughout the play. For example, the scene in which the Capulet servants prepare the hall for the party gives a vivid sense of their scramble to ready the feast in time. More noticeably, time functions as an important part of the exaggerated language of love employed by Romeo and Juliet; it is the kind of time that can turn the duration between tonight and tomorrow into 20 years in the absence of the beloved. We also get a clear sense of a generational rift, a division between the older characters and their children, a clear symbol of time's passage. And, of course, time becomes the bitter vessel of tragedy, as old Friar Lawrence's legs carry him too slowly to tell Romeo that Juliet is not dead at all, not victim to time's most painful symptom. Though the identification of the pattern is by no means easy, the real challenge is to crystallize all this textual evidence into a sharp, cogent thesis. You could synthesize this pattern of details into the following thesis: In a play where everyone except Romeo and Juliet seem to recognize that time is rushing on, the motif of time becomes an important metaphor for the way in which their model of love is unrealistic and at odds with the logic of the real world. This would make for a good but somewhat difficult essay. However, this thesis is not only inspired by the theme of time but also rooted in the play's greatest theme: love.

1. **Love:** How can the love between Romeo and Juliet be understood or characterized?

Such an essay could go in many directions and arrive at a variety of conclusions (though you should argue for one interpretation of the pair's love over other plausible interpretations). Certainly this is an issue that has excited generations of critics. The question could be crudely put as follows: Are Romeo and Juliet really as in love as they think they are? If you feel they are, then your essay will perhaps highlight the maturity and spirited rebelliousness of the lovers, their heroic standing. If you doubt it, you are most likely steering your essay toward an analysis of the play's own skepticism about the relationship. Consider some important pieces of evidence. First, what of Rosalind? What purpose does she serve, and how does her presence in the play shape your sense of Romeo? Think whether you agree with critics who argue that Rosalind functions primarily to make Romeo seem fickle and immature. Whether you agree or not, you may want to include in your analysis the Chorus from the beginning of act 2, often cited as proof that the play wants to highlight Romeo's flighty and inconstant heart. At this point it may also be worthwhile to ask if the play morally condemns excessive passions and desires; in other words, does the play agree with Friar Lawrence when he councils Romeo to "love moderately" in act 2, scene 5? Look for evidence for or against this idea. Be aware, though, that modern scholars have suggested that the sympathetic perception of Romeo and Juliet might well be a popular 20th-century invention. In the Renaissance, this argument continues, the pair would have been viewed as clearly foolish and reckless. Perhaps, then, the play mocks the impassioned idea that two young lovers can fall so swiftly and completely in love and punishes them accordingly. This is one of those essays where you "invent" the play you have just read; two potential readings offer themselves, and behind them are two radically different plays.

2. **Confusion:** What does the play's obsession with confusion and indeterminacy contribute to the philosophical worldview of the play?

The modern-day theoretical term for what you are doing in this essay is *deconstruction*. Regardless of terminology, though, the core of this essay is in the concept, often and quite deliberately employed in the play, of exploring the relationship between words and the objects they represent. Some possibly helpful theoretical terms here are *signifiers* or *signs* (the words that represent concepts or objects) and "signified" (the concepts or objects represented). Perhaps the most famous moment in which the relationship between signs and the signified is explored can be found in act 2, scene 1. In this scene, Juliet famously asks, "what's in a name?," and continues to point out that a rose by any other name would still smell as sweet. The philosophical crux here is that the connection between language and the objects or concepts it represents is weak: A rose could be called a "vomit," and it would still smell the same. The debate that triggers this deconstructive musing is, of course, Romeo's last name. What exactly does *Montague* signify? As far as the Capulets are concerned, it signifies hate, war, and generations of blood feud. The relationship between *Montague* and *hate* has been naturalized, but it is still nonetheless thoroughly constructed and artificial, as the love between Romeo and Juliet attests. Romeo then imagines that his name could be a scribbled word, one that could be torn up, and to an extent this is precisely what the lovers do by challenging the meaning of *Montague* and *Capulet*. All of this is teasingly enjoyable, but you need to do more here than philosophize; these complexities still need to be organized by the everyday demands of the essay.

First, look for other instances of confusion between signs and signified. For example, think about conversations similar to those we have just considered around the word *banishment* in act 3, scene 2 and act 3, scene 3. What do you make of the strange confusion between Romeo and Tybalt in the Nurse's account of Tybalt's death? Look for other instances of word slippage and wordplay. Next—and this is the hard part—you must formulate a thesis that organizes such observations. Why, exactly, does Shakespeare invest an apparently simple tale with such philosophical problems? There are a number of ways you could go here. Does he mean to show how Romeo and Juliet are right to fall in love as they do and that social conventions such as vendetta and feuding are no more natural than language? Could it be to show, rather, how despite all the free play of language, for all the artifice of *Montague* and *Capulet*, these concepts are real enough to cause the deaths of Romeo, Juliet, and others. Or, perhaps, could all of this philosophical quibbling be intended to show how love itself, a relationship between word and concept that the lovers never think to question, is no less vulnerable than *rose* and *Montague* to the collapse of meaning.

Character

Though inevitably the titular pairing receives the most attention, the play has a fairly deep cast of characters worthy of further study. For example, as the strange and unsettling passage cited in the "Reading to Write" section above suggests, Mercutio is a complicated figure. Like many of the minor characters in the play, he appears to function as a plot device, a catalyst for some kind of action on the part of Romeo or Juliet. However, Shakespeare invests in him much more. Indeed, an essay on Mercutio might focus on an unexpected division within his character. On the one hand, as we have seen, Mercutio is perhaps the play's dominant voice against love, and through his rhetoric love becomes not merely a childish game but a grim and ugly corner of human existence. Yet modern critics talk about the homoerotic or homosocial nature of his devotion to Romeo, suggesting that his opposition to love might simply be a manifestation of his desire not to share Romeo's affections with a woman. With this in mind, a key part of your task will be to assess how male friendships work and the expectations placed on men in the play. For example, you might want to consider how Mercutio, along with Tybalt, is conditioned to continue the feud and, above all, prize the maintenance of honor. Obviously, act 3, scene 1 will be a key scene for understanding not only Mercutio but the psychological and social codes that contribute to masculinity in Verona. Notice the changing pattern of Romeo's behavior in response to Mercutio's unwavering and self-destructive commitments to the ideals of honor and vendetta.

If Mercutio represents one of the most ferociously male figures in the text, the Nurse offers a vivid portrait of female hypersexuality; both characters operate at extremes of the gender spectrum, so to speak. While an essay on Mercutio would ultimately be an assessment of masculinity in *Romeo and Juliet,* an essay on the Nurse might study the relationship between her role as wet nurse or surrogate mother and her intense interest in sexuality. In other words, she offers a picture of femininity that appears to contrast sharply with the idealized figure of Juliet, and indeed, with her ribald talk, the Nurse offers yet another interpretation of the romantic relationship. While Romeo and Juliet talk of eternity, the Nurse equates romance and love exclusively with the sexual act; she is always pragmatic and impoliticly candid in her advice to Juliet. A good crux, indeed, for an essay on the Nurse might be to assess how the

Nurse's vision of coupling differs from Juliet's and, more important, what the implications of these very different tones might be. You might gather examples of the Nurse's interest in Juliet's sexual life, as well as what you can about the Nurse's function in the Capulet household (she is essentially a mother to Juliet, for example, and we hear open talk from her about her years of breastfeeding Juliet as a baby in act 1, scene 3). How does this symbolically situate the Nurse in relation to Juliet, or even Lady Capulet? What do you make of the so-called betrayal by the Nurse when she encourages Juliet to marry Paris in act 3, scene 5? Perhaps the question that hovers over a study of the Nurse might be one of disruption. For example, does she finally undermine the idealized talk and hopes of the young lovers with her resolute and untiring insistence on the tangible and fleshy nature of human bonding?

1. **Juliet:** Does the play encourage us to see Juliet as a strong woman?

   It is a myth that women married at a very young age in the Renaissance (probably a myth perpetuated by *Romeo and Juliet*, in fact). While some very high-level aristocratic marriages could be arranged at a young age for the future—especially international marriages that acted as cornerstones of foreign policy—the majority of women married in their 20s. As critics have pointed out, then, Juliet would certainly have been widely perceived by Shakespeare's audience as too young to marry (see, for example, her own father's declaration of exactly this in act 1, scene 2, lines 8–11). This fact makes Juliet an intentionally controversial creation and thus rich subject matter for writers. There are at least two avenues to follow here. The first is that despite her youth, Juliet matures quickly and can be viewed as a strong woman, intelligent and self-reflexive. If you favor this idea, you might suggest a turning point at which the girl Juliet becomes the woman and catalog examples of strength of character. An alternative path is that Juliet is not to be seen as strong and that the play portrays her as naive or worse (see the above section on love for further points relevant to this approach). An appealing third approach is to identify how a modern audience commonly rejects the play's intended interpretation of Juliet in favor of a postfeminist interpretation that stresses her strength. In short, using the text, show how and why Juliet has been and continues to be reinvented by modern audiences seeking positive female role models in the literature of our past.

2. **Romeo:** In what ways does the text undermine Romeo's character?

As does an essay demonstrating the text's ambiguity (or even something more negative) toward Juliet, this topic requires students to assess how and why Romeo might seem less than heroic. To put it bluntly, however, it is easier to find the flaws in Romeo's character than in Juliet's and to see how the text creates a figure of ambiguous sympathy. You might offer a thesis that posits Romeo as an immature and emasculated character, one who falls short of his society's codes of masculinity, a figure designed to win little enthusiasm from an Elizabethan audience. We have already seen how Romeo begins the play, arguably cast as a vacillating and faithless wooer of women, someone whose loud protestations of love for Rosalind are silenced all too quickly. But the opening scenes do even more to give us pause regarding Romeo. For example, what do you make of his excessive melancholy and highly stylized and rhetorical language of love? If you have read more widely in Shakespeare, you may recall the foppish and lovesick Duke Orsino of *Twelfth Night* or the benign but ridiculous Orlando from *As You Like It.* The first appears to relish and play up the pain of unrequited love, leading readers to feel that he is more in love with himself and with the conventions of love than with any woman. Likewise, Orlando's elaborate, poetic, and unrealistic statements of love for Rosalind are mocked by the play as well as by his beloved, and it is the task of the grounded and pragmatic Rosalind to bring the lyrical Orlando down to earth before they can marry. Romeo can be placed alongside these figures, and he is thus in quite dubious company. These three men speak the language of a ritualized and courtly form of love known as Petrarchism. This highly artificial and dressed-up mode of speaking about love originated in the sonnets of the Italian poet Petrarch and is characterized by a stable set of conventions. Among these are the impossible beauty of the beloved (the woman to whom the poetic expressions of love are aimed), the cruelty of the beloved in toying with or ignoring the speaker's affections, and the paradoxical pleasure found in the pain of unrequited love. With this fashionable tradition in mind, how do you assess Romeo's approach to both Rosalind and Juliet?

Alongside the problems raised by such superficial performance, the text clearly portrays Romeo as a highly feminized character. What do you make of the numerous instances where Romeo is perceived as effeminate by those around him (and by himself in act 3, scene 1, line 109) and reprimanded as such by such disparate characters as Friar Lawrence, Mercutio, and the Nurse? Look carefully at act 3, scene 3, for example, where Romeo can be found throwing a teary tantrum on the floor and is thus paralleled with Juliet. Why is Romeo emasculated in this way? How does this character detail add to the thematic fabric of the play? Can we identify these traits as Romeo's tragic flaw?

3. **Friar Lawrence:** Are we to view the Friar as a sage friend and council to the lovers or a meddling old man whose misjudgment initiates the tragic death of Romeo and Juliet?

This topic could deliver plenty of bang for your buck. This type of essay is difficult to execute yet can provide unusual and original insights. It might be called the "from edge to center" approach, as it involves taking a relatively minor character, episode, or theme and making it front and center in your essay. The advantage of this type of approach is that few other students are likely to write the same essay, so it typically evinces a strong and comprehensive knowledge of the text on the writer's part. However, such essays are often difficult to write because of limited textual material. An essay focusing on Friar Lawrence, though, might well benefit from all the advantages without the risks; while he is indeed a relatively peripheral character, there is a great deal to say about Friar Lawrence and a strong, intractable central dilemma surrounding him. In a nutshell, is Friar Lawrence a figure of wisdom attempting to check the excesses of young love, or is he a man whose decision-making powers are little better (or far worse, precisely because he does not have the excuse of youth) than those of the impetuous Romeo and Juliet?

Whichever way you lean, you will have to deal with the opposing viewpoint in your essay. So, for example, the Friar's first speech is a good example of his wisdom, and Shakespeare carefully crafts the Friar's view of the good and evil in all things to encourage respect and sympathy (2.2.1–30). In a similar vein, look for moments when the Friar seems to guide Romeo with grave responsibility (especially 2.5). On the other hand, assess his two principal decisions: marrying two plainly immature adolescents and the ill-fated poison scheme. Even though his intentions were good in both cases, critics have argued that these blunders were likely to invoke exasperation or even contempt in early audiences (often citing, too, a possible anti-Catholic bias in the Friar's ineptitude). If you do view the Friar negatively, however, you must not only judge him but assess his purpose within the play. Is he simply one more example of hotheadedness in a play that cautions against rashness, or do you see him as more central even than this? For example, might he act as a kind of moral lightening rod that conducts frustration away from the two lovers and into an older generation that fails its young charges?

Form and Genre

From the perspective of genre, *Romeo and Juliet* is a complex work (yet another way in which the play's reputation for simplicity is belied). It is, of course, a tragedy, but there are some important features that complicate and even resist that definition. First, the play does not treat the grand figures demanded of tragedy by Aristotelian decorum. Instead of a Macbeth or a Hamlet, a Lear or a Caesar, the tragedy centers on the love life of two tempestuous teenagers. Today we might argue that tragedy is no less powerful and perhaps even more so if it represents the lives of ordinary people rather than the great. (Certainly this seems to be the opinion of many filmmakers who rework Shakespeare's great tragedies into stories of ordinary people. For example, *Scotland, PA* [2002] adapts *Macbeth* by relocating the action to small-town America in the 1970s and the intrigues of a fast-food restaurant.) In Shakespeare's time, however, portraying the tragedies of ordinary people was somewhat controversial. Sir Philip Sidney, one of the great poets of the age, lamented that plays that mingled kings and clowns together on stage were guilty of mongrelizing the classical conventions of ancient drama. But many of the tragedies being written went even further down this line, overlooking the kings altogether. A genre known as domestic tragedy became popular during Shakespeare's lifetime, and critics sometimes refer to *Romeo and Juliet* as an example of this type. The form is probably best distilled in a remarkable but anonymously composed play called *Arden of Faversham.* The play follows the unfolding tragedy of an ordinary couple (perhaps upper-middle class in modern terminology) torn apart by the wife's desire for another man. Together the lovers conspire to kill the husband, Arden, though their efforts bring about their own deaths too.

However, the matter is not even as simple as labeling *Romeo and Juliet* as a certain type of tragedy. The play was written in the mid-1590s, a period in which Shakespeare appears to have been deep in thought about the limits and possibilities of genre. At roughly the same time he wrote *Romeo and Juliet,* Shakespeare composed two comedies that flirt with tragedy and mix ample darkness into the bright and festive tones of mirth. The first is *A Midsummer Night's Dream,* which in many ways seems to be almost a companion play to *Romeo and Juliet* (ideas for writing an essay on this pairing of plays are discussed in the "Compare and Contrast" section below). The second play was *The Merchant of Venice,* a comedy so stained with tragedy that its formulaic comic movements seem consciously artificial and hollow (see the "Form and Genre" section of this book's *Merchant of Venice* chapter for more on this, especially if you think you might write a compare and contrast essay about *Merchant* and *Romeo and Juliet*). At first glance, *Romeo and Juliet* might not appear to belong with these two experimental works, but on closer inspection the play has some puzzling generic qualities.

Comedy: What elements of comedy can be found in *Romeo and Juliet*?

Students writing this paper should certainly stand out from the crowd at essay-marking time. It is another example of a paper topic with a built-in surprise factor. Just as an essay on Friar Lawrence (see "Character" section above) impresses because it makes central a relatively marginal figure, this essay draws its surprise value, its uniqueness from reading against the grain, or going in the opposite direction to that which a casual reader might travel. Even a seasoned reader of student writing—someone who no doubt is aware of the generic complexities of the play—will typically be impressed by a writer's desire to challenge the obvious.

Such an essay might start by looking at the subject matter of the play. As we have seen, the theme of young lovers was not the usual subject of classical tragedy, but it is the mainstay of comedy. Indeed, everything about *Romeo and Juliet* up to a certain point in the play resembles a comedy. The story of two young lovers kept apart by a harsh law or difficult parents is the very essence of new comedy, the type of romantic comedy that dominated the 1590s. Look for other comic elements in the early scenes, especially comic characters. Look for comic tones, too, such as ample lusty talk. Then look for a turning point in the text, a moment where the forces of tragedy engulf the text. Critics cite act 3, scene 1 as just such a moment. What happens in this scene that has the power to turn the play around, so to speak? Think, too, of the frequent blurring of marriage and weddings (the principal glue of new comedy's resolutions) with funerals (definitive symbols of the destructive capacity of tragedy). Finally, think about ways in which the ending, despite the pitiful deaths of Romeo and Juliet, offers a faint vision of the comic feast, the coming together of characters, and the community that rounds off a typical Renaissance comedy.

Compare and Contrast Essays

A number of parallels discussed above might usefully be turned into compare and contrast essays. In particular, much of the material in the "Character" section could be skillfully manipulated into a compare and contrast project. For example, a writer might assess whether the play portrays one of the lovers in a more admirable light than the other (Juliet is the more likely candidate here), or whether it portrays them as alike (with all of the emasculating gender implications that has for Romeo). Moreover, you could look at each or both of the characters and compare them at the start of the play and at the close of the work. In what ways have they changed, if at all? Much of the material in Romeo's character section above invites a comparison with other men in the play, particularly Tybalt or Mercutio. The Nurse and the Friar seem made for a comparison also. And as the "Genre and Form" section above suggested, *Romeo and Juliet* is so distinct from Shakespeare's other great tragedies that you could contrast it with any of those plays, from *Hamlet* to *Othello*. A particular focal point for such essays could be the tragic vision of the respective texts. What do you learn about or see of the world in each tragedy? For example, *Macbeth* offers perhaps the bleakest tragic vision of all, summed up in Macbeth's terrifying description of life as a tale told by an idiot that signifies nothing. You might think, too, about the role of the supernatural in *Macbeth,* the way in which the universe arguably conspires against Macbeth to ensure his fall. What is the tragic vision of *Romeo and Juliet*? Why does tragedy befall the young lovers?

> **Comparing *Romeo and Juliet* to *A Midsummer Night's Dream:*** What is the relationship between these two plays? How do they explore the same material? Do their conclusions differ at all?
>
> Comparing and contrasting these two popular plays is an exciting task, one that seems to generate its own almost unstoppable energy. You might begin by assessing the thematic continuity between the two plays. What do they say about love? Think about the role of Rosalind alongside the shifting affections of the four Athenian lovers and the mercurial powers of Puck's love potion. Study the darker elements of

the forest world in *MND* that appear mirrored by the lighter elements of *Romeo and Juliet*'s tragic tale. But above all, close read and study carefully the play performed by Bottom and his troupe at Theseus and Hippolyta's wedding. The play, for all intents and purposes, is *Romeo and Juliet* by another name. What does this say about love? About comedy and tragedy? These plays are not two sides of the same coin exactly, one comic and one tragic. The relationship is more like two sides of a dollar bill: Hold it up to the light of examination and you can see both at the same time.

Bibliography and Online Resources for *Romeo and Juliet*

Brook, Nicholas. *Shakespeare's Early Tragedies.* London: Methuen, 1968.

Callaghan, Dympna. *The Weyward Sisters: Shakespeare and Feminist Politics.* Oxford: Blackwell, 1994.

Khan, Coppelia. "Coming of Age in Verona." *Modern Language Studies* 8.1 (Spring 1978). 5–22.

Knowles, Ronald. "Carnival and Death in *Romeo and Juliet*: A Bakhtinian Reading." *Shakespeare Survey* 49 (1996). 69–85.

Porter, Joseph. *Shakespeare's Mercutio: His History and Drama.* Chapel Hill: North Carolina, 1988.

"William Shakespeare's Romeo + Juliet." <http://www.romeoandjuliet.com>.

A MIDSUMMER NIGHT'S DREAM

READING TO WRITE

THE CHALLENGE of writing about *A Midsummer Night's Dream* lies partly in ordering and structuring the play's purposeful disorder. Readers and watchers of *MND* have the pleasure of losing themselves in its maze of magic and misunderstanding, but the writer must move beyond this delightful confusion toward clarity and a solid argument. This is easier than it may first appear. On first reading, the play can be as confusing as it is fun, and you might feel at times as lost in the play as the lovers are lost in the forest. But *MND* houses its motifs of confusion, blurring, and distortion in a tightly arranged and scrupulously written play, one filled with parallel movements and consistent thematic patterns, both extremely useful to the essay writer. Indeed, even the most frustrating confusion of all for the first-time reader, that of the indistinguishable lovers and the twisting movement of their affections, is actually just another part of the play's well-structured conversation on the theme of love. The interchangeable lovers and their oscillating passions become symbols for that most fickle, illogical, and bewildering of emotions. So for all its playfulness, at the core of *MND* are serious and complex ideas about human relations, romantic and otherwise. Bringing these ideas to the surface, examining and engaging them, will also be at the core of many good essays about the play.

The various interpretations of love, its characteristics and contradictions, are discussed more thoroughly in the "themes" Section below. This close reading section provides an extended consideration of love by reflecting on one of the different types of love displayed in *MND*. The following passage comes from act 2, scene 1. As Titania and Oberon argue over the guardianship of the changeling boy, Titania bases her claim on a deep emotional connection to the boy's mother.

> His mother was a vot'ress of my order,
> And in the spiced Indian air by night
> Full often hath she gossiped by my side,
> And sat with me on Neptune's yellow sands,
> Marking th' embarked traders on the flood,
> When we have laughed to see the sails conceive
> And grow big-bellied with the wanton wind,
> Which she with pretty and with swimming gait
> Following, her womb then rich with my young squire,
> Would imitate, and sail upon the land
> To fetch me trifles, and return again
> As from a voyage, rich with merchandise.
> But she, being mortal, of that boy did die;
> And for her sake do I rear up her boy;
> And for her sake I will not part with him. (2.1.122–37)

Perhaps the first things to emerge from a close reading of this passage are the twin notes of the exotic and the erotic. The "spiced Indian air by night," the yellow sands of Neptune, and the sight of trading ships hauling foreign cargos across the ocean all contribute to a lush, exotic, and fanciful pattern of imagery present in much of the play. Closely related are the powerfully erotic connotations of the passage, again striking a tone found throughout *MND*. While some critics suggest that both Oberon and Titania display an eroticized attraction to the boy himself, Titania's memory of her "vot'ress" seems unambiguously physical, fleshy, and sexual. The fairy queen's recollection of the two women carefree and sportive on the beach, her devotee's "womb then rich with my young squire," exemplifies two important trends in the play worth the writer's attention. First, of course, this relationship becomes merely one strand in the play's tangled web of sensuous, even sexual relations. Tracing these interwoven strands can reveal to the writer how dizzying, unpredictable, and even unreliable love is intended to be in this play. (Arguably, though, Titania's devotion to her disciple is the most convincing example of unwavering, honest love in *MND*. Certainly the final two lines of the passage speak to this with simple but strong eloquence.) Second, the passage provides one of several moments when the play reflects on the bonds between the female characters. Indeed, the writer could certainly develop this motif into a full-blown essay, studying closely the way in which bonds between women in *MND* are interrupted or even destroyed by men. Think, for example, about the implications of Theseus stealing his bride from a tribe of Amazon warriors, as well as the more obvious problem of Helena and Hermia's ruined friendship.

Finally, the passage succinctly illustrates the oft-ignored darkness lapping at the play's bright shores. The idyllic, sensual mood of the passage is suddenly, sharply undercut by the intrusion of the line "But she, being mortal, of that boy did die." Indeed, there is a great deal that is cynical, even ominous in *MND*. Reading against the grain, against the surface detail of the play, can provide much material for the writer. The darker shades of the play are discussed in much more detail below, but for now you would do well to recognize—and help your reader recognize—that for all its whimsy and pleasure, *A Midsummer Night's Dream* is a play rich with complicated, sometimes even unhappy ideas.

TOPICS AND STRATEGIES

Every essay requires a focus; you cannot write about everything in the play at once. The section on how to write an essay showed you a number of ways to turn a focus into a thesis, observations into arguments. However, the starting point is nearly always finding an initial focus and making first observations. What follows is a discussion of *A Midsummer Night's Dream* geared toward helping you make the most of the budding ideas you will have as you read the play. By no means should you feel limited to these topics, however.

Themes

MND is a favorite with both stage and screen audiences. Productions tend to be enormous fun, making great use of sumptuous fairy bowers and Bottom's enormous comic potential. This tradition is well captured in Michael Hoffman's lavish film version of 1999, starring Michelle Pfeiffer and Kevin Klein. Some students may be familiar with this adaptation, but delightful as the film may be, it might not offer the essay writer much inspiration. Perhaps closer to the mark for our purposes is Peter Brook's now-famous 1970 stage production. The production stripped the play's setting of its traditional extravagance, instead presenting the action on a sparsely furnished, bare white stage. What Brook and his audiences discovered was that without the luxuriant exterior, the play's provocative and engaging themes became more apparent and ready for dissection. These themes are both substantial and accessible enough to create many quality writing opportunities.

Sample Topics

1. **Love:** Does the play actually challenge the conventional, fairy-tale model of love it appears to champion? If so, what does *A Midsummer Night's Dream* offer in place of that romanticized model?

   Such an essay might begin by attempting a definition of love in the play. Unquestionably, there are many types of love in *MND* and, indeed, a number of claims about love that contradict other claims in the work. Nonetheless, you might come up with a clear statement that most closely encapsulates what the play is saying about love. For example, you might want to argue that in *MND* love is presented as an illogical, somewhat fickle force. You could decide to make your claim even stronger, suggesting that the play undermines love altogether by repeatedly showing how quickly love can turn to cruelty (or, indeed, in the case of Theseus and Hippolyta, is born of cruelty). The enigmatic moment where Hermia dreams she is attacked by a snake (2.2) provides a puzzle for you to interpret, a nightmarish vision of cruelty in the increasingly dark dreamworld of the forest. At the very least, the four lovers that readers struggle to tell apart are also caught up in the problems of their own identities. It is asked again and again, for example, how love is kindled, how one person might encounter two people of equal merit—it often appears as though the lovers are only too ready to acknowledge the homogeneity of their identities—and love one but scorn the other. Look for moments, such as act 2, scene 2, where the lovers develop such questions into fully fledged discussion about the role (or lack of it) of reason in love. Perhaps, too, include in your essay the most exaggerated example of unreasonable love, that of Titania for Bottom. Also, you might want to employ in your essay the many moments where love is forced, whether on the part of the lover or the beloved. Magic here becomes a symbol for our lack of control, and love merely a spell placed unknowingly upon a lover. If, however, you disagree with this more cynical reading of the play, you will certainly be able to make a case that a more positive understanding of love is reached by the end of the play. Of course, you would have to acknowledge—and ideally challenge—some of the above ideas, but it is entirely reasonable to interpret all of this in a more positive light. The play might be arguing that love is not a mindless and random force at all, but rather an active one that seeks to rectify and counter the blindness of the lovers. For example, Demetrius did love Helena before the play's action begins (1.2.242), so the confusions of the forest might be said to correct romantic mistakes, binding every Jack to his rightful Jill. Alternatively, Demetrius is to be pitied when the play's curtain falls as he marries a woman he no longer really loves. It is entirely possible that as you write you will get lost in the woods yourself, and like the lovers you will have a change of heart as to what love means and who loves whom in *MND*.

2. **Gender:** What kind of relationship exists between the sexes in *MND*? How might the balance of power be described within those relationships? In what ways are these power dynamics repeated throughout the play?

An essay of this kind need look no further than the opening scene for strong material. Indeed, the control of women by dominant male characters seems to be stressed so robustly in act 1, scene 1 that the reader can be left in little doubt that this will emerge as a major theme in the play. Pay close attention to the details of Theseus's forceful wooing of Hippolyta, for example, as well as the cruel, controlling demands of Egeus over his daughter Hermia. Pay close attention to how Theseus responds to the complaints of Egeus, developing a sense of how the laws of Athens enforce a patriarchy. Think, too, about the significance of making Theseus's wife a captured Amazon, a domesticated member of a wild tribe of women warriors known for their independence from (and aggression toward) men.

If you make a case for the existence of a patriarchy in the play, one that is quite severe, you will want to establish that this is in evidence not only in the court of Theseus but also in the woods outside Athens. This is vital because in the magical, somewhat chaotic world of the forest it seems that the harsh laws of Athens should disappear or even be reversed. Look for ways in which patriarchy is maintained in the woods no less strictly and troublingly than it is in Athens. Most obviously, perhaps, assess the treatment of Titania at the hands of Oberon. Less apparent but no less worrisome is the way in which female friendship and communities in the play are consistently disrupted by men. We have seen something of this already in the passage quoted in the "Reading to Write" section, but another passage rich in the pathos of ruptured female friendships can be found in Helena's complaint in act 3, scene 3, lines 193–220. Given all of this, you might also suggest a connection between the themes of love and gender, perhaps exploring the idea that the failures of love in *MND* are frequently caused by the abusive control of women by men.

Character

Writing about individual characters in *MND* is a slightly more difficult prospect than it is in other Shakespeare plays. The four young lovers are not well-rounded, multidimensional characters (though this fact itself can be fertile ground for the writer). Moreover, the pairings of Oberon/ Titania and Theseus/Hippolyta are so thoroughly interconnected and parallel that individual treatments of the characters might ultimately be less fruitful than a careful study of one or both couples.

1. **Bottom:** What function does Bottom serve in the intellectual
   fabric of *MND*? Does the play merely mock him, or is its treatment of him more generous?

As much or more than any other of Shakespeare's comic creations, Bottom can still elicit deep belly laughs from audiences
today. His two most memorable scenes, the ass's head sequence
with Titania and his bravado performance at court, are the
humorous highlights of the play—and, if done well, are among
the funniest in Shakespeare. But does the audience laugh at or
with him? You can take either side here, but it may be easier to
explain how Bottom is victimized by the aristocrats of the play.
Indeed, students interested in the theme of oppression more
broadly might choose to connect the mistreatment of Bottom
by his social superiors (primarily Theseus and King Oberon)
with the abuse of the female characters by the same male, aristocratic characters. And there is certainly more to Bottom than
meets the eye. After all, you should always pause and take stock
whenever Shakespeare represents any kind of theatricality in
one of his plays. Bottom is, in this sense at least, the representative of Shakespeare, a writer and actor seeking to please his
audience and gain stature through success. Louis Montrose
has written memorably about social fantasies sublimated deep
inside *MND,* and much of his hypothesis rests on Bottom as a
hapless social climber who is loved by a queen and rewarded by
the state. For all his social aspirations, however, Bottom also
has profound artistic ambitions. Consider whether Shakespeare
is an established member of the stage elite making fun of a theatrical novice or a self-reflexive artist having a laugh at his own
expense. Either way, you might also use Bottom as a gateway
into an essay on art in *MND.* Theseus, in his famous speech at
the beginning of act 5, scene 1 suggests a link between the artist
and the lover (and the lunatic) that makes the symbolic connections between Bottom and the four young lovers deep and
wide. An essay evaluating this link between art and the reality
of the play—with all its love juices and spells—might certainly
discover a unique way into the text. Look for characters who

control the action of the drama, like playwrights. Puck, Peter Quince and his troupe, Oberon, and Theseus all exert some influence over the action of a play, controlling other characters and directing the action toward a conclusion.

2. **Oberon and Titania:** Is the resolution between Oberon and Titania powerful enough to undo the couple's earlier divisions?

Such an essay could begin with the sources of discord between the pair early in the play, move on to Oberon's strategies to defeat Titania, and finally address the quality of their restoration at the play's close. This essay will inevitably overlap with material in the "Gender" section above and broad gender concerns could form the backdrop for an essay that deals in detail with Oberon and Titania specifically. A close reading of act 2, scene 1, for example, offers you an opportunity to work carefully with the complicated causes of the rift. We have already seen that at the center of the argument is the disputed Indian boy, but evaluating the volatile mix of anger, jealousy, attraction, desire, and aggression on display is no simple matter. Pay special attention to the darker components of what can be presented on stage as a lighthearted spat. For example, what do you make of the consequences of this conflagration for the mortals of Athens (2.1.81–118)? Consider, too, that while Titania's infatuation with Bottom may provoke laughter from audiences, the mirth is at the expense of both these unlikely lovers; Oberon's significant cruelty (not to mention the joy he seems to take in that cruelty in 2.2 and 3.2) is a source of serious concern for many careful readers. Finally, then, try to evaluate the means by which the dispute is ended. Do you feel that the resolution is nothing more than the total defeat and humiliation of Titania?

Form and Genre

Much of what we have discussed so far challenges the notion that *A Midsummer Night's Dream* is a purely joyous, happy comedy. We have found philosophical and social struggles casting a long shadow over the beginning, middle, and end of the play. As in other Shakespearean comedies, the thematic tensions of the work have significant implications for the form and genre of the play. However, in this regard *MND* is unlike many other plays in Shakespeare's canon. Unlike his later comedies, as well as his earlier *Merchant of Venice*, *MND* takes its comic pretensions seriously. In these other plays, the darker notes sound unmistakably and very uncomfortably—the tension at the end of *Merchant* or *All's Well That Ends Well*, for example, is palpable and prevents comic satisfaction being taken in the obviously hollow "happy ending." In many of Shakespeare's earlier comedies, on the other hand, such as *The Comedy of Errors*, *Two Gentlemen of Verona*, or *The Taming of the Shrew*, threats to the comic resolution are either faint or the product of anachronistic thinking. *MND* seems to occupy a middle ground between these two approaches to Shakespearean comedy. Its dark matter is not so obvious that it can be found without looking, but at the same time the search for shadows in this play is not difficult. Therefore, you might relish the challenge of appraising this interesting species of genre.

1. **Comedy:** What structural, thematic, and tonal elements undermine the comic movement of *A Midsummer Night's Dream*?

Not surprisingly, much of the material we have already discussed could find a home in this essay. In particular, it would be difficult to imagine a paper dealing with the play's darker tones that did not mention some of the gender issues discussed above (though the risk here is always that 21st-century readers are seeing problems that Elizabethan audiences would not have). Moreover, the play's representation of love as an illogical bewitchment hardly leads us to embrace the comic conclusion wholeheartedly; the coming together of the lovers is only obtained by the shiftiest of methods. But these are only a few of the points this essay could offer to support its claim. You might do well, for example, to linger on oddly, inappropriately chilling moments in the midst of festivity. Think, for example, about Hermia's frightening dream or Puck's peculiar evocation of lions, corpses, and screeching owls in the final scene. And while Puck's memorable quip that every Jack may have his Jill seems to be the unambiguous embodiment of the comic spirit, all of this is placed alongside another play, the rude mechanical's *Pyramus and Thisbe,* that depicts both its Jack and Jill, much like Romeo and Juliet, suffering the tragic fates of separation and death.

2. **Festivity:** What is the relationship between *A Midsummer Night's Dream* and the festive or holiday world evoked in its title?

It has long been believed that in the ancient world dramatic plays grew out of ritual activities. The genres of drama, in fact, originated in different types of ritual activity in ancient Greek society: Tragedy was born of somber ceremonies, while comedy emerged from celebratory festivities. This is all too simple, but the fundamental connection between theatrical and ritual practice is certain. With this in mind, a number of critics during the 20th century and beyond studied the connection between Shakespeare's works and the festive world in which he lived. The 16th and 17th centuries enjoyed and participated in holiday festivals and celebration with a frequency and fervor entirely lost to us. Perhaps the most popular text in this scholarly tradition is C. L. Barber's *Shakespeare's Festive Comedy. A Midsummer Night's Dream* has a particularly strong link with festivity because it is an occasional drama—written for a wedding, it seems—but also because its title and its action evoke the summer celebrations of the rites of May, so familiar to all of Shakespeare's audience. These celebrations (which could be held at any point through the summer) were characterized, as many holiday and festive occasions were, by the suspension of normal order. The flight of young people into the woods for a night of revels was a notorious component of these celebrations. Predictably enough, then, during Shakespeare's lifetime conservative forces mounted a sustained attack on such festivals, and the result was a slow but palpable decline in festive celebrations of holidays. Because *MND* reveals Shakespeare's clear interest in the subject of festival, an essay that explores the role of festival in the play and the conditions of ritual activity when Shakespeare wrote it would certainly be rewarding. The topic has consequences for the play's form and genre because of the connection between comedy and the types of ritual evoked by the play. But there is also an important element of historical research too, as you would need to consider what the rites of May were like in Shakespeare's time. It seems clear that such research might be compared to the events and setting of the play (François Laroque's book on Elizabethan festivity, listed in the "Bibliography" section, is the standard work to consult here). Finally, and perhaps with more difficulty, you might explore the connection between the Renaissance playwright and the world of festivity in which he lived. Both were under attack by similar critics for similar reasons, and it is not unreasonable to suggest that Shakespeare and his contemporary dramatists would have felt a keen kinship with festivity and a sharp sadness for its steady decline. You might reflect on what Shakespeare is using *MND* to say about the holiday world.

Compare and Contrast Essays

Again, *A Midsummer Night's Dream* is structured symmetrically enough to present many compare and contrast opportunities. The "Character" section above discusses possible approaches to writing about Titania and Oberon, but it is a natural extension of that idea to compare this pair with Theseus and Hippolyta, the fairy royals' mirror image in the human court. Equally, the play is topped and tailed by scenes from the court of Athens, inviting comparison of these with the forest world of the middle scenes. As in many of Shakespeare's comedies, the heroes flee a strict and harsh society to a place of freedom known as the Green World. Within the Green World, characters have the social and emotional freedom to discover themselves and to solve problems and tensions rooted in their former court lives. Typically, the comic movement drives toward a reconciliation of characters in the reformed court setting. So the obvious essay here would appear to be a contrast between the conservatism of the court and the liberality of the Green World setting. However, it can often be interesting, having established the basic expectations of the Green World/court divide, to explore the more unexpected similarities between the two spaces. In the case of *MND*, this is a particularly promising approach. Begin by brainstorming as many similarities and connections as you can, ranging from the parallelisms of Oberon/Titania and Theseus/Hippolyta to the questionable quick fix in the Green World that unsatisfactorily reconciles the lover's problems before they return to court.

> **Contrasting the play-within-a-play to *A Midsummer Night's Dream:*** In what way does the play staged by Bottom and his fellow actors help you better understand *MND*?

Whenever Shakespeare stages a play-within-a-play, it is always worth asking why. This popular device, much like having a movie-within-a-movie today, was a clever, winking in-joke for regular theatergoers to enjoy. But it was also a philosophical conceit, one that asked audiences to consider the laws of representation and, ultimately, of the divide (or lack of it) between reality and artifice. Furthermore, the playwright employing such a technique is often asking the audience to make connections between the larger and smaller plays. An essay that explores these links would have a wonderful structure and relatively contained focal point (a close reading of the play-within-a-play), but it would still require a strong knowledge of the larger play as you "make the connections" between the two texts. First, you may want to approach *Pyramus and Thisbe,* the play the amateurs stage for the nuptial celebrations of Theseus and Hipployta in act 5, scene 5, much as you would approach Shakespeare's plays: by identifying themes and characters. You will find that both the play-within-a-play and *MND* take love as their theme. The trick is to see the two plays in conversation with each other.

Your thesis might well be based on a key similarity or difference or, even better, what effect *Pyramus and Thisbe* has on *A Midsummer Night's Dream.* Think, for example, about the issue of genre. Bottom and his friends stage a tragedy at the moment of comic resolution; a bloody tragedy at a wedding banquet seems a jarring moment of incongruity. Does this undermine the comic conclusion of *MND,* even though everyone—not least Theseus—is trying to turn *Pyramus and Thisbe* into a comedy? As some critics have noted, the workers' drama resembles *Romeo and Juliet,* a play almost exactly contemporaneous with *MND.* Why combine a tragic vision of love with a comic vision of love? What might be the intended moral or meaning behind this juxtaposition? Think about what separates the ill-fated Pyramus and Thisbe from the ostensibly "happy ever after" pairings of Athenian lovers. Pay close attention to their fates, of course, but perhaps more to how they arrived there, what did or did not help them through their obstacles. Again, having contemplated this, reflect on whether this difference undercuts the comic resolution of *MND* yet further. And, finally, if you are interested in the theatricality of staging a play within a play, you might further speculate on another staging matter. Many critics believe that *A Midsummer Night's Dream* was written to be staged at an English aristocratic wedding, though there is no record of whose wedding it was. What, then, do you make of a wedding party watching a wedding party watching a play about two lovers who die tragically?

Bibliography and Online Resources for
A Midsummer Night's Dream

Barber, C. L. *Shakespeare's Festive Comedy: A Study of Dramatic Form and Its Relation to Social Custom.* Princeton, N.J.: Princeton UP, 1959.

Laroque, François. *Shakespeare's Festive World: Elizabethan Seasonal Entertainment and the Professional Stage.* Tr. Janet Lloyd. Cambridge: Cambridge, 1991.

Legatt, Alexander. *Midsummer Night's Dream. Shakespeare's Comedy of Love.* London: Methuen, 1974. 89–115.

"*Midsummer Night's Dream:* Directors' concepts." Updated 24 Mar. 2005. Retrieved 14 Mar. 2007. <http://www.lib.washington.edu/subject/Drama/msndconcepts.html>.

Montrose, Louis. *The Purpose of Playing.* Chicago: U of Chicago P, 1996.

Nelson Garner, Shirley. "*A Midsummer Night's Dream:* 'Jack Shall Have Jill; / Nought Shall Go Ill.'" *A Midsummer Night's Dream: Critical Essays.* Ed. Dorothea Kehler. New York: Routledge, 1998. 127–45.

Taylor, Michael. "The Darker Purpose of *A Midsummer Night's Dream.*" *Studies in English Literature 1500–1900* 9 (1969): 259–73.

THE MERCHANT
OF VENICE

READING TO WRITE

THOUGH *THE Merchant of Venice* is dominated by the figure of Shylock, and the tragedy of the Holocaust and continuing discord in the Middle East make the play's discussion of Judaism especially resonant to modern audiences, *Merchant* also offers many other exciting prospects for the writer. The play has a deep cast of characters whose actions and motives are intriguing. It functions as a snapshot of changing economic realities in early modern Europe. Moreover, it has significant formal consequences for Shakespeare's future career, especially his comedies.

Merchant also has one of the dramatist's finest set pieces. You could write an essay entirely about the trial scene of act 4, scene 1, analyzing the virtuoso display of dramatic action and characterization on display, as Shylock pushes ahead with his claim on Antonio's flesh, while the entire judicial and political authority of Venice presses back against him. Although Shylock trusts in nothing more than the letter of the law, you could construct an essay by observing the ways in which the accumulated machinery of the state works consciously and deliberately against him. Particularly worth noting and incorporating into your essay are any shifts in sympathy you sense as the scene progresses: While you might begin the scene resenting Shylock for his unrelenting malice, by the end of the scene a modern audience might find it difficult to take any pleasure in the thwarting of Shylock and the punishment meted out to him. The scene concentrates the play's action, skillfully condensing so many of the work's core themes and concerns. As a result, a close reading of it will allow you to synthesize many broader elements of the play. What might such an essay consider? Here is perhaps the most memorable and often-quoted passage from the scene. Portia, disguised as a learned doctor called to adjudicate on the dispute between Shylock and Antonio, lectures Shylock on the need to be compassionate and release Antonio from the bond.

> The quality of mercy is not strained.
> It droppeth as the gentle rain from heaven
> Upon the place beneath. It is twice blest:
> It blesseth him that gives, and him that takes.
> . . . It is an attribute to God himself,
> And earthly power doth then show likest to God's
> When mercy seasons justice. Therefore, Jew,
> Though justice be thy plea, consider this:
> That in the course of justice none of us
> Should see salvation. We do pray for mercy,
> And that same prayer doth teach us all to render
> The deeds of mercy. I have spoke thus much
> To mitigate the justice of thy plea,
> Which if thou follow, this strict court of Venice
> Must needs give sentence 'gainst the merchant there.
> (4.1.179–200)

You might begin by observing an obvious point about the passage as a whole: It is profoundly eloquent. Without question, the speaker, Portia, is a remarkably intelligent and assertive woman. As these are probably Portia's most recognizable lines of the play, a close reading of them could be a starting point for character analysis. Besides displaying rhetorical skill, consider what these words say about their speaker. Traditionally, Portia was viewed as one of Shakespeare's most admirable heroines, but her currency dipped in the late 20th century. Why? Compare this speech to Portia's treatment of Shylock moments later. Also, what does it say about the socially constructed limits of Portia's authority that she must speak these words disguised as a young man?

The opening lines of the speech praise the value of mercy, implicitly contrasting this value with Shylock's remorseless determination to execute Antonio. But as Portia gives her argument a religious turn, she sets up another contrast that goes straight to the heart of the play's action. Comparing Christian to Jew in Shakespeare's Venice might make for a very strong essay indeed. Here Portia proposes a Christian model of mercy, acknowledging that no person can be saved without the ultimate mercy of God, thus urging compassion among humans in their worldly affairs. If this sentiment is supposed to represent the Christian species of forgiveness, what is implied (or assumed) about the Jewish model? Commentators have traditionally viewed this as a conflict between two interpretations of law: the Christian one focusing on the spirit of the law, with the Jewish one bound to the letter of the law. You might look for evidence of this dualism throughout the play. However, it might be wise to ask if this really is the full extent of what Shakespeare has in mind. After all, such a theological statement would be little more than an eloquent voicing of stereotypes. To look for more than this in the play, you should contextualize Portia's speech, locating it within the scene and within the play as a whole. After all, the most important thing to seek out in this play might be irony. Look for ways in which the Christian characters of the play say one thing and do another; they are so often guilty of the same practices for which they hate and condemn Shylock. Portia's speech here is followed almost immediately by an extremely harsh and merciless punishment of Shylock, one that both denies him his bond and strips him of his identity and dignity. From this perspective, Portia's famous speech on mercy is a fake, a cruel trick no less disguised than its speaker.

Finally, this speech raises an important point about Shakespeare's authorial presence and intention. It is, of course, impossible for us to know what the dramatist wanted to say, what he thought and felt. Nonetheless, for centuries writers have spent ink and paper attempting to do just that. *The Merchant of Venice* provides you with a truly magnificent opportunity to participate in this time-honored tradition. To what extent are the lines quoted above—and others like them throughout the play—ironic, or to what degree do we as modern readers and writers insert that irony because we wish to find it? In other words, what balance should we strike between what we hope is the spirit and what we can see is the letter of the play?

TOPICS AND STRATEGIES

Every essay requires a focus; you cannot write about everything in the play at once. The section on how to write an essay shows you a number of ways to turn a focus into a thesis, observations into arguments. However, the starting point is nearly always finding an initial focus and making first observations. What follows is a discussion of *The Merchant of Venice* geared toward helping you make the most of the budding ideas you will have as you read the play. By no means should you feel limited to these topics, however.

Themes

When approaching some of the themes in this play, first look to see if Shakespeare appears to make the theme you are considering a point of contrast between Shylock and the Christians of Venice. Next, you might strongly consider asking whether any simple dichotomy (Christian mercy versus Jewish cruelty, for example) is undermined by the actions of Bassanio, Portia, and the others.

Other themes, of course, will not necessarily invite that exact approach. However, there is far more to this play than meets the eye. For example, think about the theme of love in *The Merchant of Venice*. On the surface, this play would appear to celebrate love and make use of it to shape the comic movement. But look closely at each of the couplings in this play, and you may find that the relationships in each case have question marks lingering over them. You might also extend your essay to cover different forms of love, such as the relationship between Shylock and Jessica (a potential source of sympathy for Shylock) or Antonio's love for and devotion to his friend Bassanio. Are any idealized forms of love present in this play? Or, once you have scraped at the surface with a pointed reading of the text, can you see this as a text governed by cynicism and irony rather than romance and love? Indeed, it might even be possible to turn the answer to this question into a thesis statement. An essay assessing the role of irony as a theme might provide you with a focused way of discussing *Merchant* as a whole while still allowing wide discussion of the play's characters and themes.

Sample Topics

1. **Money and wealth:** Does money mean different things to the Venetian Christians than it does to Shylock? How much of the play's action is motivated by money?

For many critics, money is what makes the world of Shakespeare's Venice go round. It seems to motivate many of the choices made by characters, from Bassanio's quest for Portia to Lancelot Gobo's desire for a better livery. Look for ways in which money and wealth structure other characters and their actions. Assess, too, whether there are differences in how money is valued and treated between Belmont and Venice. What does money mean to Shylock? Look for parts of the text that hint at other factors motivating him, even while money continues to play a central role in his character. What does the play seem to say about usury, the act of charging interest on a loan? Compare Shylock's zeal for money to the Christians' financial dealings. Also, you might try to connect the theme of wealth and money to another reoccurring motif, that of "hazarding," or gambling. These two closely related themes overlap in parts of the text, especially the casket scenes in which Portia tests her suitors. Love and business perhaps become connected by the notion of gambling and risking all, just as Antonio does first with his ships and then with his dangerous bond to Shylock on Bassanio's behalf.

2. **Fidelity:** This is a play that seems obsessed with bonds of different kinds, as well as the consequences of not honoring those bonds. What does the play say about faithfulness? How might this theme influence your evaluations of other thematic areas of the play?

Such an essay might establish a connection between the action surrounding Shylock's bond and the subplot of Portia's ring in act 5. While the final act can seem at first glance unnecessary, a strong case could be made for its integral place in the play. Look for interconnecting issues raised by the two trials, that of Shylock in court and Bassanio in Belmont. In this essay, you might let the unexpected connection between the two plot lines suffice as your thesis, allowing room in your essay to show and explain similarities and meaningful points of difference. For example, the marriage bond represented by Portia's ring is obviously one that should be kept, while Shylock's bond is one that the play wants to see broken. Perhaps you might expand your essay to include other signs and symbols of faithfulness, from Jessica's sale of Shylock's wedding ring to the statements of religious devotion that reappear throughout the text; you might certainly extend the discussion to the infidelity of the Venetian Christians to their much-professed and -flaunted moral creed. Finally, try to cement your discussion together by asserting what faithfulness or fidelity finally means in the play. Are there any faithful characters? What are they faithful to? Does the play value fidelity?

Character

All of the main characters in this play deserve and can support their own essays. While not drawn with the psychological complexity of Macbeth or Hamlet, for example, the characters in *The Merchant of Venice* are nonetheless fascinating, not least because of the gap that exists between so many of their statements and actions. Take Bassanio, for example. An essay on this character might turn on the question of his motives: Why does he pursue Portia? Is he a gold-digging playboy or a romantic hero in the traditional vein? Begin by outlining what you learn of Bassanio's past in the opening acts. Assess his relationship with Antonio and closely examine his reasons for seeking Portia (look, for example, at his ordering of Portia's qualities in 1.2.161–76). Look for irony, too, in Bassanio's victory in the casket scene. What is the relationship between the moral of the lead casket and what is known of Bassanio's history and character?

An equally rich essay could be written about Shylock's daughter, Jessica. Like Bassanio, she is a character we seem asked to admire, but we might not be able to. Such an essay would begin by establishing the relationship between father and daughter, noting Jessica's various complaints but also carefully observing Shylock's treatment of and feeling for his daughter. Then ask yourself what motivates Jessica to elope with Lorenzo, sifting through her escape scene to assess again the role of money and wealth. You might proceed by looking at how Jessica's flight influences your sympathies for Shylock as he discovers her loss (and the loss of his stolen money).

Character study, then, even of the minor characters, seems to be a productive way to approach *Merchant*. Many students, however, will choose to focus on one of the three main characters.

Sample Topics

1. **Shylock:** How do you view Shylock's character? What are his redeeming features, and how might you assess his function and meaning in Shakespeare's play?

There is so much to say about Shylock that you could very well write a book about him. Indeed, John Gross has done just that with his very readable and well-researched *Shylock: A Legend and Its Legacy.* The first challenge of dealing with Shylock, then, is to focus your essay on a specific aspect of him. One thesis might concentrate on his redeeming characteristics, showing how a man who is clearly the antagonist of the play is also a victim. Once you have established this sympathetic position, the next move might be to show how Shakespeare slots Shylock into his complex system of meaning. Both of these steps might involve pinpointing Shylock's position within the culture and society of Venice.

First, what picture of Shylock emerges in the opening scenes? Look for any evidence of how he is treated and viewed by Venetians, including Antonio. Equally, assess how Shylock views the citizens of Venice. Try to piece together Shylock's philosophy of money and wealth, looking in particular at any justifications he offers for his usury. Consider, too, his domestic life with Jessica. Look very closely here for details that might endear you to Shylock, especially in his response to Jessica's flight. Why does he pursue his revenge against Antonio? How do you feel about him once he has been defeated in the court, stripped of his money and religion?

This final question urges you to reflect on Shylock's function within the play's production of meaning. Try to think why Shakespeare creates such an ambiguous and rounded figure where other lesser artists might have settled for a stock Jew to vilify. This approach puts Shylock at the heart of the play's moral compass, again encouraging you to question the differences between Jew and Christian in Venice.

2. **Antonio:** Why is Antonio marginalized by the play, left out of the comic resolution? What is the cause of his unexplained melancholy voiced in the play's opening line?

Antonio is a somewhat obscure figure who has received considerable critical attention in recent years. Much of that interest has centered on his relationship with Bassanio, as critics have commented on the homosocial nature of his love for the young man. This affection and the despondency caused by Bassanio's quest for a profitable marriage are suggested as the roots of Antonio's famous sadness. If you wished to pursue this aspect of Antonio's character, you might marshal other works of Shakespeare's canon to your side. Shakespeare treats the importance of male friendship in his early play *The Two Gentlemen of Verona*, but this idea is more readily available and interestingly rendered in his sonnets and the (coincidently named) figure of Antonio in *Twelfth Night*. Critics Bruce R. Smith and Valerie Traub have led the way in considering these issues in Renaissance drama, and their work would be of help if you wish to bolster your writing with reference to outside sources.

More traditional approaches to Antonio focus on his financial dealings and what some critics refer to as his martyrdom. Compare Antonio's handling of money to Shylock's. Equally, however, you might find that Antonio can be contrasted to many of the play's characters in other ways, not least by way of his faithfulness to Bassanio. If you can arrive at a distinction or difference that separates Antonio from the other characters, see if you can use this to explain why Shakespeare leaves Antonio noticeably out in the cold as the comic feast of resolution closes the play.

3. **Portia:** While Portia is an admirably strong and intelligent woman, how does she employ these virtues in controversial ways?

Such an essay should unquestionably consider points already discussed in the "Reading to Write" section of this chapter. More than this, however, you might explore the function of Belmont, Portia's home, to which she is symbolically conjoined. Shakespeare's comedies typically feature a "Green World," a setting in which characters escape the rules and logic of the court in order to find themselves and resolve problems that are rooted back in the real world of the city. While Belmont is the Green World of this play, assess whether it serves the typical function of such a setting. How similar or different is Belmont from Venice? Again, the role of money and wealth may be your starting point here.

Finally, look critically at the ring plot that occupies the fifth act. While Portia's trick with the ring and barely veiled threats of infidelity are bawdily funny, how do they further threaten the already compromised comic ending and connect back to themes of trial and fidelity set out by the play earlier?

History and Context

As discussed in the "Character" section, a study of Antonio might take your writing down a distinctly historical route. To understand the implications of a homosocial love between Antonio and Bassanio, you must bring to the table more than our 21st-century notions of sexuality. An essay treating this aspect of Antonio or this theme in Shakespeare generally must attempt to understand the historical context. Although historians disagree on how the Renaissance perceived intimate, even sexual relationships between men, it is certain they did understand them differently than we do today. Many argue that the category "homosexual" did not even exist in the Renaissance, and it appears that it was common for some men to speak of a male friendship as idealized, better than a relationship with a woman precisely because it lacked the complicated and potentially ruinous sexual dimension. This theme was of enormous interest to Shakespeare and appears frequently throughout his work, so it is clear that a reading of Antonio might benefit from historical research.

If a character study of Antonio could be redirected by complementary historical research, the theme of money and wealth is unquestionably another essay topic that could likewise benefit. Historians talk of the early modern period as witnessing the birth of what we call capitalism. The way wealth and status were generated changed during Shakespeare's lifetime. Medieval economic practices such as the feudal system receded and were gradually replaced by early free markets. New attitudes to private property and consumerism radically changed the meaning of wealth, and some critics have suggested that in *The Merchant of Venice* Shakespeare breathes a sigh of disappointment and disapproval with the emerging ethos of capitalism. Find ways in which Shakespeare's play seems to speak out against a culture preoccupied with mercantilism and profit, forging from these a reading of Shakespeare's play as satire or social commentary. Lisa Jardine's excellent book on consumption and business in Renaissance Europe, *Worldly Goods: A New History of the Renaissance,* is an excellent place to begin research in this area.

Sample Topic

Judaism in Renaissance Europe: Does Shakespeare use *The Merchant of Venice* to condemn anti-Semitism, or at least to challenge some of its harsher commonplaces?

Such an essay would attempt to see Shakespeare's text as social commentary, a document in which the dramatist contemplates the figure of the Jew in his time. Obviously, the important thing here is to recognize that you are no longer treating Shylock as a self-contained character in a self-contained play but as a creation pieced together out of cultural tradition and historic moment. Asking what Shakespeare does with that mix, how he processes the ideas, beliefs, and images of his age, is the key to this essay. James Shapiro's *Shakespeare and the Jews,* a seminal work in this particular field of Shakespeare studies, would make an excellent point of departure for such research.

It will be helpful if you are aware of the literary tradition forming the backdrop to Shakespeare's play. In early modern Europe and earlier, anti-Semitism was rooted in biblical accounts of the death of Christ. It was this perceived blame for Christ's death that spawned popular resentment of Jews and a virile tradition of folk belief and literature peopled by countless variations of the murderous Jew. This culture of hatred can be found even in the works of Chaucer, whose "Prioress' Tale" tells the story of a young Christian boy killed by envious Jews. As is discussed in the "Compare and Contrast" section below, this tradition was alive and well in Shakespeare's day, most visibly in Christopher Marlowe's play *The Jew of Malta* (a work certainly at the front of Shakespeare's mind as he wrote *Merchant*).

Though Shakespeare was surrounded by stock representations of Jews, he probably never encountered an actual flesh-and-blood Jewish person. The number of Jews in Shakespeare's England is difficult to estimate but probably numbered only in the low hundreds. Jews had been expelled from English soil in 1290, and the remaining small number was made up mostly of immigrants from southern Europe who did not openly practice their faith. It might seem, then, as though Judaism was hardly a topical matter for Shakespeare to pick up, but Marlowe's play and the arrest and execution of Roderigo Lopez gave the subject contemporary resonance. Lopez was a Jewish doctor accused of plotting to kill Queen Elizabeth, and his traitor's death—hung, drawn, and quartered—in 1594 would have stoked anti-Jewish sentiment enough to make Shakespeare's play very much of the moment.

You might wish to investigate this cultural and historic context further, assessing Shakespeare's response to it. An essay could usefully be structured by a provocatively simple question: Is this an anti-Semitic play? You should answer this as you wish, but a safe path to steer might be the predictably qualified answer "yes and no." As many commentators have noted, it would have been impossible for Shakespeare to discard the intellectual baggage of his time entirely; look for ways in which Shylock retains some of the elements of the stock Jew, and examine how Shakespeare's play employs them to bring paying customers into his theater. But equally seek ways in which Shakespeare, even if he does not reject the anti-Semitic tradition of his culture, at least reconsiders and revises it. Your task as writer here is to catalog your evidence on either side but then assess the balance that Shakespeare strikes.

Form and Structure

The Merchant of Venice is a comedy, but an essay exploring the problems of this definition might be extremely rewarding. Most critics do not label *Merchant* as one of the "problem comedies," a small group of later comedies that explicitly and innovatively challenge the meaning of comic drama. In many ways, however, *The Merchant of Venice* anticipates the challenges to comic form offered by later plays such as *All's Well That Ends Well* and *Measure for Measure.* When Shakespeare challenges comedy, the approach he seems to favor most is to have all the required sweet ingredients of comedy present yet still produce a bitter flavor. One of Shakespeare's problem comedies may well end in marriage, as a comedy should, and avoid death as it must, yet its resolutions appear intentionally incomplete, its air tainted by the breath of tragedy.

Sample Topic

The Limits of comedy in *The Merchant of Venice:* Despite the comic closure of the play, does *Merchant* function successfully as a comedy? What elements of the play question or hinder its comic movement, even after the union of lovers in marriage?

Such an essay might start by looking at the end of the play, the moment in which a comedy should offer resolution and hope. Regardless of the appearance of unity, look for sources of discord and dissent in the final acts. The most obvious character to start with might be Shylock, but note also how Antonio, despite the return of his ships, seems excluded from the festivities at the close of the play. How are these two figures marginalized? Consider the impact of the ring plot on the comic movement as well. While it is funny, its consequences are far from comic in the formal sense of that word. Think about how Portia's threats of infidelity undercut the reconciling comic power of marriage. The thing to consider as you write this essay is effect. How does this play, regardless of its comic promise, finally manage to spread a little of Antonio's enigmatic sadness to its audience?

Compare and Contrast Essays

As discussed above, one of the most prominent approaches to this play, the weighing of Shylock against the Venetian Christians, inherently takes the form of compare and contrast. Be alert to the way Shakespeare draws parallels where audiences would have only expected distinctions. An essay comparing Belmont to Venice might also encourage you to find unexpected similarities. Look for ways in which the magical, carefree Belmont is as focused on money and superficiality as Venice, the city that embodied luxurious excess and wealth for the early moderns. Approaching comparison and contrast from a character perspective, you might look for yet more unanticipated common ground between Shylock and Antonio. While the play hinges on Shylock's antipathy for Antonio, what do they have in common? Look for ways in which they are both cogs in the wheel of Venetian capitalism, and perhaps explain how both characters seem to lead marginal lives despite their wealth. Yet another approach might be to look elsewhere in Shakespeare's canon for related works. *The Tempest* and *Othello* are major plays that also treat "otherness," exploring the confrontation between white Europeans and people of different religions or races. Such an essay might turn on a comparison of Shylock with Othello or Caliban, arguing as you see fit for similarities or differences in Shakespeare's level of sympathy for these characters. However, perhaps the most attractive compare and contrast opportunity would be to link *The Merchant of Venice* to a text by another great playwright of the English Renaissance.

Sample Topics

1. **Comparing Shylock to Christopher Marlowe's Barabas (*The Jew of Malta*):** While both Shakespeare and Marlowe base plays

on a Jewish antagonist, how much do Shylock and Barabas have in common? Despite their differences, how might Shakespeare and Marlowe finally use these central characters from *The Merchant of Venice* and *The Jew of Malta* to create related effects and social commentary?

Marlowe's play came first, so a good approach might be to assess how Shakespeare builds on *The Jew of Malta* to create his play and his representation of Shylock. You might first consider the differences between Barabas and Shylock, some of which should be quite clear. Marlowe seems to rely far more on the stereotypical figure of the villainous Jew, much like the one found in Chaucer's "Prioress' Tale" and countless vulgar ballads and stories (but perhaps he is doing so ironically). Find examples of this tradition in Marlowe's portrait, looking at moments like the slave market scene, in which Barabas boasts of his astonishingly prolific evil. Contrast this to Shylock's altogether subtler villainy. However, you may find a few ways in which Barabas is less stereotypical. For example, critics have observed that while Shylock earns his money through usury, Barabas has earned his great wealth primarily through long-distance business ventures like Antonio's. Other distinctions can be found, for example, in the relationships Barabas and Shylock have with their daughters, Abigail and Jessica.

Having found similarities or differences, you might turn to a consideration of what effect each dramatist seeks through his central Jewish figure. Look especially at how both Marlowe and Shakespeare set up divisions between Jewish and Christian communities that essentially become engines for satire and comparison. Although vastly different, what might connect, say, Ferneze in Marlowe's play with Bassanio in Shakespeare's?

2. **Contrasting Shakespeare's play to Michael Radford's film adaptation of *The Merchant of Venice* (2004):** What strategies does Radford use in adapting Shakespeare's play? What are

the most significant interpretive moves made by the film, and what are the effects of these choices?

With its star cast and lavish production, Radford's film adaptation of the play will surely feature regularly in classroom discussions of *Merchant* for a good many years to come. While it is faithful to the play to a great extent, it does offer some interpretations beyond the text, primarily through visual additions to the original text. One of the great opportunities of cinematic adaptations are the shots that, without adding a word to the dialogue in Shakespeare's play, can radically alter the play. Pay close attention to such moves made by Radford. For a start, what is the effect of staging Antonio's spitting on Shylock, only mentioned in the play? Why does Radford show a number of early scenes, entirely absent from Shakespeare's play, of Christian victimization of Jews in Venice? Such an essay might reflect, too, on the visibly eroticized relationship between Antonio and Bassanio. Most important, however, think about the effect and meaning of the final montage. Consider the effect of shots showing Shylock and Antonio alone as the play closes, but especially think about what might be Radford's most daring visual invention: a closing shot of Jessica and the ring she was rumored to have sold for a monkey. What implications does this proof she did not sell the ring have for Jessica's character? Try to characterize early in your essay, as your thesis, the governing logic or pattern of Radford's interpretive choices in *The Merchant of Venice.*

Bibliography and Online Resources for *The Merchant of Venice*

Gross, John. *Shylock: A Legend and Its Legacy.* New York: Touchstone, 1992.

Edelman, Charles. "Which Is the Jew That Shakespeare Knew? Shylock on the Elizabethan Stage." *Shakespeare Survey: An Annual Survey of Shakespeare Studies and Production* 52 (1999). 99–106.

Jardine, Lisa. *Worldly Goods: A New History of the Renaissance.* New York: W. W. Norton, 1998.

"The Merchant of Venice. Shakespeare and the Players." Retrieved 14 Mar. 2007.
  <http://shakespeare.emory.edu/playdisplay.cfm?playid=18>.

Orgel, Stephen. "Shylock's Tribe." *Shakespeare and the Mediterranean.* Ed. Tom
  Clayton et al. Newark, DE: Delaware, 2004. 38–53.

Sinfield, Alan. "How to Read The Merchant of Venice without Being Heterosex-
  ist." *Shakespeare, Feminism and Gender.* Ed. Kate Chedgzoy. Basingstoke,
  England: Palgrave, 2001. 115–34.

Shapiro, James. *Shakespeare and the Jews.* New York: Columbia UP, 1996.

"William Shakespeare's *The Merchant of Venice:* Official Teacher's Guide."
  Retrieved 14 Mar. 2007. <http://www.sonypictures.com/classics/merchan-
  tofvenice/SONY=VEMI=04/TeachersGuide. pdf>.

1 HENRY IV

READING TO WRITE

SHAKESPEARE'S HISTORY plays present several specific challenges to the reader. First, they tend to have relatively large casts of characters who are embroiled in often difficult-to-follow plots and networks of allegiance. Second, by definition, they are not really self-contained plays like a *Hamlet* or *Othello;* rather, Shakespeare's histories are groups of plays that come together to dramatize quite lengthy historical narratives. The action staged in *1 Henry IV,* for example, follows on from the events Shakespeare represents in *Richard II* and precedes the dramas of *2 Henry IV* and *Henry V.* These are quite burdensome problems in Shakespeare's earliest history cycle, a string of plays dealing with the life of Henry VI (the son of Prince Hal, or Henry V as he became; even more confusingly, the plays about Hal's son were written by Shakespeare before the plays that treat Hal himself). In *1 Henry IV,* however, these obstacles are more negotiable. First, while an encounter with the play is certainly illuminated by a solid knowledge of *Richard II,* there is merely one detail from *Richard* that readers must know in order to understand and work with *1 Henry IV:* that Henry IV deposed Richard II and took the crown of England from him. It is important to keep this detail vividly in mind, even if it happened in a play you have not read. Moreover, the problem of convoluted plotting (associated with the histories by beginning readers and many seasoned scholars alike) is far less severe in *1 Henry IV* than in many other Renaissance history plays; indeed, at its heart, the play is driven not by historical narrative at all but by the creation of memorable and complex characters. The result of all this is that while *1 Henry*

IV may intimidate you at first, your confidence will grow as your focus shifts from the sweeping and historical to the immediate and human.

One of the most frequently cited passages from the play demonstrates exactly this kind of personal rather than historic content. Here is Hal's famous soliloquy from act 1, scene 2:

> I know you all, and will awhile uphold
> The unyoked humour of your idleness:
> Yet herein will I imitate the sun,
> Who doth permit the base contagious clouds
> To smother up his beauty from the world,
> That, when he please again to be himself,
> Being wanted, he may be more wonder'd at,
> By breaking through the foul and ugly mists
> Of vapours that did seem to strangle him.
> If all the year were playing holidays,
> To sport would be as tedious as to work;
> But when they seldom come, they wish'd for come,
> And nothing pleaseth but rare accidents.
> So, when this loose behavior I throw off
> And pay the debt I never promised,
> By how much better than my word I am,
> By so much shall I falsify men's hopes;
> And like bright metal on a sullen ground,
> My reformation, glittering o'er my fault,
> Shall show more goodly and attract more eyes
> Than that which hath no foil to set it off.
> I'll so offend, to make offence a skill;
> Redeeming time when men think least I will. (1.2.173–95)

The passage is jarring and unexpected, at odds with everything up to this point in the scene. Thus far, the second scene, set in Hal's private apartment, has depicted the prince at ease, lightly carousing with his friends, poking fun at the incorrigible Falstaff. The mood is carefree, but the spirit of waywardness is clearly established by the introduction of the plot to rob travelers of their money. The overall effect is of misguided youth and boyish misadventures, harmless enough though anything but admirable. Readers, like Falstaff and Poins, may think they know Hal already, know that he is far from what he should be, far from an ideal heir to the throne. This perception of Hal as a lightweight and a waster, however, is shattered with just the first two lines of this soliloquy, and a sudden darkness eclipses the preceding jollity.

Soliloquies, like this one, are passages spoken by a character alone on stage. They afford the audience powerful insight into the character's psyche and motivations because they are private reflections, manifestations of whatever truth inhabits the character. It is common, then, for a character's soliloquy to contrast sharply with what he says and does elsewhere, but Shakespeare uses the device here to suddenly imbue a simplistic sketch of a character with depth and dimension, with the power to create itself.

This is a play of many such dualities, and you could develop an analysis of one or more of these divisions into the foundation of a paper. The division of Hal so strikingly rendered by this passage, for example, is mirrored by the division between court and tavern, the apparently divergent spheres of politics and mirth. But, as outlined in this passage, it is precisely the reconciliation of these two worlds that Hal seeks, the "reformation" of a life of "idleness," "sport," and "holiday" into a "glittering" ascendancy. Look for the many ways in which this is a play about containing rupture, of holding things together that appear to be irreconcilable or at a breaking point.

Related to the theme of division but distinct nonetheless is that of counterfeiting, of pretending or acting. Note how the passage foregrounds the idea of imitation. When Hal tells his absent friends, "I know you all, and will awhile uphold / The unyoked humour of your idleness," he initiates a sequence of role-playings that will continue through to the final moments of the battle at Shrewsbury. Notice, too, that another closely related theme emerges here, also of great potential for an essay. Hal is talking about inventing himself, but he is talking about political strategy more than he is about personal identity; the "reformation" Hal speaks of is a political triumph rather than a personal salvation. As are all of Shakespeare's history plays, *1 Henry IV* is rich in political philosophy, so essays that attempt to discern an ideology behind the play are likely to be successful. Look for ways in which the play attempts to understand the way power works, pulling aside the curtains to reveal the mechanisms that animate authority.

TOPICS AND STRATEGIES

Every essay requires a focus; you cannot write about everything in the play at once. The section on how to write an essay shows you a number of ways to turn a focus into a thesis, observations into arguments. However, the starting point is nearly always finding an initial focus and making first observations. What follows is a discussion of *1 Henry IV* geared toward helping you make the most of the budding ideas you will have as you read the play. By no means should you feel limited to these topics, however.

Themes

Just as he does with his literary source texts, Shakespeare mines and alters historical sources to create philosophical explorations of theme. Shakespeare is no historian and is not interested in accurately recounting what happened in the past. Instead, his goals lie in the present and the general—using history to make important points about his own time and, more broadly, about human experience.

Certainly one of the most prominent themes considered in the history plays is politics. As is discussed in the "Reading to Write" section above, *1 Henry IV* is concerned with exposing the calculation that operates in the shadows of power. While traditional views of royal power stressed the natural and the inevitable, the Divine Right of rulers ordained by God, Shakespeare's play is part of an early modern body of work based on the premise of realpolitik, the study of politics as it really is. Indebted to the early 16th-century Italian writer Niccolò Machiavelli (see the chapter on *Julius Caesar* for a more detailed discussion of Machiavelli's ideas), Shakespeare considers the way power is gained and maintained through the use of manipulation, deception, and ingenuity. An essay on this topic would seek out examples of such tactics. As well as Hal's gambit to lower public expectations and then vault to glory, look at the moments where his father instructs and advises him on such things as developing a public persona, stage-managing the monarchy. Ask, too, what Henry's usurpation of the crown in *Richard II*, the event that hangs heavily over *1 Henry IV*, says about the nature of royal power. Think also about the function of Mortimer, a relatively minor character, but one who has a claim to the throne stronger than Henry's. You might also make something of the contrast between Hotspur's chivalric but outmoded ideals and the "new" methods for political success employed by Henry and Hal. Hotspur may be an unsustainable character, destined to lay cold in his own hot blood, but does the play mourn this passing of an old political ideal or simply accept the changing of the political order? In addition, an essay on the political philosophy of this play would probably overlap with and use material from character studies of Hal and Hotspur, as well as thematic essays on artifice and honor.

Do make sure, however, that if you approach the broad topic of politics, you do so from a specific starting point, such as tracing the influence of Machiavelli on *1 Henry IV* (Machiavelli's basic principles are easy to grasp, so do not be put off from trying this rewarding angle) or exploring the events of *1 Henry IV* as the inevitable fallout from Henry's act of seizing the crown.

1. **Artifice:** Why are there so many examples of role-playing or pretending in *1 Henry IV*?

   Such an essay presents a fine topic but also a common writing trap. Reading the play, a student might be excited and intrigued as a pattern of role-playing emerges. After all, spotting patterns in a work of literature is an excellent way to read with writing in mind. Many good students at this point might think, Aha! I have spotted a number of instances of pretending or counterfeiting in the play, too many to be accidental, and will therefore make this the topic of my paper. As they then set about the task of writing, the essay quickly turns into a laundry list of episodes from the play that highlight different types of role-playing. This is only half the job, however. In fact, it is perhaps a little less than half, because the most difficult question is still to be asked: So what? The essay has pointed out that role-playing appears many times in *1 Henry IV*, but the best essays will also tell the reader why there is so much role-playing. In other words, the essay as it stands offers only observation; to soar, the essay needs both observation and significance. What is the significance or meaning of role-playing in this work? At this point, the essay grinds to a sharp halt for the best of students; coming up with the significance to accompany an observation will take time.

What might a viable significance look like? Ask questions of your observation, brainstorm around it. Here is one option and how you might arrive at it: What is role-playing? It is a type of acting. What philosophical implications surround acting? For one, there is the issue of reality versus artifice, doubts about what is real and what is not. At this point you might set up another line of thought about the broadest concerns of the work, such as politics. If this is a play about kingship, what happens when you talk about acting and politics together? Politics is implicated in the unreality of acting, perhaps. You are getting close to a thesis now. By tying the two themes of acting and politics together, you have arrived at the possibility that all this role-playing might be used to suggest how politics itself, or the nature of kingly power to be precise, is in some ways illusory, in some ways an act. With a little more thought and fine tuning, you will be ready to formulate a thesis, something like the following: In *1 Henry IV* the many examples of role-playing become a commentary on royal power, urging the audience to consider monarchy as a contrived and constructed institution rather than the pinnacle of a natural social order.

Once the essay is rooted in this idea, the body of the paper can more or less present and interpret the numerous examples of role-playing seen in the play. The idea is strong enough to form a glue to bind it all together, but do refer back to the thesis throughout the essay, reminding the reader of what your analysis of role-playing is achieving.

Some examples of role-playing most germane to this political application might be Hal's famous soliloquy, Henry's battlefield tactic of having many men dressed as the king in act 5, scene 3, and Falstaff's counterfeited death in act 5, scene 4.

2. **Honor:** How many models of honor are presented in the play? Does the play favor one version of honor over others?

As Shakespeare does with many subjects in his drama, he approaches honor in *1 Henry IV* by offering different pictures or versions of it side by side. Look for these different models of honor and identify the characteristics of each. The writer might start with Hotspur, a character who seems to belong in an age of knights and chivalry rather than a time of clandestine political intrigue. Ask what honor means to Hotspur and what he fights for. In particular, pay close attention to his sense of what exactly a king should be and how the king should accommodate and in a sense share power with his nobles.

Another model of honor, one that sharply contrasts with Hotspur's, is in the Machiavellian plotting of Hal and Henry. The subterfuge of this pair, their use of disguise and deceit, is in direct opposition to Hotspur's exaggerated openness and honesty. Look for examples of Hotspur's inability to conceal or contain his opinions and desires, and perhaps set these alongside the measured and staged actions of the king and his heir.

Yet another version of honor, one that has more in common with Hal than Hotspur but that ultimately lampoons both men perhaps, is Falstaff's. Compare Falstaff's speech on honor (5.1.127–39) with his character and anarchic function in the play, especially his performance on the battlefield.

When you are ready to arrive at a sense of what the play might be saying about honor, the choices are numerous and entirely your own. Do you feel that the play mocks Hotspur or lauds him? Your answer to this question will allow you to make logical deductions about the model of honor Hotspur represents. Notice that it is Hal and Falstaff who flourish at the close of the play, but are they meant to be admired or not? Pay special attention to Falstaff's triumph, something that appears morally undeserved perhaps.

Character

This is a play about four men that is disguised as a drama about English history. Much of what is interesting within the play results from the multiple lines that join the four points of Henry, Hal, Falstaff, and Hotspur.

Predictably, then, there are a number of good combinations for character-based comparative essays, which will be addressed in the "Compare and Contrast" section below. For individual character studies, the four central characters offer plenty of scope, especially Hal and Falstaff. Ironically, given that the play carries his name, Henry is perhaps the least prominent of these four points (and in the sequel, *2 Henry IV,* Henry is even less of a presence, doing little more than dying at the end to allow Hal to complete his journey from tavern to throne). A character study focusing on Henry might explore the anguish that haunts the king. A complex mix of emotions in Henry, from guilt to fear, could be explored in an essay that mixes psychological analysis with a study of the play's political preoccupations. Try to understand the paradox of kingship as Henry sees it, a prize he sought but wears almost as if it were a curse.

1. **Hal:** Is Hal's transformation complete by the close of the play?

> It is tempting to ask whether we should like Hal or not, but the question seems to be the wrong one to ask. Hal's complexity reaches beyond simple labels like good or bad; his subterfuge is no more "bad" than Hotspur's exaggerated chivalry is "good." Though we are prone to see deception as inherently bad, the key principle of Machiavellian philosophy is that princes and rulers operate within a different ethical code, one where the ends justify the means. Perhaps the best path to take is one that seeks to understand Hal's transformation rather than judge it. What exactly is he trying to become? The soliloquy that opened this chapter is a good place to start, but it is just a start. Consider his desire for a connection with all types of men, as outlined in act 2, scene 5, lines 4–29. It might be useful, too, to read closely the telling role-play between Hal and Falstaff (2.5.340–440). Especially, what do you make of Hal's response of "I do; I will," to the notion of rejecting Falstaff? Ask how fully the king and his son are reconciled in act 3, scene 2, and examine Hal's apparently comprehensive turnaround at the battle of Shrewsbury. Some critics have suggested that Hal's compliance with Falstaff's lies is puzzling, suggesting that his transformation might be incomplete and ambiguous.

Do you see this as a minor concession to an old friend or a symbolic failure by Hal to turn his back on the temptations of youth and festivity?

2. **Falstaff:** Falstaff is often talked about as Shakespeare's greatest comic creation; but why, exactly? What distinguishes Falstaff from Shakespeare's other clowns?

Such an essay should probably be founded on Falstaff's multidimensionality. Look for as many different "sides" to Falstaff as you can. Know that Shakespeare scholars have long linked Falstaff to several traditions, all of which help explain his character but fall short of saying everything. First, Falstaff appears in part to be an example of the *miles gloriosus* or braggart soldier figure, a familiar presence in ancient drama. The braggart soldier is a cowardly creature who nonetheless boasts of his (usually nonexistent) military achievements. Next, he clearly resembles the vice tradition in the medieval morality play. The vice was a one-dimensional figure who symbolized a particular sin or temptation, such as greed, lust, envy, and so on. What sin does Falstaff represent exactly, or is he more complex than that? Finally, Falstaff invokes the role of Lord of Misrule, a carnival figure associated with certain early modern festivities and celebrations. Part of the carnival ethos was the inversion of existing order, and the Lord of Misrule was a fool or peasant temporarily promoted to a position of make-believe authority. What authority does Falstaff have or believe he has in *1 Henry IV*? Think about how each of these traditions informs the character of Falstaff. Think also about the prominence of Falstaff compared with other comic creations or clowns in Shakespeare's drama. Why does Shakespeare make Falstaff so large a presence, literally and figuratively? Interpret Falstaff's importance in the various triangulations offered by the play, in particular, the way he functions as an alternative father figure to Hal. You might also sketch the ways in which Falstaff appears to be a creature outside of humanity (this way of thinking dovetails nicely with views of him as a vice figure or as a festive presence). For example, Hal's statement that Falstaff has no need of the time of day depicts Falstaff as a figure so independent, so subversive, that he functions outside of time. However you approach an essay on Falstaff, it is important to recognize that for all his humorous value, there is a disturbing, lawless, even chilling side to him. For example, think carefully about the troubling elements in Falstaff's account of the men he leads into battle (4.2).

3. **Hotspur:** What function does Hotspur's excess serve in the moral order of the play?

An essay focusing on Hotspur's character and function would employ much of the material in the section on honor above. Here, of course, the essay should pay particular attention to more of Hotspur's scenes, such as his confrontational encounter with Owen Glyndwr (3.1) and his tender but mistrustful scenes with Kate (especially 2.4). Hotspur's opinions on other characters will be of great help in establishing his own character too. For example, what do you learn about Hotspur's political ideals from his labeling of Henry as the "king of smiles"? If Falstaff is a symbol of excessive pleasure and ease, it is quite clear why Hal must shun Falstaff's example. However, how can there be an excess of honor, and why must Hal steer away from Hotspur's example as much as Falstaff's? Interpret the symbolic configuration staged in act 5, scene 4, as Hal stands between the corpses of Hotspur and Falstaff, but also try to account for the trickier issue of why Hotspur must die but Falstaff can be raised.

Form and Genre

What makes a play a history play rather than a tragedy or comedy set in the past? This is a very difficult question to answer, and it is potential material for a fine essay. In *Macbeth*, the story is historical and comes from the same chronicle source from which Shakespeare took his English history plays. But *Macbeth* has always been understood as a tragedy rather than a history because it sets out an unmistakably tragic view of the universe. History as a whole, moreover, is neither comic nor tragic but a continuum that contains comic and tragic episodes in no particular order or pattern. Thinking of a person's life can be somewhat helpful here. Overall, most people's lives cannot be termed tragic or comic in particular; rather, their lives are sequences of events, some happy and some sad. Such is history. Indeed, history is even more neutral because it has no imaginable end, whereas the human life moves toward inevitable death in something that resembles a tragic movement. Depending on which moment a playwright chooses to dramatize, at which moment he picks up the action and at which he brings down the curtain, a history play could be a comedy or a tragedy. But there is one more complication. Despite the dramatist's stopping of time at the end of the fifth act, for the real historical figures represented on stage, time did not stop at all. Not for them was the comic resolution a lasting one, perhaps. As mentioned in the "Reading to Write" section above, that is very much the case with Shakespeare's story of Hal's transformation into the victorious and legendary Henry V. Despite his glorious victory over the French as staged in *Henry V*, Henry inevitably died and was succeeded by a son whose monarchy was a failure and whose reign was exceedingly troubled. This historical knowledge, then, cannot but loom troublingly over the celebrations of *Henry V*; history shows that the best of times eventually give way to the worst, and that, in turn, those terrible times are shaken off as a lucky generation reemerges back into the sun.

1. **History and comedy:** Can *1 Henry IV* broadly be called a comedy?

   Perhaps a good way to approach such an essay is through the lens of moderation. It might be an effective strategy to argue that while the shape of the play is broadly comic, there are some important ambiguities and uncertainties that need to be addressed. For the play to be seen as a wholly comic, self-contained play, you would need to assert that Hal's redemption is achieved and that the forces of good vanquish the forces of evil. Do you agree with one or both of these statements? Neither? One way to undermine the stability of the comic movement would be to illuminate some similarities between the two factions, or at least to suggest that one side has no particular moral advantage over the other. In terms of Hal's progress toward redemption, you could argue that it is only imperfectly achieved or that the whole notion of a redemption story is flawed in the first place, a fabrication of Hal's Machiavellianism.

Compare and Contrast Essays

The construction of *1 Henry IV* allows for a number of important character-based compare and contrast essays. In some ways Hal is at the center of the play's creation, and the other characters form symbolic magnets that compete to pull Hal into their hold. One possible essay to emerge from this formulation is a study of Henry and Falstaff as competing father figures for Hal. The key to this essay might be to acknowledge that it is not enough to label Henry as a good father and Falstaff as a bad father (in fact, to say that this play is not a story of choosing the good father and rejecting the bad father might make for an excellent thesis statement). Rather, what does each offer Hal, and what does Hal ultimately take from each? Also, you should avoid saying that Hal rejects Falstaff in favor of Henry. While Hal certainly will reject Falstaff in the sequel to this play, it is far from clear that he does so here. It is also not entirely clear that Hal unconditionally embraces his father, either, despite the son's rhetoric. Another essay from this mold is a comparative study of Falstaff and Hotspur (discussed in the "Character" section above). It might also be fruitful to compare Hal at the start of the play and at the end; in other words, track carefully his much-discussed reformation in order to highlight key moments in his progression and to characterize specifically the nature of the transformation, using the milestones you identify as evidence to support your characterization.

1. **Contrasting the world of the tavern and the world of the court:** What does Shakespeare's use of diverse geographical spaces, from the lowly tavern to the royal court, contribute to the thematic concerns of the play?

   Such an essay might draw the reader's attention to the full range of geographical spaces and places that appear in the play, even if it focuses primarily on the contrast between the Cheapside Inn and the royal palace. The play ranges far and wide, from London to Wales to Coventry to Shrewsbury, among other places. More important, Shakespeare guides his readers to places high and low, sharply contrasting places of ordinary, everyday life with the immediate environs of the most influential and powerful. First, think about the breadth of the geography involved. Consider how the decision to show so many locations around the British Isles complements or becomes part of the conversation about politics and government. How does representing so much of the nation make Henry's task seem more real and more difficult, perhaps? Connected with this issue of space, but also somewhat separate, is the social diversity of the spaces staged. Most memorably there is the Cheapside Inn, but another inn is represented in act 2, scene 1 as well as a highway in Gad's Hill and a road on the way to Coventry in act 4, scene 2. What do you notice about the way Shakespeare portrays the inns in particular? For example, what do you make of the attention to detail, the rich depiction of ordinary folk and ordinary ways? This is certainly wrapped up with the issues emerging from the breadth of geographical space, but you could also see in this social diversity something of Hal's attempts to reach out and appeal to all of his future subjects. In essence, you might reflect on how space becomes a powerful symbol for both political division and unity in *1 Henry IV.*

2. **Comparing *1 Henry IV* to *2 Henry IV:*** As the sequel seems to be unnecessary from a narrative point of view, what other intentions might Shakespeare have had for the second play?

The second play adds almost nothing to the story of Hal's progress toward becoming Henry V, and the essential elements it does contain (Hal's final rejection of Falstaff and Henry IV's death) could have been tagged onto the beginning of *Henry V* or left undramatized. Instead of thinking in narrative terms, then, look for other components of the play that might have motivated Shakespeare to compose this underrated sequel. In particular, study the differences in tone and mood between the two plays. What new themes emerge in the second play? Time is an especially visible concern, and you might think about what this means in a history play. Pay close attention to the melancholy qualities of the play, its intense interest in aging and declining. Evaluate the changes in Falstaff's character too. While he is far more central to the latter play, think about the newly acquired tragic streak that runs through him (and through the play as a whole). Finally, you might cement all of your observations by leaning toward either the notion that the two plays complement each other in some fundamental way or that they function more like discrete dramatic works.

Bibliography for *1 Henry IV*

Bloom, Harold, ed. *William Shakespeare: Histories and Poems.* New York: Chelsea House, 1986.

Bradley, A. C. "The Rejection of Falstaff." *Oxford Lectures on Poetry.* London: Macmillan, 1909. 247–79.

Holderness, Graham. *Shakespeare's History.* New York: MacMillan, 1985.

Jardine, Lisa. *Reading Shakespeare Historically.* New York: Routledge, 1996.

Wells, Stanley, ed. *Shakespeare Survey 48.* Cambridge: Cambridge UP, 1995.

Wood, Nigel. *Henry IV Parts One and Two.* Buckinghamshire: Open UP, 1995.

JULIUS CAESAR

READING TO WRITE

WRITING AN essay on *Julius Caesar* gives you a chance to participate in the play's open-ended debates. So much of *Caesar* is uncertain; Shakespeare never clearly endorses one character over another, never gives a single notion of what is best for Rome over any other. Therefore, the play becomes a conversation about the relationship between states and citizens, leaders and populaces, with no evident authorial guidelines for what the audience or readers should think or feel. As you read the play, carefully consider the ideas voiced by each character. You will see an urgent political debate in progress. Read the dialogue closely not only for developing oppositions between characters but also for contradictions made by individuals.

The following passage comes from act 1, scene 2. Using carefully crafted rhetorical gambits, Cassius persuades Brutus to join him against Caesar. After recalling a swimming race in which the apparently mighty Caesar needed to be rescued by him, Cassius continues:

> Why, man, he doth bestride the narrow world
> Like a Colossus, and we petty men
> Walk under his huge legs, and peep about
> To find ourselves dishonorable graves.
> Men at sometime were masters of their fates.
> The fault, dear Brutus, is not in our stars,
> But in ourselves, that we are underlings.
> Brutus and Caesar: what should be in that "Caesar"?

Why should that name be sounded more than yours?
Write them together: yours is as fair a name.
Sound them: it doth become the mouth as well.
Weigh them: it is as heavy. Conjure with 'em:
"Brutus" will start a spirit as soon as "Caesar"...
When could they say till now, that talked of Rome,
That her wide walls encompassed but one man?
Now is it Rome indeed, and room enough
When there is in it but one only man.
O, you and I have heard our fathers say
There was a Brutus once that would have brooked
Th'eternal devil to keep his state in Rome
As easily as a king. (1.2.136–62)

The opening image of this speech is perhaps one of the most memorable of the play. Cassius paints the dramatic picture of a gigantic Caesar towering over Rome, a monstrous, unnatural threat that could squash the insectlike citizens who flit around his giant steps. But how is this reconciled with the image of a weak and feeble Caesar offered by Cassius in his speech moments earlier? When Cassius adds that the rest "peep about / To find ourselves dishonorable graves," he suggests that an unrestrained Caesar poses not merely a physical threat but a social and cultural one also: The small things under Caesar's feet do not just live powerless like insects, they die like them, unremembered and unmarked. It is this threat to honor that makes the risks of Caesar so great. But Cassius quickly builds on this image, shifting slightly to the philosophical idea that men, and not the stars, make their fates. The first image stresses the powerlessness of the citizens against a tyrant Caesar, while the second offers a stirring counter to the threat. Cassius asserts that no man is destined to be lowly; rather, an individual chooses to be so by not making it otherwise.

This line of thought might encourage you to reflect on the tension between individual and state throughout the play. An essay on this topic could explore ideas of equality and freedom in the text. What is it about Caesar's power that seems to threaten the conspirators so much? However, you might also consider the possibility that when a character voices an apparent concern for the state, rhetoric may be masking nothing more than the desires of that individual to maintain political prominence.

As the passage continues, Cassius returns to his central thesis that all Romans are equal. However, he frames this argument within a comparison of Brutus and Caesar. This is rhetorically clever, of course—Cassius knows his mark is Brutus and attempts to appeal directly to him—but it is more than that. For the first time, through Cassius's rhetorical devices, the relationship that, for many readers, structures the play is introduced: the opposition of Brutus and Caesar. Although Cassius is attempting to make the point that Caesar should not hold sway over Brutus, he is also setting up the important idea that these two men have much in common. After all, the final invocation of a grand Roman history is in reality nothing more than another personalized appeal to Brutus, a reminder of his own family history more than that of his city.

Another topic question could be taken from this passage: What is the symbolic relationship between Brutus and Caesar? This essay would consider the motivations of Brutus, suggesting ways in which he is as interested in personal authority as Caesar is, but it might also look at the way Shakespeare makes both characters fatally flawed.

TOPICS AND STRATEGIES

Every essay requires a focus; you cannot write about everything in the play at once. The section on how to write an essay shows you a number of ways to turn a focus into a thesis, observations into arguments. However, the starting point is nearly always finding an initial focus and making first observations. What follows is a discussion of *Julius Caesar* geared toward helping you make the most of the budding ideas you will have as you read the play. By no means should you feel limited to these topics, however.

Themes

Caesar is thematically quite focused: It is a play primarily about politics. A chief concern of the work is political systems, the way humans organize their societies into governed communities rather than the chaotic free-for-all of a natural state. How should this be done? What form of government is best? Should power be shared among many or concentrated in the hands of a few or even one? The section "History and Context" below discusses these as pressing questions in Shakespeare's time.

A close reading of *Caesar* will offer potential themes that might be developed in essay form. Using the passage studied above, for example, think how you might write an essay on the theme of honor in *Julius Caesar*. Having selected the theme, ask how it functions in the world of the play. Cassius suggests that being stripped of political power is like a dishonorable death, but power may be just one component of honor in the play. Asking how the theme functions will lead you to seek a definition of honor in the play and then to find parts of the text that support that claim. What actions do you believe Shakespeare portrays as honorable? Of particular interest here might be moments in the text where there is a potential gap between an action or act and its motivation. For example, the killing of Caesar might be a dishonorable act brought to pass by nonetheless honorable intentions (or vice versa). A similar problem could be also found in the suicides of Cassius and Brutus, perhaps.

Sample Topics

1. **Tyranny:** How dangerous is Caesar to Rome? Is he the monster that Cassius claims he is?

   An essay on this theme might naturally begin with a careful look at what Caesar says and does. Compare his actions to the complaints of the conspirators. Do you think the murder is justified? The other component of this essay might be a close look at the motivations of the conspirators. What do they want and why? Be careful, though, because you certainly should not take any of the characters in *Caesar* at their word. When characters talk about helping Rome, are they actually talking about helping themselves?

2. **The crowd:** How important is the crowd, or the "rabblement," as they are less favorably termed during the play, to the control of political power?

   An essay on this theme might start at the beginning of the play. In the opening scene, the Tribunes, a group of men charged with looking after the interests of the working class, are rudely abusing and harassing the very people they are supposed to represent. What do you make of this? Isolate other scenes in which the crowd is depicted and see if you can build up a profile of them, of what function they serve. The key task might be to determine whether Shakespeare is sympathetic to the crowd or not. This is no easy matter. For example, why does the poet Shakespeare have the crowd unjustly murder the poet Cinna? Look closely, too, at how the crowd functions during the funeral scene. Try to assess whether they are portrayed favorably or not in this key episode.

3. **Rhetoric:** How reliable is rhetoric, the art of persuasion, in *Julius Caesar*? Can words be trusted, even if crafted elegantly and elaborately by brilliant speakers?

This essay will rely especially on close readings of key rhetorical moments. You might ask, Is there any relationship between language and truth in this play? Find moments in the text where one character persuades others to do something they may not otherwise have done. Look carefully at these scenes to assess the consequences of rhetoric in the play. Shakespeare uses flourishes of linguistic brilliance, such as Antony's funeral oration, to study how language helps build and organize human relations and political power. He wants his audience to think carefully about the art of language, to question it and look beneath the surface to understand its workings. What do you think he is encouraging us to see when we do so?

Character

Caesar has a relatively small cast of important characters, and the dramatic energy of the play comes from the tensions between the characters as much or more than the events of the plot. Indeed, critical approaches to *Caesar* have had a particular interest in pairings of characters (Brutus and Antony, Brutus and Caesar, Cassius and Brutus, etc.). But while you might find yourself naturally drawn to working with two characters from *Caesar* (see the section "Compare and Contrast" below), each of the principle figures provides ample scope for a strong essay. Especially helpful to students writing about this play are character transformation and character duality. Antony, for example, is first seen as an athletic hero, quick of mind and rhetorically gifted, who seeks to avenge a murder. However, do you view him in this heroic light at the end of the play? Caesar, on the other hand, may not be in the play long enough to go through significant transformation, but his character is divided between the giant monster about whom Cassius cautions and a rather feeble old man who is hard of hearing.

Sample Topics

1. **Brutus:** Though he claims to be motivated by a love of Rome and a desire to protect it from tyranny, to what extent is this motive mingled with or overshadowed by more selfish ambitions?

   This essay might start by asking how sympathetic Brutus is supposed to be. It goes without saying, of course, that in writing this essay you should focus on scenes in which Brutus is central to the action, but three episodes in particular might underpin the whole essay: the scene in which Cassius seeks to enlist Brutus, the murder of Caesar and the assassin's oration immediately after, and Brutus's suicide. To what extent does Cassius manipulate Brutus in their first conversation, and to what extent is Brutus a cautious but willing conscript? What does his funeral speech reveal about his character? What do you think we are supposed to feel at his death? This essay will need to address the ambiguity of Brutus as a tragic hero. Do not let the complexity of the character become an obstacle; try to spot as many different (and, no doubt, contradictory) elements of his character as you can.

2. **Antony:** Can Antony be regarded as the play's hero? Is his revenge entirely driven by love for the dead Caesar?

   This essay, like an essay on Brutus, must confront a nuanced character. He possesses a magnetic rhetorical power, but Shakespeare seems to caution that Anthony should not be embraced unreservedly. Perhaps your thesis might reach for a multidimensional attempt to characterize Antony. Try to find scenes that reveal different sides of him, and place them alongside each other in your analysis. You should be able to find radical extremes of behavior. For example, you might consider Antony's chilling conversation with Octavius at the beginning of act 4 alongside his apparently touching devotion to Caesar.

3. **Caesar:** What in Caesar simultaneously provokes such intense love and fear?

This essay might begin by assessing who thinks what about Caesar at the beginning of the play. There is clearly a difference of opinion in Rome, and the split seems to run along class lines. Consider why the masses might be infatuated with Caesar while the patricians seem possessed by a malignant mix of fear and contempt. Make a list of Caesar's qualities and characteristics before you begin writing, and then see if you can use your list to formulate a thesis that characterizes him. Pay equal attention to his strengths and weaknesses. It might be profitable to ask how much Caesar is really in control of his actions, let alone the action of the play that bears his name. Consider, for example, his decision to go to the Senate. Finally, it will probably be necessary to think hard about the accuracy of the charges made by the conspirators, comparing them to what is known of Caesar's government of Rome. Again, the division between what the masses feel and what the elites perceive may be very telling.

4. **Portia/Calpurnia:** Can these seemingly marginal figures facilitate your understanding of the characters of Brutus and Caesar? More important, how do they function as interesting and significant characters in their own right?

If the play gives little room to its two female characters, you can go some way to correcting that imbalance. To counteract the lack of time these women spend on stage, you might consider treating both Portia and Calpurnia in the same essay: the women of *Julius Caesar.* Certainly Portia seems to know that she inhabits a man's world, even going as far as challenging her own gender during her conversation with Brutus. Study the exchange closely, drawing significance from as many elements of it as you can. See if you can assess the type of marriage the pair have, focusing in particular on any mention of gender. Also, try to arrive at a symbolic or psychological meaning of Portia's wounded thigh. Moreover, why does she later take her own life in such a brutally unusual manner? Do not overlook the scene in which Portia waits to hear the outcome of the plot. If writing a comparative piece, how does Portia differ from Calpurnia? How much control does each woman have over her respective husband? Is there a difference between the way Caesar treats Calpurnia in public and the way he treats her in private? Gender may be a theme buried deeply in the play, but through study of these two characters, the political sphere of the play can be extended to the relationship between the sexes.

History and Context

While Shakespeare sets his play in ancient Rome, he is a poet and not a historian. Unlike the historian, whose task is to reconstruct the past as accurately as possible, the artist is more likely to seek moral or aesthetic meaning. Therefore, in writing *Caesar,* Shakespeare would have been responding to questions and issues surrounding him at the close of the 16th century. The implication here is that Shakespeare's play about ancient Rome says more about Elizabethan England than it does about antiquity. But how does the play reflect the concerns of Elizabethan England? Literary critics have written a number of interesting essays about *Caesar* and Shakespeare's world. For example, Barbara Bono has suggested that in the debate over Caesar's murder can been found anxieties surrounding the impending death of Queen Elizabeth, while Wayne Rebhorn has written on the relationship between *Caesar* and the crisis in the Elizabethan aristocracy. Needless to say, these are highly specialized arguments, but you could certainly find ways to approach *Caesar* historically. As it is principally a play about politics, one way to approach a historical essay might be to assess the relationship between Shakespeare's text and the political landscape of his day.

Sample Topic

Tudor and Stuart politics: In what way does *Julius Caesar* reflect the political tensions and concerns of Renaissance England? How might Shakespeare be using a play about ancient Rome as a safe arena for topical debate?

Written in 1599, *Julius Caesar* was composed literally on the eve of the most turbulent century of English political history. By the midpoint of the 17th century, England would enter into civil war, the most critical moment of which was the execution of Charles I. Such things seemed cataclysmic at the time, and Robert Miola has suggested that *Julius Caesar* is an important part of the intellectual background of these events. Moreover, Shakespeare was living through an age of increasing state power, as the machinery of power became more efficient and centralized. Elizabeth's government tried to exert control over many areas of an individual's life. For example, laws demanded church attendance on Sundays and dictated what clothes could be worn by each class of person (though historians disagree over how successfully such laws were enforced). If you are interested in researching this topic, Andrew Hadfield's *Shakespeare and Renaissance Politics* provides a lucid introduction.

An essay of this type would find an initial focus, such as the debate over concentrating power into the hands of a single figure such as an emperor or monarch. After you have identified as many strands of this debate as possible in *Julius Caesar*, isolating key scenes and speeches for use in the essay, research into Tudor and Stuart political life might show how these debates were being conducted. You might then compare the play to the historical record, asking how Shakespeare edits the debate for his text, what ideas he includes and excludes. Pay special attention to the different models of government offered in *Julius*

Caesar, from monarchy to aristocracy to popular participation of sorts.

Philosophy and Ideas

Julius Caesar is an intellectual play, interested especially in the way power operates. As a writer, you can focus on at least two currents of this intellectual energy. The principle focus of this debate is the way humans construct political power, the different visions the play offers for how Rome might be best governed. But power is not only something that the characters in *Caesar* contest for; it is also something that is exercised upon them. As you read the play and prepare to write, think carefully about how power circulates through the work. Look closely at scenes where the balance of power changes or, more troubling still, where human power appears to be an illusion, an impotent talisman that does little to protect Caesar, Brutus, and others from forces larger than themselves. The ultimate questions you address in this style of essay might be quite simple: What is true power in *Julius Caesar*? Where or with whom does it lie?

1. **Predetermination/free will:** What does the play say about the role of fate in the lives of its characters? How much control do individuals in *Caesar* have over the events that befall them?

   A paper approaching this debate in *Caesar* might begin by assessing the philosophical alternatives found in the play. In part, you could focus on the power of fate and its dramatic agent, the supernatural. Consider the different ways supernatural events might be understood to direct the characters' fortunes: Calpurnia's dream, the soothsayer's vision, the remnants of an animal sacrificed the morning of Caesar's murder, and the strange portents the night before. However, do not forget that alongside this motif the play also treats the role of decision making very seriously. Characters are frequently faced with pivotal, stark choices that have enormous implications. Look for the many instances where supernatural omens foreshadow these key moments of decision making. Further, consider the final implications of each major decision and assess in your essay how inevitable or avoidable each link of the play's tragic chain is. For example, could Caesar have avoided his assassination?

2. **Machiavelli:** Which character in *Julius Caesar* is the most Machiavellian?

This essay would begin with some reading from Machiavelli's principal work, *The Prince.* Writing almost a century before Shakespeare, Machiavelli argued that for leaders to be successful, they should appear to be good but never shy away from almost any kind of evil in order to hold on to power. This sounds like devilish excess, and that is just how Shakespeare's England understood Machiavelli. But for all the bad press, his ideas are more subtle than they first appear. In fact, Machiavelli argues that the goal of a leader is simply the creation of a safe and stable state. To achieve this, he will have to lie, cheat, and even kill while all the time trying to appear honest, good, and pious.

Look for scenes in *Caesar* where the patricians adopt the key Machiavellian strategy of saying one thing while intending or doing another. You could do so character by character, in fact. Pay attention especially to the role of soliloquies, moments where the characters speak alone on stage to reveal their true thoughts and motives. Scenes of rhetorical performance would also be of great value to this essay, from Cassius's attempt to enlist Brutus in his plot through Antony's funeral speech initiating the counterplot.

Form and Genre

Thinking about *Caesar* explicitly as a piece of literature rather than as a living, breathing world inhabited by its characters will take your essay in a new direction. When you choose this approach to the play, you are looking not so much at what *Caesar* says but at how it says it. The difference may sound slight, but it dramatically changes how you read and write about the text. Shakespeare, as the author of *Julius Caesar,* comes to the foreground, and your task is no longer to assess the choices of

Brutus or Caesar but to examine those of the playwright as he goes about his job. This play is a tragedy, and Shakespeare wrote it against a backdrop of expectations about what such a play would contain and do. Consider what Shakespeare might want his audience to take away from *Julius Caesar,* and offer evidence of how he is manipulating his drama and its spectators through his art. As you do so, consider how *Caesar* works in comparison with other Shakespearean tragedies you have read or with what you understand by the basic idea of tragedy in general.

To do this, you must consider key structural moments that determine not only what happens in the drama but the tone produced as a result. In addition, you could ask why Shakespeare makes certain structural decisions in *Caesar.* For example, you might ask why, in a work titled *Julius Caesar,* Caesar himself appears relatively little, and his death, which could have been the tragic end of the play, occurs in the middle.

Sample Topic

Tragedy: How cathartic is *Julius Caesar*? Is there an adequate sense of resolution at the close of the play?

Writers addressing this topic should pay especially close attention to the final act of the play. Catharsis is the idea that a play ends with a sense of release, the final events cleansing the reader emotionally and the world of the play literally. Reflect on what the characters of Cassius and especially Brutus have come to mean by the close of the play, reflecting then on what is accomplished by their deaths. You could ask a similar question about Caesar's death too. Has Rome been purified by any of the tragic deaths? Is it any better off at the end than it was at the beginning? Consider also that Shakespeare assumed that some of his audience knew that the real-life Octavius lived to be made Emperor Augustus (and, as staged by Shakespeare in *Antony and Cleopatra,* to become Antony's enemy). Judging the cathartic value of the play, therefore, is difficult and requires you to assess carefully the outcome of the play in relation to the tensions and problems raised by the work as a whole.

Compare and Contrast Essays

As mentioned above, *Caesar* is a play that seems to welcome compare and contrast essays, particularly those focusing on character. The characters overlap and oppose each other in interesting and often unexpected ways, uniting members of rival factions and even murderers with the men they kill. The play works hard to create symmetries between characters that deserve a reader's attention. For example, both Brutus and Cassius conspire to kill Caesar, tussle for the right to define the behavior of the anti-Caesar camp after the murder, and commit suicide at the close of the play. An essay focusing on this relationship should capture its intensity (witness, for example, the emotional fervency as the pair iron out their differences before battle), though perhaps the essay's principal energy would come from identifying the differences that exist amidst all this similarity and apparent brotherhood.

Caesar also invites many connections with other works in Shakespeare's canon. Not least, of course, students could make use of the sequel to the play, *Antony and Cleopatra*, comparing how characters (Antony and Octavius) develop from one play to the next or how Shakespeare continues to work with similar themes. However, perhaps the closest play in terms of political tone and theme would be Shakespeare's *Richard II*. Both plays ask what right powerful aristocrats have to overthrow their rulers under extreme circumstances, but do both plays take this debate in the same direction? Assess how much Caesar is similar to the equally ill-fated Richard or what, if anything, distinguishes Brutus from Bolingbroke.

Sample Topics

1. **Comparing Brutus and Caesar:** Are these two characters linked by shared weaknesses?

   You might structure this essay by first treating Caesar's weaknesses, then Brutus's before offering a third section that reflects on the relationship you have suggested. A little more challenging, perhaps, would be an approach that moves from fault to fault (the desire for power, susceptibility to flattery, failure to take good counsel from their wives, and so on), considering both characters simultaneously. Do not feel obligated to argue that Brutus and Caesar are identical, even as you argue that they are similar. Within the process of demonstrating shared weaknesses, you can reveal even greater sensitivity for the characters by showing the reader important distinctions between the two men.

2. **Contrasting the tragedies of** *Julius Caesar* **and** *Macbeth:* How are these two Shakespearean tragedies about killing kings different? Although the action of both plays centers around the plot to murder a ruler and the unhappy consequences of the deed, do the plays finally say different things about the same theme?

   This essay would take the structural similarities of both plays and consider both the differences and the meaning or import of those differences. For example, Duncan in *Macbeth* is an idealized, good king, while Caesar is arguably a tyrant in the making. The effect of this is to make Macbeth's deed seem more obviously despicable than Brutus's, but it also opens up two very different thematic concerns. Because of this key difference, *Macbeth* becomes a play about the tension between the natural and unnatural (focused on this most unnatural murder of the fatherlike King Duncan). In contrast, by making Caesar a more ambiguous figure and the motives for his murder cloudier, Shakespeare takes the action of regicide as the focal point for a complex discussion of political alternatives.

3. **Comparing the domestic scenes of the play:** Shakespeare portrays two parallel scenes in *Julius Caesar*—one showing Brutus and Portia in private conversation, the other, Caesar and Calpurnia. In what ways do these scenes mirror each other?

   Such an essay would begin with careful scrutiny of these two scenes alone (using the kind of close-reading skills stressed throughout), though ultimately it would need to make connections between the words and actions of these two limited portions of the text and the themes of the play as a whole.

Think about what the scenes reveal about the male figures and the female characters individually, as well as assessing the dynamics of their relationships. Look for differences in the way Caesar interacts with Calpurnia when the two are alone and how he treats her during more public moments. Think carefully about the qualities displayed by Caesar and Brutus during these scenes, comparing them to their characters as a whole. Do the two men seem fundamentally the same as they are elsewhere in the play, or are there differences in this more intimate setting?

Bibliography and Online Resources for *Julius Caesar*

Bloom, Harold. *Julius Caesar.* New York: Penguin, 2005.

———, ed. *William Shakespeare's "Julius Caesar."* Modern Critical Interpretations. New York: Chelsea House, 1988.

Bono, Barbara. "The Birth of Tragedy: Tragic Action in *Julius Caesar." English Literary Renaissance* 24 (1994): 449–70.

"Julius Caesar: An Annotated Guide to Online Sources." Retrieved 14 Mar. 2007. <http://virgil.org/caesar>.

"The Julius Caesar Site." Retrieved 14 Mar. 2007. <http://www.perseus.tufts. edu/JC>.

Kahn, Coppelia. *Roman Shakespeare: Warriors, Wounds, and Women.* New York: Routledge, 1997.

Marshall, Cynthia. "Portia's Wound; Calpurnia's Dream: Reading Character in *Julius Caesar." English Literary Renaissance* 24 (1994): 471–88.

Miola, Robert. *Shakespeare's Rome.* Cambridge: Cambridge UP, 1983.

AS YOU LIKE IT

READING TO WRITE

*A*s You Like It might be Shakespeare's most joyous play. Though not without darker elements, this is a comedy that glows with wonderful characters—one of Shakespeare's very finest, indeed, in Rosalind—enchantment, and good humor. Savoring the sheer pleasure of this play is the key to reading and writing about it successfully too. While other Shakespeare plays may principally engage readers on ideological, intellectual, or aesthetic levels, *As You Like It* tempts them first to feel more than to think, to embrace warmly rather than analyze coolly. If you can initially connect with this play as a source of delight, the kind of awareness of character and theme required for successful writing becomes much easier and more effective. While the bleaker Shakespearean visions you may have encountered in class, a *Macbeth* or a *Hamlet,* may for some readers wear their greatness prominently and in intimidating style, *As You Like It* wears its illustriousness lightly.

However, do not mistake this felicity for shallowness. *As You Like It* is rich with topics for discussion, complex ideas, and ample room for interpretation. Indeed, it is one of Shakespeare's most profound engagements with the great human themes of love and time, for example. The following passage from the play shows how Shakespeare nimbly weaves pleasure and meaning. Here is the celebrated response of Rosalind, disguised as Ganymede, to Orlando's claim that he will die if Rosalind does not return his love for her.

> . . . The poor world is almost six thousand years old, and in
> all this time there was not any man died in his own person,

videlicet, in a love-cause. Troilus had his brains dashed out with a Grecian club, yet he did what he could to die before, and he is one of the patterns of love. Leander, he would have lived many a fair year though Hero had turned nun if it had not been for a hot midsummer night, for, good youth, he went but forth to wash him in the Hellespont and, being taken with the cramp, was drowned; and the foolish chroniclers of that age found it was hero of Sestos. But these are all lies. Men have died from time to time, and worms have eaten them, but not for love. (4.1.81–92)

First, you might notice that this quote looks different from most of the other passages cited in this book's "Reading to Write" sections. See that it continues across the page and does not start each new line with a capital letter. These hallmarks indicate that here Shakespeare is writing in prose, not verse poetry as he often does. This difference matters, and you should note when poetry is used and when prose is used. What is the effect of Ganymede/Rosalind's prose speech here? Perhaps it is to naturalize Rosalind, to make her more real and less theatrical. This significant detail of form opens up at least two possible avenues for essay writing.

First, how might Rosalind's rejection of poetic speech be connected here with a larger theme? Look always for links between content and form, what is said and how it is said. If Rosalind spoke these lines in poetry, she might lay herself open to charges of literary hypocrisy. Her whole purpose here, after all, as it is elsewhere, is to dismantle hyperbolic and idealized notions of love. Orlando, despite his dramatic protestations, will not die of unrequited love. She attempts to make Orlando aware of a more realistic and true form of love, one more organic than ornate. This attempt is mirrored in the distinction between poetry and prose speech, revealing how a careful reading of Shakespeare's form can illuminate thematic concerns.

Merely the form of this passage, then, might serve as a springboard for an essay on love. It might also prompt consideration of Rosalind as a character. If the effect of prose instead of poetry here is to connect Rosalind more immediately with an audience, to strip away one important element of theatrical artifice, how does this knowledge help you understand her character more? From this perspective, you might see in this passage some contradictions. For a start, while the passage argues in both form and content for honest estimations of love, it is spoken by someone in disguise and having some slightly less than honest fun. Moreover, the simpler, more natural prose style—often reserved by Shakespeare for his clowns and peasants—is in direct contrast to the classical allusions that denude Rosalind's uncommon and deeply attractive intelligence. Rosalind is a remarkably complex character, and writers should seek this complexity, looking for the paradoxes and dualities surrounding her. Some of this is evident in the mix of harmony and discord between content and form in this passage.

TOPICS AND STRATEGIES

Every essay requires a focus; you cannot write about everything in the play at once. The section on how to write an essay shows you a number of ways to turn a focus into a thesis, observations into arguments. However, the starting point is nearly always finding an initial focus and making first observations. What follows is a discussion of *As You Like It* geared toward helping you make the most of the budding ideas you will have as you read the play. By no means should you feel limited to these topics, however.

Themes

Over the last several decades especially, Rosalind's disguise as a young man, Ganymede, has developed into a major thematic concern. Writing on the role of gender in *As You Like It*, critics have discovered many implications beneath the multiple layers of Rosalind's disguise. Certainly, gender will play a role in a number of the essay topics considered in this chapter, so (as with, say, race in *Othello*) the important thing is to refine a broad, central theme into a specific statement or argument. For example, assess how the basic speech and action of the play are changed, subjected to new and hidden meanings, by Rosalind's male disguise.

Shakespeare has enormous fun in several of his plays with the dramatic, comic, and philosophical potential of cross-dressing; always follow carefully the dizzying sleights-of-hand he employs to get his audience thinking about gender. Ask what it means, for example, that Orlando is wooing Rosalind dressed as Ganymede pretending to be Rosalind. Examine the consequences of such distortions not only for Rosalind's gender role and sexuality but also for those around her. Perhaps, however, the simplest way to clear your head after all of this might be to consider Rosalind as a woman speaking up for women and for honesty in love; she is arguably the most admirable woman conceived anywhere in Shakespeare's work. Fueled in large part by the intelligence of its central character, then, *As You Like It* pursues a number of debates that students may participate in through their writing.

Sample Topics

1. **Love:** What different models of love are offered in *As You Like It*? How would you describe the play's favored idea of love?

   This being an example of new comedy, the most popular comic style of the 1590s, the expectation is that lovers will overcome obstacles in order to marry at the close of the play. However, as a variety of commentators have suggested, in *As You Like It,* the chief obstacle to the lovers is not the interference of a spiteful parent or harsh law but the need to clarify what love is before the play can be resolved. There are a number of competing definitions, and a good start to your prewriting process might be to attach to each character a particular model of love. For example, Silvius displays a decidedly pathetic form of love, committing himself to the service of Phoebe even in her act of wooing another man (or what Phoebe thinks is another man) on her behalf. This is an example of a kind of courtly love made commonplace in the Renaissance by writers of sonnets in the style of the Italian poet Petrarch. The speaker in these sonnets, just like the lovesick Silvius, often stressed the pain of unrequited love and the highly exaggerated beauty of the beloved—as well her cruelty. Look at Orlando and consider if his model of Petrarchan love differs from Silvius's. Most important, look for moments when these stylized expressions of love are challenged. Look at Phoebe in act 3, scene 5, but especially at Rosalind's rebuffs of Orlando's idealism in act 3, scene 5 and act 4, scene 1. Think, too, about the problems of attraction. What does the play say about love at first sight, for example? Think about Celia's dismissal of it early in the play, but perhaps place this early rejection alongside her rather hasty pairing with Oliver. Also consider, as mentioned above, the implications of cross-dressing for physical attraction—both Phoebe and Orlando woo the disguised Rosalind.

2. **The forest:** In what ways is the Forest of Arden different from the court setting at the beginning of the play? What is life like for the exiled characters in the forest, and what threatens the sense of idealism that at first seems to surround the forest?

Many of Shakespeare's comedies are structurally organized by the contrast between a court setting and a pastoral or idyllic setting, often labeled by critics the "Green World." Along with *A Midsummer Night's Dream, As You Like It* features Shakespeare's most concentrated examination of the power and possibility of the Green World space. The play begins with scenes from the court, revealing a number of political and personal troubles that drive the protagonists into the Forest of Arden. Look carefully at these opening scenes, identifying the central problems of the court. You may also find that these problems have a common nature, finding a relationship between Oliver's mistreatment of Orlando and Duke Frederick's usurpation of Duke Senior's authority. Think, too, about the political undertones of Frederick's decision to banish Rosalind but also the nature of the relationship between Rosalind and Celia that helps explain why the banishment of the former also necessitates the flight of the latter.

Traditionally, the Green World space is a setting from which the rules of the court are absent, and a kind of free play allows characters a broad liberty to learn and develop. Try to assess the conditions of the forest. Look at the banished duke's idealism in act 2, scene 1, but also note the darker tones immediately following in the talk of hunting. Indeed, you might want to follow the recurring use of hunting. What effect does it have on the sense of idealism? How does Jaques equate the hunting of deer to the problems of the court? Think, too, about the curious episode of the lioness and the snake, identifying what effect the presence of these creatures has on your perception of Arden. Finally, follow the debates over the merit of court versus country life between Touchstone and the rustic inhabitants of the forest. In your opinion, who has the upper hand in these discussions?

Character

Rosalind may steal the limelight, but there is much to say and write about her companions in the forest. For example, while many critics have suggested that Orlando is an amiable but inadequate partner for Rosalind, he is by no means without substance. Think about the gendering of Orlando, for example. Assess the strange juxtaposition of masculine and feminine attributes, such as his wrestling prowess alongside his tender, maternal care for Adam. Think, too, about Orlando's ideas of love and why these must be overturned by Rosalind. Duke Senior, along with his woodland courtiers, might make a good character study choice if you are interested in the theme of the Green World. Charles the wrestler says that the duke is like Robin Hood of old, but you may come up with a more complex (and accurate) portrait of this man and his followers. With most of the characters in *As You Like It*, however, a good point to keep in mind is that of transformation. The forest changes many of the characters significantly—the immediate transformation of Frederick as he enters the fringes of Arden makes the most striking example—and that movement can usefully underpin a number of character studies.

Sample Topics

1. **Rosalind:** In what ways can Rosalind be considered Shakespeare's surrogate in *As You Like It*?

   It is perhaps proof of Rosalind's vitality and centrality to the play that some critics have talked about her as Shakespeare's representative in *As You Like It*. Exploring this idea gives you a good point of focus through which to approach Rosalind's extremely layered character. As your task is to show how Rosalind not only is central to the dramatic action of the play but also essentially controls and drives the action, you might begin by broadly assessing her character in the early scenes. Think about her relationship with Celia, along with her head-over-heels attraction to Orlando. She is a figure of intense emotional capacity, characterized most, perhaps, by her ability to love. But think about the apparent contradictions between her intensity of love—be that love for Celia or Orlando—and the bubble-bursting challenges she offers to Orlando's expressions of high romantic love. Although it will be difficult, such an essay might even assess any subtle distinctions that exist between Rosalind and Rosalind as Ganymede.

With all this as important background, how does Rosalind become the voice and spirit of the play (if you agree that she does)? How does she become the narrative engine of the plot? You might find this role most prominently staged in the final act of the play. But by this point you may be ready to question how successful Rosalind has been as the playwright's stand-in, even perhaps asking the difficult question whether Shakespeare in the end pokes gentle fun at his heroine's capabilities?

2. **Jaques:** What is the function of Jaques? What is his philosophy, and how does it challenge or complement other ideas in *As You Like It*?

Jaques is an example of the malcontent figure, a person on the fringes of the community who uses his removal to comment on the behavior within his society. An essay might try to examine Jaques's observations on life in the forest, processing them into a sense of his philosophy. Pay close attention to the way he introduces melancholy or darker tones to the activities of Senior and his followers, noting how the courtiers have imported the problems of the court to the pastoral setting. Again, think especially of his sympathies for the deer killed during hunts. Certainly look at the conversations he has with other characters, which generally seem to take the form of challenges and disagreements. Can you spot a pattern or governing logic in his arguments? What sentiments does he challenge? Notice, too, the role of time in many of his musings (also see the section on time in "Philosophy and Ideas," below). Finally, search out moments when he talks about himself, such as his explanation to Rosalind of his particular breed of humorous melancholy.

History and Context

As You Like It is a play with no clear historical or geographic setting. There are traces of England in the supposedly French scene, and a nostalgic but timeless world of trees and animals rejects any fixed temporal location. None of this means that historical interpretations of the play are impossible; the marks of Shakespeare's time and world are etched onto his plays like Orlando's poems on the trunks of Arden's trees. Louis Montrose, for example, has written powerfully about the role of primogeniture in *As You Like It*. This dominant legal and social convention insisted on the passing of inheritance to the first-born son, a tradition abused by Oliver. Montrose argues that anxieties about potential faults in this system would have given Orlando's plight a very strong relevance to many in Shakespeare's audience.

Sample Topic

Cross-dressing in Shakespeare's England: How does Shakespeare handle this subject, controversial in his day? Indeed, how does the English theatrical convention of boy actors playing women's roles form an important dimension of this play?

As is our own place and moment in history, Elizabethan England was the site of culture wars. This took the shape, broadly, of contention between puritanical forces bemoaning the collapse of order and progressives who sought to push social boundaries. Clothing was an important focal point for this contest. After all, in early modern Europe, clothing acted as a symbol of order, demarking rich from poor, servant from master, and especially male from female. Sumptuary laws were implemented to ensure that people could not dress above their station, to prevent the blurring of clear social categories.

As consumerism developed strongly in the economic markets of Europe, clothing became more available and diverse. As a result, it was increasingly difficult to enforce strict codes of dress. Conservative commentators, aside from the troubling class implications of finer clothes being worn by middling sorts, were distressed by the effeminacy seen in some of the more popular styles of dress for men. Perhaps an even greater source of concern was the phenomenon of women dressing in more masculine attire. In his *Anatomie of Abuses*, Phillip Stubbes (a kind of Elizabethan equivalent to today's talk radio hosts) ranted against such acts of cross-dressing, labeling women who wore manly clothes as monstrous aberrations of nature.

Stubbes was also a prominent opponent of the theater, and the issues of clothing and playgoing were closely linked for him. It was, he argued, on stage that audiences saw the potentially corrupting sight of males dressed as females, a spectacle that might ignite strange and unusual sexual impulses. The tradition of boy actors playing women's roles contributed significantly to the moral depravity such critics saw in stage plays. For a fuller account of these and related issues, see Ann Rosalind Jones and Peter Stallybrass's book *Renaissance Clothing and the Materials of Memory*.

These debates fascinated Shakespeare and are obviously reflected in *As You Like It*. Think about how Shakespeare plays with the concept of gender, a set of clearly fixed, identifiable, and natural categories to people like Stubbes. Suddenly gender becomes a construction, a fluid marker that to a certain extent can be blurred and distorted. Look for scenes highlighting this potential: for example, the moments when Rosalind as Ganymede is courted by Phoebe and Orlando toy with gender boundaries and stimulate, as Stephen Greenblatt has argued, sexual friction through misunderstanding.

Think, too, about the effect of using boy actors to play female parts. How does this intensify the sexual and gendered complexity of the Rosalind/Ganymede figure?

Philosophy and Ideas

Through cross-dressing, *As You Like It* enters into the philosophical debate of essentialism versus constructivism. When Rosalind/Ganymede offers to cure Orlando by posing as Rosalind, the resulting construction is a boy playing a woman playing a man playing a woman. This multiplicity of identities surely serves as a challenge to the idea that a person has one fixed, concrete identity beyond his or her control. This kind of thinking is very much at home in a twenty-first century philosophy prone to questioning absolutes, but shows, more importantly, how the history of ideas is not necessarily a story of progress but one of reinvention. Moreover, before we cite this philosophical dexterity as one more reason to embrace the idea of Shakespeare's universal genius, it should be noted that Shakespeare was by no means alone in working with this theme. Indeed, essay writers seeking a challenge might head to John Middleton and Thomas Dekker's early 17th-century play, *The Roaring Girl.* An essay might examine how *The Roaring Girl* develops the delicate philosophical implications of *As You Like It* into a radical social and moral commentary.

Shakespeare explores the idea of identity in *As You Like It* alongside contemplation of another entity typically perceived as natural and beyond our control.

Sample Topic

Time: What does Shakespeare say about time in *As You Like It*? Is Rosalind anything more than just literally correct when she says there are no clocks in the forest? Where are the clocks in this play, and what power do they have over the characters?

The most memorable speech in *As you Like It*—and one of the most recognizable in all of Shakespeare's writing—is Jaques's moving, melancholically beautiful depiction of the Seven Ages of Man. Time is, of course, a philosophical theme that has endured and will continue to endure; our fear of and fascination with time are timeless traits of a thinking human race. Yet in Shakespeare's day, time was not merely a phenomenon to meditate on; it was a cultural, social, and economic construct being revised, designed anew. In short, the early modern period witnessed the steady transformation of time from a natural, cyclical sense of existence to the precise, quantifiable, and demanding sense of time most of us have today. The title of Ricardo Quinones's book, *The Renaissance Invention of Time*, says it plainly enough.

So Rosalind's observation that there are no clocks in the forest may be rooted in a collective desire to return to a time when people were less reminded of the quick evaporation of our hours, days, and lives. Look for evidence of the play's obsession with time. Be careful to note that it offers different models of time. For example, how would you describe Jaques's understanding of time, including his account of Touchstone's anxious fretting about rotting (see, in particular, the entirety of act 2, scene 7)? Ask, too, whether time is truly absent from the forest. Again, reflect on the hunt motif as a source of contrast to the duke's idyllic dream of Arden. Finally, consider the characters of Corin and (especially) Adam, two men who have experienced much passing time. How are these characters used? What contrasts do they offer to events and characters in the play?

Form and Genre

Perhaps nowhere else does Shakespeare handle with such skill the traditional comic model as he does in *As You Like It.* In subsequent plays, Shakespeare has no interest in writing pure comedy; his output darkens into the problem comedies and great tragedies. So for lovers of happy comedy, *As You Like It* is probably Shakespeare's greatest achievement in this genre, artistically superior to his early comedies and lacking the cynicism and satirical tone of a work like *The Merchant of Venice.* But is it free of these darker notes? Many critics have found in *As You Like It* evidence of a more cynical play buried beneath the mirth. Joining these commentators in their search for concealed generic problems can be an excellent approach to the play and can generate an essay that allows for wide coverage of the play.

Sample Topic

Comic failures in *As You Like It:* What details do you find in Shakespeare's play to make you question its apparently exuberant comic outcome? How are traditionally comic movements and devices undercut in *As You Like It*? Do these "problems" finally challenge your categorization of the play as a comedy?

Such an essay might begin by exploring some of the darker qualities of Arden, the play's apparently idealized pastoral setting. Again, the hunting motif and fascination with time will be of use here. However, perhaps the bulk of this essay will focus on the final act. After all, it is in the final scenes that comedies tend to solidify their generic outcome, almost universally through weddings and community feasts uniting characters and resolving earlier difficulties. *As You Like It* appears to offer an ideal comic finale, blessed, indeed, not just by four weddings but an appearance by Hymen, the god of marriage. What could be more suggestive of pure comedy than this? There are three things to pay especially close attention to here. First, examine in your essay the quality of the relationships that end in marriage. Of particular concern, perhaps, are the unions of Silvius and Phoebe and of Touchstone and Audrey. Surely, marriages can only be truly comic if they are good matches. Why might you question not only these pairings but even the marriage of Oliver and Celia? You might even extend this line of analysis to include problems with the pairing of Rosalind and Orlando; these tend to focus on uncertainties raised by the text's playfulness with gender and identity. Second, the ease with which everything is resolved appears almost to mock the conventions of comedy—the conversion of Duke Frederick seems the most guilty twist, but Rosalind's conveniently quick solutions to the lovers' problems may be another. Next, consider whether you find satire or parody in four weddings and the appearance of Hymen. Is this perhaps Shakespeare winking at his audience, gently teasing them for their comic desires? Finally, you might ask what the cumulative effect of all of this is. Do you still find this to be a delightful comedy with necessary splashes of contrast, or is it an exercise in subverting the generic conventions of comedy?

Compare and Contrast Essays

First, an essay on the Green World might be structured as a compare and contrast essay, perhaps finding unexpected similarities between the Green World and the court. The theme of love, also, could be structured around a comparison and contrast, perhaps usefully shaped by the central division of male visions of love contrasted with female models. Notice that Silvius and Orlando seem to approach love as an idealized and highly aesthetic form of worship, while Phoebe and Rosalind appear to debunk such fanciful notions. There are also Celia's doubts over Rosalind's love at first sight for Orlando, to add another example of feminine pragmatism. However, as in any compare and contrast essay, within the overall movement of your main argument—here the division between male and female visions of love—try to add some intriguing complications. You can do this either in a paragraph or two near the beginning or end of the essay or as a second clause to your thesis. In the first scenario, you might say, "In *As You Like It* there is a clear difference between how men and women imagine love, though there are some potential complications to this argument, which I will summarize so you, the reader, can see that I know them." In the second case (the more sophisticated and more difficult option), you would layer your thesis, creating a self-contained debate within it, something like this: "In *As you Like It*, it appears there is a clear difference between male visions of love, which seem to be governed by poetic ideals, and the more pragmatic, realistic model envisioned by the female characters. However, a more careful investigation of the play reveals that in fact there is no such distinction. Instead, the play offers a model of love as a shifting and inconstant phenomenon." What would be the evidence for such a counterclaim? You might, for a start, consider Touchstone's far from admirable or idealistic reasons for marrying Audrey. Perhaps more significantly, you should think about the way in which all of the female characters actually do succumb to or espouse a more starry-eyed vision of love, despite their protestations against such a definition of love.

A good comparison text for *As You Like It* might be *The Roaring Girl*, but students wishing to stay within Shakespeare's canon might find an obvious candidate for comparison in *Twelfth Night*. While the two plays have a number of similarities, complex differences can be found both in the tone or mood of the plays and in the way cross-dressing is employed to create confusion in the gendering and identities of characters. In many ways, *Twelfth Night* takes these ideas much further than *As You Like It*, arguably intensifying the philosophical impact of the cross-dressing motif.

Sample Topics

1. **A comparison of Rosalind to Portia from *The Merchant of Venice*:** Are Rosalind and Portia, traditionally labeled as two of Shakespeare's greatest heroines, in fact more different than alike?

   Needless to say, you could write your essay either way, but the more promising path might lie in arguing for difference rather than similarity. Certainly, though, the similarities are quite striking, at least on the surface: two enormously intelligent women who cross-dress in order to carry out a plot that will set up an apparently comic resolution to their respective plays. However, the differences are meaningful. For example, you might talk about the different ways that the cross-dressing motif is used in each play. Portia primarily uses her cross-dressing as a disguise that grants the legal and social status of a man, while later she uses her disguise to gain moral authority over her husband Bassanio. Consider how this compares to Rosalind's use of cross-dressing. The kind of authority she seeks and gains through cross-dressing appears quite different. Such an essay might consider how each of these strong heroines uses her authority within the play, what outcomes they engineer, and what motivates them to these actions.

2. **Contrasting Touchstone to Jaques:** While both these figures act as commentators on the action and behavior of the play's other characters, how do their observations and philosophies differ?

The fool and the malcontent, in Renaissance drama, are in many ways two sides of the same coin. Their positions often enable them to speak truthfully and insightfully, unencumbered by the social restrictions holding the tongues of others. Consider Touchstone's dalliance with Audrey, as well as his rejection of country ways and abuse of country folk. Compare these to Jaques's concerns with time and justice, as well as his final decision to stay in the forest. Such an essay might usefully structure all this around the notion that Jaques is a true outsider, someone who finally rejects the ways of the court in favor of a more organic life. His insights perhaps reflect this genuine antipathy for courtly conventions. On the other hand, Touchstone perhaps rejects only the conventions that are inconvenient to him—such as the idea that a marriage should be lasting and binding—while broadly embracing the principles and comforts of court life. Touchstone's cynicism and Jaques's melancholy finally allow them both, however, to offer rebukes and challenges to other characters. Focus on these debates with other characters, and analyze occasions where Touchstone and Jaques meet or we hear an account of them meeting (as happens in act 2, scene 7). Finally, your essay might consider whether either of these figures provides an effective challenge to the dominant ideas and ideals of other characters, or even of the play itself.

Bibliography and Online Resources for *As You Like It*

"*As You Like It*." Royal Shakespeare Company. Retrieved 15 Mar. 2007. <http://www.rsc.org.uk/asyoulikeitpack/students/directing1.html>.

Gay, Penny. *As She Likes It: Shakespeare's Unruly Women.* London: Routledge, 1994.

Greenblatt, Stephen. "Fiction and Friction." *Shakespearean Negotiations.* Berkeley: U of California P, 1988. 66–94.

Jones, Ann Rosalind, and Peter Stallybrass. *Renaissance Clothing and the Materials of Memory.* Cambridge: Cambridge UP, 2000.

Quinones, Ricardo J. *The Renaissance Discovery of Time.* Cambridge, MA: Harvard UP, 1972.

Shapiro, Michael. *Gender in Play on the Shakespearean Stage.* Ann Arbor: U of Michigan P, 1996.

Stubbes, Phillip. *The Anatomie of Abuses.* Ed. Margaret Jane Kidnie. Tempe: Arizona Center for Medieval and Renaissance Studies, 2002.

HAMLET

READING TO WRITE

HAMLET IS probably the most celebrated piece of literature in the Western tradition. Familiarity with the text crosses many boundaries, from educated to uneducated, nation to nation, those who have read the text to those who have not. The figure of Hamlet and his soliloquies are iconic, recognizable in some form to virtually all Western minds. This prestige makes reading *Hamlet* exciting in the way it is exciting to tour one of the world's great cities. The "To be, or not to be" soliloquy rises up and catches the breath like the first glimpse of the Eiffel Tower; "Alas, Poor Yorik" impresses us with the awe of the Empire State Building as we find ourselves directly in its shadow. As we read and turn the page, we come across yet another landmark of literature, already so familiar to us from representations but all the more stunning encountered in the flesh of the text. This is the excitement and thrill of reading a text located at the heart of our culture. However, it is exactly the things that make reading *Hamlet* so electrifying—the vastness of the play, the intellectual and philosophical depth, and above all, the enormous tradition of performance and criticism grown thick around the play—that make writing about it such a worry.

However, keep in sight the fact that because there is so much in the play, the task of writing should be made easier, not harder, if you are diligent at the prewriting stage about reading carefully and identifying and tracking themes or issues that you might like to write about. One of those celebrated speeches by Hamlet comes from act 2, scene 2, as the luckless Rosencrantz and Guildernstern question Hamlet over the root of his melancholy:

> This most excellent canopy the air, look you, this brave
> o'erhanging firmament, this majestical roof fretted with
> golden fire—why it appears no other thing to me than a foul
> and pestilent congregation of vapors. What a piece of work
> is man! How noble in reason, how infinite in faculty, in
> form and moving how express and admirable, in action how
> like an angel, in apprehension how like a god—the beauty
> of the world, the paragon of animals! And yet to me what is
> this quintessence of dust?

While this passage appears to be about such universal, infinite subjects as the world itself and the people who live in it, the precise matter at
hand is rather the mind of Hamlet, his perception of these great things.
The play and the consciousness of its main character are indivisible, the
latter taking the former to places that could not be reached without it.
This might sound like a grandiose thing to write about a fictional character, but Hamlet is a truly remarkable and innovative presence, and most
of the essays you could write on the play will sink or swim based on how
much effort you give to understanding his character, the world of the
play as it exists through him.

It is exactly Hamlet's imaginative power that is encountered in this
passage. While most people are content to be shaped by their world,
Hamlet represents a kind of super-being whose mind and imagination
are powerful enough to shape the world in which he lives. Here, no less,
Hamlet is revising and subverting the very principles on which the Elizabethan world was founded. Faced with such an unbounded consciousness, then, is it any wonder that most of the essay suggestions below will
become essays on Hamlet as much as on *Hamlet*?

The passage can be split into two halves, each forming one component of a remarkable argument. In the first, Hamlet envisions the wonder
of the world, its awesome natural beauty and power, as "a foul and pes-
tilent congregation of vapors." Aside from the transcendent capacity of
Hamlet's mind, two key themes emerge from this chilling phrase. First,
in the rankness of what Hamlet perceives, there is a recurring image
of disease and decay. From the first scenes, the play evokes images of
the "rot" in Denmark, a pestilence that Hamlet suggests several times
is by no means contained by the borders of his country. Many critics

have attempted to diagnose the diseases of the play, and you might marshal this pattern of imagery in essays ranging from character studies of Claudius to thematic essays on gender or politics in *Hamlet*. But with the word "vapors," Hamlet goes further still. Here he invokes a sense of nothingness that becomes one of the most recognizable philosophical notes of the play. The world is not only foul but is no more substantial, no more real than a mass of vapors evaporating into the air. This urges you to consider the play's obsession with undermining reality, whether that is through radical thought, as in this passage, or through the act of putting on a play.

Hamlet then turns his attention away from the stage of mankind's existence to the species itself. As he describes the virtues of man, you might think of Hamlet himself. Not only does Hamlet's intelligence and consciousness seem to represent human faculty at its most acutely developed, but his description notably encompasses both "reason" and "action," two qualities infamously opposed to each other as Hamlet's psyche is confronted with the task of murdering Claudius. But it is the inevitability of the closing image, life reduced to "dust," that catches the eye and the mind sharply. Again, this moment becomes just one point in a sequence of images and thoughts connected through the play. This time the theme is death, and you might be drawn by this line to write an essay touched by or directly engaged with the play's remarkable and extended meditation on this most unhappy and universal of concerns. But certainly what will be clear by now—if it was not before—is how dark and deep this text is. That sounds unnerving, but do not forget that dark and deep makes for very good essays.

TOPICS AND STRATEGIES

Every essay requires a focus; you cannot write about everything in the play at once. The section on how to write an essay shows you a number of ways to turn a focus into a thesis, observations into arguments. However, the starting point is nearly always finding an initial focus and making first observations. What follows is a discussion of *Hamlet* geared toward helping you make the most of the budding ideas you will have as you read the play. By no means should you feel limited to these topics, however.

Themes

While the character Hamlet looms large over *Hamlet,* essays could certainly be written that minimize his role or contextualize him. In other words, the essays in this section will include Hamlet, but they will not necessarily be dominated by him in the way that the "Philosophy and Ideas" or "Compare and Contrast Essays" topics below are. For example, the play forms a political parable charting the evolution of the state of Denmark from an old, chivalric order to a new system driven by the methods of realpolitik (for important background on this term, see the section on Machiavelli in the *Julius Caesar* chapter). The writer treating this historicized theme could begin by looking at representatives of the old way of political life: Old Hamlet and Old Fortinbras. Read the early scenes of the play to establish a picture of how the previous generation approached international relations. How would you describe the code of conduct in which the two kings duel for supremacy rather than commit to all-out war? Assess the characteristics of Old Hamlet in the ghost scenes. Pay close attention to the demands he makes of Hamlet, noticing the special request to leave Gertrude alone.

Having established a picture of the old order, the essay would naturally proceed to the larger task of mapping out the political system that appears to have replaced it. Look for small clues, of course, such as the court parasites and climbers (Rosencrantz, Guildernstern, and Osric), who suggest a world in which superficial pandering reaps rewards. You might employ some of the metaphors of disease and decay (like those highlighted in the "Reading to Write" section above) to demonstrate how the play appears not to endorse the processes of political change forced on Denmark. Useful as such motifs and details may be, however, the bulk of the study should focus on the way in which ambassadors of the new political order (Hamlet, Claudius, and Young Fortinbras) approach domestic and international politics. Try to define their styles and outline their ethics. Of course, there will be differences in the way they do things, but the key to this essay might be in identifying the core principles of the new order replacing the old.

Such an essay would reflect a good historical approach, but other thematic avenues take the writer directly to the universal qualities so celebrated in the play.

1. **Death:** In what ways does death occupy and influence the living in *Hamlet*?

   This question encourages you to arrive at a tentative idea of what deaths means in the play. Once you have crystallized your thoughts into something like a definition, you will be ready to produce a thesis statement on the play's darkest of themes. Notice, first, that death is not a distant or removed event in the play. You might begin by identifying the ways in which the dead make their presence felt. For example, even before he sees the ghost of his father, Hamlet is engaged in an intense and over-whelming process of mourning (think, too, about Hamlet's dying request to Horatio at the close of the play, taking it full circle). Compare this to the advice of Claudius and Gertrude that death is natural and inevitable and should not preoccupy the living (1.2). Certainly, Hamlet refuses to dismiss the subject of death from his mind, and as the play progresses his thoughts dwell increasingly on the subject. Scrutinize the great soliloquies (3.1.58, etc.), but look for contrasts in Hamlet's own thinking. For example, though Hamlet's meditations seem to conclude that death is unknowable to the living, an undiscovered country populated by shadowy prospects and dangers, this kind of philosophical dread is paralleled by frequent images of death as a tangible force of equality and realism cutting through the feeble constructions of human society. It is sober and serious at the same time as it is a vulgar joke; it is nowhere (a place yet to be discovered), and it is everywhere (there are countless skulls beneath our feet). Key scenes for this latter, almost blackly comic vision of death are act 4, scene 3 and act 5, scene 1.

2. **Drama and theater:** In what ways is *Hamlet* a study of the practice of drama? What is the relationship between the stage and the real world of the play?

   Such an essay might focus on one of at least three areas. First, you might consider the way in which characters act their parts. For example, Claudius is a man performing the role of bereaved brother who inherits the throne. In other words, he is presenting to the world a version of reality that is false. Even Rosencrantz and Guildernstern, the court lackeys who seek Claudius's favor, are playing the part of interested friends of the troubled prince—a sordid performance that Hamlet sees right through. But, of course, the true actor par excellence here is Hamlet. Much has been written about Hamlet's performances through the play, especially the oft-debated issue of his pretended madness and his trouble assuming the popular role of revenge hero. This all resonates with the idea, discussed above, of a corrupt state; the business of acting, of performing, of staging is as important to the business of daily living here as it is to theater. Are there any characters who do not act, however? If so, what do they contribute to the play's discussion of artifice and illusion?

The next strand of this complex topic to consider is the remarkably overt discussion of theatrics found throughout the play. From the recurring references to Polonius's theatrical past to the elaborate, frequently cited sequence of Hamlet's advice to the players (2.2), you should analyze both the details and the effects of the ever-present use of metadrama, or meta-theater (terms given to components of a play that make drama the subject of the action rather than just the medium for it). In particular, act 2, scene 2 reveals Hamlet to be a connoisseur of the stage, with an elaborate set of opinions and preferences about how actors should best approach their lines and performances. One way to approach this scene is to think about Hamlet's advice in relation to his own acting elsewhere in the play. More generally, why does Shakespeare foreground the illusion of drama, the fact that *Hamlet* is a play, not a snatched vision of reality, so explicitly and deliberately here?

Finally, consider the use of the play within the play (see the chapter on *A Midsummer Night's Dream* for further discussion of the philosophical implications of staging a play inside another play). Always consider the relationship between the layers of staging. For example, what do you make of the fact that in

The Murder of Gonzago it is the nephew of the king who commits the murder? Think especially about how this detail helps you make new connections between Claudius and Hamlet.

Character

Character criticism has traditionally formed the foundation of writing about *Hamlet*. Even the slightest of characters seem to offer substantial opportunities. For example, Young Fortinbras is mentioned early in the play and glimpsed briefly several times in the second half, but he could be the subject of a good essay nonetheless. He is one of the play's symbols of a new age in political life, but you could certainly draw out his qualities and contemplate his actions at length. Pay close attention to Fortinbras's intentions to go to war against Denmark, his motivations for doing so, and finally his "Plan B" campaign against the Polish when his thoughts of invading Denmark are thwarted by his father. The "Compare and Contrast Essays" section below discusses another function of Fortinbras's character, his parallels to Hamlet. Consider in some detail the brief appearance of Fortinbras in act 4, scene 5, asking about the ethics of his campaign against the Polish as it is related by one of his captains. Finally, assess the meaning of his centrality at the close of the play: How should the prospect of Denmark under Fortinbras be viewed? Similarly, the minor characters Rosencrantz and Guildernstern (as well as Osric) could be the focal point of a character study approach to the political sphere of Hamlet's Denmark. They show in miniature the vices of Claudius, Fortinbras, and (arguably) Hamlet.

Why is Hamlet lumped in with Claudius? His character is so expansive and multidimensional that so many colors of life and feeling can be found there, including the darkest. Critics have never tired of the melancholy Dane or run out of fresh things to say about his 400-year-old angst. While some scholarship has fought against the current of elaborate awe (T. S. Eliot famously wrote that Hamlet's character was flawed by an excess of emotion in relation to the situation he faces at the start of the play), the majority of writers have attempted to comprehend rather than refute Shakespeare's singular creation. Harold Bloom suggests that Hamlet is nothing less than "the most comprehensive of all literary characters." Strong praise indeed, but it seems wholly justified.

One of the best ways to approach the character Hamlet is to view him in relation to other characters in the play; they appear at times drawn not as independent characters at all but rather as reflections and inversions of Hamlet. If you choose to work primarily with Hamlet, endless routes are available. You might begin by asking a question such as "Is Hamlet a misogynist?" or "In what way is Hamlet less than an ideal hero?" Both of these questions offer examples of precise and narrow approaches to Hamlet's character. There are broader questions, too, that allow you a freer reign across the wide horizons of Hamlet's psyche.

1. **Hamlet:** Is Hamlet feigning madness, or is he driven to it by circumstances? What does the play say about the division between madness and sanity? Can the difference even be determined in *Hamlet*? If it can, on what terms could such a distinction be made?

In such an essay, you will naturally draw on some of the material in the section on drama and theater above. After all, insofar as he is feigning his madness, he is acting it. In this way, Hamlet's character becomes an entry point into a meditation on human character or identity in general; as Hamlet performs his role we—and, it seems, he—hopelessly struggle to distinguish where natural identity ends and invention begins. The key to this essay is to recognize that Hamlet himself may not be in possession of any answers here. You should build on the idea that there may be a wide gap between Hamlet's real character and what Hamlet tells us about his character. There may be ample textual evidence to support the idea that, as Guildernstern puts it, Hamlet is suffering from nothing more than "crafty madness" (3.1.8). For example, you could marshal evidence to this effect from act 1, scene 5, line 171; act 2, scene 2, line 347; and act 3, scene 4, line 138 among many other places. Indeed, so much suggests that Hamlet is feigning madness that centering your essay on such a claim might not be the most exciting or revealing move. Instead, you might see if there is a friction or tension between such details and Hamlet's behavior. You might argue, indeed, that there is a moment at which the pretended madness is, unknown to Hamlet himself, overtaken by more real madness. Another way to frame this is by asking if Hamlet is always in full control of his actions. For example, the scene in which Hamlet interrogates Gertrude raises this question. However, there is a problem—one that might itself make a good foundation for an essay—in that the Hamlet of act 5, scene 2 seems to have acquired (how?) a remarkable calmness and resolution. Critics have long sensed that at the close of the play Hamlet has grown or developed in some way, though identifying the precise nature of the change is difficult (but worth attempting).

At this point, it is appropriate to make a brief diversion into that other classic puzzle of Hamlet's character: the divide between action and thought. For a long time, readers and writers have approached the dilemma of Hamlet's inaction, exploring psychological and emotional reasons for his delay in avenging his father. The formulaic response is that Hamlet is an intellectual hamstrung by too much thinking. This statement may or may not be true—or may just be part of the truth—but it is well worn and in need of revision. There is certainly room in this conundrum for many a good essay to tinker with—or, even better, completely overhaul—this argument. After all, as A. C. Bradley asserted in the early 20th century, Hamlet actually leaps into action (quite literally on the pirate ship and at Ophelia's grave) a number of times throughout the play. Therefore, if by offering and supporting a more specific reason for Hamlet's very specific inaction (that seems to be limited to the action of killing Claudius), you could improve the portrait of Hamlet as a somewhat wishy-washy, too-cerebral young man more inclined to acting than to action. For example, perhaps Hamlet struggles with killing Claudius because, consciously or not, he recognizes himself in his uncle (see the "Compare and Contrast Essays" section below).

2. **Gertrude and Ophelia:** Does the play *Hamlet* endorse the character Hamlet's disturbing view of women?

Individually, each of the two women characters could support her own essay. The most obvious example—and one much revisited over the years—is the issue of Gertrude's complicity with Claudius, extending into a wider consideration of the play's matriarch as mother (and Hamlet as son). Ophelia, too, provides an interesting parallel to Hamlet's madness, one that is fatally, unambiguously authentic. If so much energy has been invested in exploring Hamlet's troubled psyche, then why not explore Ophelia's psychological decline too? However, the two female characters are together here because of their telling similarities and differences. Certainly, in effect, Hamlet makes no distinction between the two women, tarring all of womanhood with the same brush (3.1.135, for example). Look at this moment in the text, as well as others in which Hamlet rails against the inconstancy and impropriety of women. Is there a symbolic pattern to his comments? Does the play give just cause to agree with Hamlet? Does your response differ from Gertrude to Ophelia? For any differences you might find, it is impossible to deny that both Ophelia and Gertrude are doomed to the same fate; the play punishes both equally. Do you agree with critics who suggest that the abuse and condemnation of the female characters, along with their tragic ends, encourages the audience to interpret the women as helpless victims of a male-dominated court? Or do you side with those who argue that Gertrude's muddied moral position in the play, along with, to a lesser extent, Ophelia's vulnerability and passivity, in fact requires the audience to accept Hamlet's famous condemnation of woman's frailty as the play's position too?

Philosophy and Ideas

Hamlet provides an unrelenting attack on the unified concept of reality. By offering so many levels of reality, so many alternative variations of the real, the play undermines any single notion of what is real and what is not. Essays treating this theme might focus on Hamlet's foregrounding of theatricality, acting, and dissembling (see the "Themes" section above). It seems that everyone is playing or acting a role, and Hamlet himself has numerous roles or identities that finally make impossible any clear sense of who the real Hamlet might be (or even that such a singular identity could exist). Look at the myriad of parallels and echoes that further add to the sense of fragmented identities scattered across the play—there are splinters and reflections of Hamlet in Ophelia, Claudius, Fortinbras, Laertes, and even that theatrically inclined lover of words, Polonius. Look for other ways in which reality might be problematized, such as the shadowy alternative reality suggested by the presence of the ghost (a presence that itself is open to question when the ghost appears to Hamlet but is invisible to Gertrude). Philosophically minded students can not only explore this dissolution of the boundaries between reality and artifice but also look for other divisions interrogated or dissolved by the play, such as madness and sanity. To do so, in fact, is to follow in Hamlet's footsteps.

> **Existentialism:** Does the play finally suggest that people can construct their own realities through philosophy? Is this what Hamlet does? What is the relationship between Hamlet's interior world (his psyche) and the exterior world around him? Is that boundary ultimately dissolved too?

In the speech quoted in the "Reading to Write" section above, Hamlet redefines his universe, distorting and diminishing the wonders of the natural world into a dead and decaying space. Denmark and the world can be transformed from vast expanses into confining prisons, all through the will and perception of the individual mind. Perhaps at the philosophical heart of such an essay, then, would be an assessment of how much power the play assigns to Hamlet's imagination. A good place to start this essay might be act 2, scene 2, in which the hapless Rosencrantz and Guildernstern are befuddled when they attempt to match wits with Hamlet. Try to puzzle through a statement like this one from Hamlet: "O God, I could be bounded in a nutshell and count myself a king of infinite space, were it not that I have bad dreams" (2.2.248–50). What does it seem to suggest about physical space, the world outside the individual, in relation to the inner existence of the self? Once more, the theme of acting and stagecraft might be useful as an example of the play's deep-rooted interest in the way humans create and script their own reality. But it is important to remember that against this current of thought and meditation is set a countercurrent of action and events: Does the play finally suggest, given the wave of death, accident, and mischance that sweeps across its conclusion, that reality—whatever that might be—does finally assert itself even on the most contemplative of souls? Look, too, for other limits to the power of thought. Think, for example, about Hamlet's famous rejection of suicide precisely because his imagination cannot comprehend it. Indeed, in a variety of ways, Hamlet's soliloquies will furnish this essay well and give writers the opportunity to work closely and at length with complicated, dense passages.

Form and Genre

The *Hamlet* story seems to have been a popular one with Elizabethan audiences, as there was another, now lost version of the play (perhaps authored by Thomas Kyd) staged a few years before Shakespeare's. But though the exact evolution is not clear—the lost *Hamlet* is a kind of missing link that prevents us from knowing exactly how Shakespeare made the story his own—it is absolutely certain that Shakespeare worked exceedingly hard to make this play a terrifying and pitch-black tragedy. After all, in the story as it was found in Scandinavian folk tradition, the hero Amleth (Hamlet) avenges his father by killing Feng, the usurping, brother-murdering king who becomes Claudius. Amleth then becomes king. In other words, the original tale is hardly tragic, as justice is fully served, the state purified, and order restored in the form of a triumphant revenge hero. Hamlet should be so lucky. As the dark, existential tones of the play suggest, *Hamlet* aspires to be more than the tragedy of an individual or small group of people. A version of the essay on existentialism could certainly be written from the angle of *Hamlet* as universal tragedy, the tragedy of existence as it is presented in the play. Another essay might consider the implications of the tragedy for the play's world. Always look for the ironies and uncertainties among the corpses of Shakespeare's tragic resolutions; ask what, if anything, has been achieved. What has been gained and what lost? As many critics have pointed out, one particularly striking irony is that by compelling Hamlet to have his revenge against Claudius, Old Hamlet ensures that Denmark will fall into the hands of his old rival, Norway, thus canceling out Old Hamlet's previous victories. Contemplate, too, the meanings of such apparently indiscriminate death in the final movement of the play. From the minor specks of Rosencrantz and Guildernstern through the middling figure of Polonious to the great majority of the principal characters, it seems that Shakespeare's tragic vision is total and encompassing. An essay might attempt to assess exactly what the sum of that vision might be—recognizing that the play seems to resist single, clear answers on anything, of course. Is the great tragedy of Hamlet simply death, the shuffling off a mortal coil? Or is it more about the way we live than the way we die, perhaps?

Revenge: Does the play endorse or denounce revenge?

Revenge appears here rather than in the "Themes" section because revenge tragedy was an extremely popular genre on the Elizabethan stage, and because Shakespeare subverts that genre so completely in *Hamlet.* It will not be necessary for writers to know much about the revenge tradition in order to tackle revenge as a topic, but a little background will be useful nonetheless.

Obviously, the Elizabethans did not invent revenge tragedy; it was in many ways the staple of ancient Greek drama. Equally, it is an important motif in contemporary film and television. What Shakespeare and his fellow 16th-century playwrights did do, however, was to revitalize and even reinvent the tradition. After all, as citizens of the early modern world, Shakespeare's contemporaries were witness to a time of transition during which social and legal conventions shifted and changed. While in ancient societies revenge was not only acceptable but essential to the maintenance of individual honor and collective justice, by the 16th century revenge was increasingly outlawed and replaced by the ideal of a state justice system. If a man's father was killed, it was not his but the state's role to avenge the death. Of course, it is impossible to know if there was a general consensus among Elizabethans that this change was a good thing or even if the change had occurred with any evenness by the time of *Hamlet.* Certainly many of Shakespeare's contemporaries wrote against individual revenge, most famously Francis Bacon, who dubbed it "wild justice." The intellectual, state, and religious institutions of Shakespeare's time all viewed revenge as not only imprudent but dangerous, a crime in and of itself. But what of the ordinary people who largely made up Shakespeare's audience? What of *Hamlet*?

You might begin this essay with an examination of act 1, scene 5. Analyze the conversation between Hamlet and his father's ghost, studying the ghost's advice to Hamlet (his tone, his expectations, etc.) and Hamlet's response. Pay close attention to Hamlet's speech beginning around line 92. What does he claim will be his approach to the task of revenge? Given Hamlet's character, is such an approach possible? Is there anyone in the play who does take this approach to revenge? Look at the way Young Fortinbras intends to avenge his father by launching war against Denmark and how Laertes becomes a vengeful fury in the name of Polonius. In contrast to these other characters, as well as his own frequent hot and bloody words about revenge (some critics have suggested that Hamlet, being such a fan of the stage, is at times performing the stereotypical role of the theatrical revenge hero, bombastically launching into formulaic promises of vengeance), how does Hamlet actually approach the act of revenge? What psychologically or emotionally separates Hamlet from Laertes? For example, you might argue that Hamlet consistently seems to require proof or knowledge of something and will not act without it; Laertes does not wait for certain knowledge before stirring up a riot in the name of revenge. The backbone of this essay, perhaps, will be an attempt to link Hamlet's character (whatever that is to you) to his execution of the avenger's task. You might also consider whether the play judges Hamlet's failings: Is the audience encouraged to regret his inability to avenge his father or prompted to some other, more complex moral response?

Compare and Contrast Essays

The very subject of revenge creates a number of compare and contrast possibilities among Shakespeare's works. Whatever you conclude *Hamlet* says about revenge, you could write an interesting essay comparing your findings for *Hamlet* with your assessment of another play. Of the plays treated in this volume, points of comparison or contrast might be found in *Julius Caesar, The Merchant of Venice,* and *The Tempest.* Is Shakespeare saying similar things, for example, in *Hamlet* and *The Tempest* if the latter is a play strongly condemning revenge in favor of reconciliation and forgiveness? Alternatively, a comparison of Hamlet to other Shakespearean tragic heroes will offer a wealth of material. A close parallel might, for example, be found in Brutus from *Julius Caesar.* Something in Brutus's nature (in this case, his commitment to old-fashioned ideals of honor that make him prey for a new breed of political machines like Octavius and Antony) makes him an ill fit for the task of political intrigue and machination, as is Hamlet. However, Hamlet belongs precisely to that same new breed of political animal as Antony, while Old Hamlet resembles the anachronistic Brutus. Comparisons of Shakespearean heroes can bend in many ways. Think about a comparison of Othello and Hamlet, for another example. An essay could be grounded in the notion that while Othello demands proof of Desdemona's infidelity, just as Hamlet seeks proof of the ghost's honesty or Claudius's guilt, the pair must finally be contrasted because Hamlet ultimately rejects the idea of truth while Othello falls victim to the illusion of truth.

Of course, *Hamlet* alone can generate a great many compare and contrast essays. Indeed, a consistent theme of this chapter has been the way in which themes and characters are mirrored and paralleled throughout. Think, for example, about a comparison between the situations of Hamlet and Laertes and the stark contrast in their responses to those similar situations. Again, even within the character Hamlet you can find enough progression and change to create a compare and contrast model of character essay by assessing the differences between Hamlet at the beginning and end of the play. What has he learned about the world and about himself? What in him has changed?

1. **Comparing Hamlet and Claudius:** How much does Hamlet resemble his enemy?

   The way to go here is with similarities rather than differences. The surprise value of this essay is in showing how these two enemies and mortal rivals have much more in common than their antipathy for each other suggests. This essay could go two ways, then—and probably both will be useful, though the second should probably form the bulk of the essay. First, you could suggest ways in which Claudius, despite his act of primal evil, can be seen in sympathetic ways. Some critics have pointed to his self-reflexive examination of his guilt, for example, or the way he appears to be in tune with the cycles of nature when he lectures Hamlet on the inevitability of death. On the other hand, and much more effective, is to show how Hamlet resembles Claudius. The bulk of the essay might bring together and contemplate moments in which the darkest components of Hamlet's character are denuded. For example, look at his murder of Polonius and its immediate aftermath, his harsh and heartless treatment of the blundering Rosencrantz and Guildernstern, his abusiveness to Ophelia and Gertrude, and—the episode that seems to disturb critics the most—the unthinkably cruel desire to consign Claudius not only to death but to eternal torment. Look, too, for other parallels, such as Hamlet's strange casting of the nephew of the king as killer in the play within the play.

2. **Contrasting Hamlet and Fortinbras:** While Fortinbras seems to impress Hamlet greatly (and vice versa, as we learn at the end of the play), how do you interpret the play's comparison of these two young men?

If the preceding essay has a surprise element, this one should win praise for the way it foregrounds a seemingly minor figure. Both essays show that you are thinking outside the box. First, assess the relationship between the pair as it is constructed early in the play. Both are young men who desire revenge for wrongs against their fathers. From this point on, however, the dominating perspective appears to be mostly one of contrast. Consider Hamlet's attempts at revenge alongside those of Young Fortinbras. What do you learn of Fortinbras's ambitions to attack Denmark and then of the replacement campaign against the Polish? A close reading of act 4, scene 5 will be at the heart of this essay. Consider Hamlet's response to Fortibras's military campaign, but also consider whether the audience is supposed to admire Fortinbras or not. Think carefully about the apparent pointlessness and recklessness of the forthcoming battle with Poland. If what separates Hamlet from Fortinbras is action, what does the comparison in this scene suggest that the play has to say about action after all?

Bibliography and Online Resources for *Hamlet*

Bloom, Harold. *Hamlet: Poem Unlimited.* New York: Riverhead, 2003.

———, ed. *Hamlet.* Philadelphia: Chelsea House, 2004.

Bradley, A. C. *Shakespearean Tragedy: Lectures on* Hamlet, Othello, King Lear, Macbeth. 1904. 3rd ed. Basingstoke, England: Macmillan, 1992.

Bristol, Michael D. *Carnival and Theater: Plebian Culture and the Structure of Authority in Renaissance England.* New York and London: Methuen, 1985.

Garber, Marjorie. *Shakespeare's Ghost Writers.* New York: Methuen, 1987.

"Hamlet on the Ramparts." Shakespeare Electronic Archives. Retrieved 15 Mar. 2007. <http://shea.mit.edu/ramparts>.

OTHELLO

READING TO WRITE

ALTHOUGH THERE are many possible approaches to writing on *Othello*, one of the most interesting is to examine the role of race. As you read this play, then, be sure to follow carefully the complex meanings and function of race. Do not fall into the trap of seeing this play as simply a black man victimized by the racism of a white society. While it is this to an extent, what the play has to say about Othello's relationship with the white Venetian community, as well as his own sense of racial identity, is far more intricate.

A passage from the play illustrates this point more clearly. The following lines come from an early key moment in act 1, scene 3. Othello is trying to convince the court that he has won the hand of Desdemona honestly, explaining how she came to love him.

> Her father loved me, oft invited me,
> Still questioned me the story of my life
> From year to year, the battles, sieges, fortunes
> That I have passed. . .
> Wherein I spoke of most dangerous chances,
> Of moving accidents by flood and field
> Of hair-breadth scapes i'th' imminent deadly breach,
> Of being taken by the insolent foe
> And sold to slavery, of my redemption thence . . .
> And of the cannibals that each other eat,
> . . .the Anthropophagi, and men whose heads
> Do grow beneath their shoulders. . . .

She [Desdemona] loved me for the dangers I had passed,
And I loved her that she did pity them.
This is the only witchcraft I have used. (3.1.127–68)

This short passage reveals an enormous amount that could form the foundation for an essay. Notice that the passage begins with a significant clue to Othello's status in white Venice. Brabanzio, Desdemona's father, now outraged by the marriage of Othello to his daughter, was once comfortable inviting Othello to his house. At this point, you might reflect on the degree to which Othello has been accepted by and welcomed into Venice, asking perhaps if that welcome is unconditional.

Othello continues by recounting how he entertained those gathered at Brabanzio's house with stories of his past. The content of these stories opens up one of the most important concepts in the play: the conscious and unconscious ways Othello's actions are determined by his race. Notice the exotic sights and curiosities populating his tale, the fantastic and monstrous symbols of a dark world away from the civilization of Europe. Is Othello merely recollecting things he has seen and done, or is he wittingly using his otherness to appeal to his audience (and, perhaps, Desdemona)?

So far, race seems to be playing a powerful though benign role in Othello's Venetian life. It grants him a difference that he uses to his advantage for public and, as Desdemona comes to "pity" him, private gain. (And do not ignore Othello's use of the word *pity* in describing Desdemona's responses to his tales. Take this as a cue to think carefully—as Othello himself will do to a fatal extent—about the roots of the play's central marriage.) But notice how the final lines of the passage disrupt this complicated but largely benign interpretation of race. Consider the implications of Brabanzio's accusing Othello of employing "witchcraft" to woo Desdemona—he is at a loss for other ways to explain what is to him and his society such an inexplicable decision on his daughter's part. The dark and mystical elements of the story Othello told to his advantage are reflected in the preexisting cultural imagination of white Venice. They are brought to the surface when Othello wants to be more to Venice than a fascinating sideshow, when he wants to become a member of the European community. As you write, focus on other ways in which racially motivated feelings emerge from hidden places in unexpected ways.

As this small cross section of the play's racial discourse suggests, you should resist the assumption that because Shakespeare's play is four centuries old it is from a simpler time. The best way to approach the social issues contained in *Othello* is to recognize that while different, the racial relationships in Shakespeare's lifetime were as fraught and complex as they can be today.

TOPICS AND STRATEGIES

Every essay requires a focus; you cannot write about everything in the play at once. The section on how to write an essay shows you a number of ways to turn a focus into a thesis, observations into arguments. However, the starting point is nearly always finding an initial focus and making first observations. What follows is a discussion of *Othello* geared toward helping you make the most of the budding ideas you will have as you read the play. By no means should you feel limited to these topics, however.

Themes

While many students will be drawn to the theme of race in *Othello,* many alternative avenues are available. For example, there is in *Othello* a stark and frightening contemplation of the nature of evil, of unlimited hatred. A paper treating gender in the play, focusing perhaps on Desdemona's restricted control of her fate and person, might not include analysis of race. But as race is a particularly popular choice among student writers working with this play, it is discussed at some length here. Clearly, the key to writing about race in this play is to have a sharp focus on a specific aspect of that theme. You should use a thesis statement to make sure your essay avoids becoming merely a broad discussion of race in the play.

In a close reading of the passage above, the opening and closing lines suggest how Othello is viewed by the white denizens of Venice. This perspective on race in the play might make for a good, sharp essay. What exactly does Othello mean to the state he serves? You should certainly consider the hypocritical opinions expressed by Brabanzio but also the seemingly different point of view held by the duke. Why does the duke defend Othello against Brabanzio's charges? Look closely, too, at Lodovico's response in act 4, scene 1 to Othello's violence. Of course, as in any paper, you must think about what limits to place on your study. For example, should Iago be included in such an essay? What about Desdemona?

Regardless, this essay would clearly have a more or less limited scope. The limit is created when you say, "I will think only about how Othello is viewed by other people and in that way build an understanding of the society in which Othello lives." You could also achieve a similar effect without placing such rigorous textual limitations on yourself, however. To do so, think about questions offering the chance to discuss race in the play more broadly while still ensuring a tight focus. For example, you ask some variation of the following question: To what extent is this play racist? To write this essay, you would look for evidence of Shakespeare's sympathies for Othello or, conversely, the playwright's reliance on and perpetuation of racial stereotyping.

Sample Topics

1. **Race:** How central is race to the play's action? To what extent is the action driven by race?

   Such an essay might begin by identifying explicit statements of racism in the play. Do not simply list them, however. See if you can characterize the patterns and central principles of racial discord as they appear in *Othello*. For example, Brabanzio naturally slips into identifying Othello as a magical, witch-like figure born of some otherwordly place. Look, too, at the opening exchange among Iago, Roderigo, and Brabanzio. Try to spot commonalities of image and metaphor that shape the racist slurs abounding in the first scene. How does society perceive the marriage between Othello and Desdemona? Read for patterns of language and symbolism invoking the unnatural or the bestial.

   Perhaps, however, the most intriguing element of this theme can be found in Othello's own conflicted sense of racial identity. Try to gain psychological insight into Othello's perception of himself by locating passages in which he expresses anxieties about his marriage that are anchored in his racial identity. Identify the ways in which Iago brings these deep-seated anxieties to the surface in Othello. Then find evidence of a growing division in Othello's sense of self. How might Shakespeare be intending his audience to see Othello's transformation in the second half of the play through a racial lens? Be sure to include a discussion of Othello's final speech, unraveling the complex layers of racial metaphor and meaning that surround his suicide. The key to such an essay might lie in identifying the nature of Othello's divided self. How does this split personality stem directly from the racial conditions of the life he tried to lead in Venice and the social anxieties that appear to have weighed heavily on him all along?

2. **Love:** Although we hear much from the Venetians condemning Othello and Desdemona's marriage, how does Shakespeare represent the love between a white woman and a black man?

Again, a good place to begin this essay might be the opening scene, in which Iago's vulgar jibes caricature the physical relationship between Othello and Desdemona. Compare this view from the outside to moments where the lovers characterize their marriage. What is the dynamic of the marriage as the play opens? What kind of husband is Othello? What, for him, appears to be the correct way to love Desdemona? What draws Desdemona to Othello in the first place? As you write, you might then work backward from Othello's final observation that everything has gone wrong because he "loved not wisely but too well" (5.2.353). Was excessive love really the root of Othello's fall? The most important thing might be to recognize that love here does not exist in isolation from the social and psychological ghosts that haunt Othello from the start. Try to identify the various pressures exerted on the love between Desdemona and Othello, perhaps finding scenes that challenge Othello's final, too-neat judgment of what went wrong.

Character

A character essay on Othello might obviously draw on many of the same questions and textual moments as an essay on the theme of race. A character study of Iago, moreover, while allowing the student to move away from the theme of race somewhat, presents clear problems of its own. Principally, the main appeal of Iago for many students is precisely what makes him difficult to write about; he is an enigmatic presence about whom there is arguably little concrete to say beyond a few textual clues to his purposes. Certainly none of this means that you should avoid character analysis essays on *Othello*. On the contrary, such an approach opens up different aspects of Othello's character for study or might provide a good way to narrow the focus of an essay on race or some other theme. For example, an essay asking whether Shakespeare's presentation of Othello is sympathetic, given the absolute centrality of race to an understanding of Othello's character, is a very specific reformulation of a thesis seeking to evaluate how Shakespeare handles race. The key to a character essay on this play, then, is recognizing that each character is a product of his or her society, as mired in the same swamp of conventions and prejudices as the next character.

1. **Othello:** How would you explain Othello's transformation from military hero, darling of the Venetian elite, to a murderer who appears to kill his wife over nothing more substantial than a handkerchief?

   As discussed above, such an essay will use many of the same concepts and textual moments as an essay on the theme of race. A good structure for this essay might be to start by briefly showing the reader Othello as he is at the beginning and then proceed to a more substantial analysis of the character at the end of the play, focusing on the idea of Othello as a divided, torn man. The remainder of the essay would cover the middle portion of the play, detailing the complex mix of social and psychological elements that lead to his transformation. Do not forget, though, that the seeds of this transformation might not be found in Iago's machinations but in the workings of European society and Othello's attempts to belong within it.

2. **Desdemona:** Is Desdemona merely a passive victim of the tragedy that overcomes her? Or does she help bring disaster on herself, as some critics have suggested, through her desires?

As you read, look for ways in which Desdemona is marginalized. There seem to be similarities between Othello's status as a black man in Venetian society and Desdemona's as a woman: Both are clearly outside the authoritative heart of the community. Pay close attention especially to the early scenes in which she is argued over as if a belonging, an object whose ownership is contested between father and husband. Even more controversially, is Desdemona portrayed as being "punished" for her desires, succumbing to erotic fantasies centered on the other? Look for ways in which she is increasingly associated with images of darkness and evil instead of the language of purity and whiteness that surrounds her at the start. Try to wrestle meaning from the link between Desdemona and the servant Barbary (almost certainly intended to have been black), emphasized by the "Willow" song moments before Othello kills Desdemona. Remember that in Renaissance symbolism, whiteness was understood to represent goodness while blackness was a metaphor for evil. Has Desdemona finally undergone a transformation that mirrors Othello's progression to a divided racial identity?

3. **Iago:** What are Iago's motivations as a villain? Are they substantial enough to give meaning to his character and the actions he takes?

Many students are drawn to this essay, but exercise care; this is a difficult one to write well. The romantic poet and critic Samuel Coleridge complained that Iago's motives were inexplicable and insufficient to make the action of the play believable. Look carefully through the early scenes of the drama, in which Iago offers a number of explanations for what he is about to do. Do you find these convincing? If not, you should embrace Iago's lack of dimension; think about Iago as a symbolic character, a representation of evil rather than a well-rounded, multidimensional figure. This approach connects him to the medieval stage tradition of the vice, a character who simply represents a negative quality such as greed or lust, for example. If you view Iago as symbolic, what exactly is Shakespeare saying about evil?

You should certainly not hesitate to differ in your essay with this take on Iago if you do not agree; this will take you in a different but no less profitable direction. If you accept Iago's early justifications as substantial enough to propel him forward, you might claim that his jealousy mirrors that of Othello and thus shapes the play into a warning against excessive envy. This approach argues for Iago's complexity and humanness, perhaps the most frightening of all possible interpretations of this character. If Iago is more than a symbol, how might you begin to explain a figure of such unmitigated evil?

History and Context

Much of the intellectual energy surrounding *Othello* in recent decades has been generated by a school of criticism known as postcolonial studies. Along with several other Shakespeare plays, *Othello* has received attention from these critics, who hope to obtain a better understanding of Europe's encounter with the ever-growing outside world in the early modern era. From this perspective, *Othello* becomes a historical document of considerable importance because it takes as its thematic focus precisely this encounter.

This type of approach gives the student an opportunity to write about and participate in the very latest critical trends. As in any historically minded essay, you will need to follow the basic strategy of researching the historical moment and comparing it to the episodes and characters of the play.

Sample Topic

The African or Moor in Europe: What was the relationship between Europeans and the Africans, or Moors, existing on or within their borders? In what ways does Shakespeare engage real issues and anxieties of his time in *Othello*?

There were relatively few people of African origin living in Shakespeare's England. However, their presence was enough of an issue for Elizabeth I to give a proclamation that they should be removed from the land. To the east of Europe, the Turks represented a grave military threat to Christendom. Finally, of course, the empires of Europe in the New World were being built by the muscle of enslaved African labor, whose lives were so cheaply expended to make colossal profit from crops such as sugar in the West Indies. In short, there was a mix of fear and subjection that in many ways is replicated in Othello's story. G. K. Hunter's classic study *Dramatic Identities and Cultural Tradition* is a slightly dated but nonetheless good place to begin research in this area. More contemporary but perhaps less accessible is the impressive body of work being written by postcolonial critic Ania Loomba.

As you write this essay, compare the historical record to two components of the play. First, look at what characters say and do throughout the play. You will find many of the same anxieties and prejudices in the words of the characters as you do in the historical record. Then try to view the play as a statement about the European encounter with the African (or Moor) distinct from the sentiments of its characters. Ruth Cowhig argues that in writing *Othello,* Shakespeare breaks new ground of sympathy and tolerance for a black character. She points out that regardless of Othello's flaws, Shakespeare consciously avoids the otherwise inevitable stereotype of the villainous black man that audiences would have expected. Indeed, Shakespeare seems deliberately to soften his version of Othello compared with the more sinister Othello character found in his source material. Assess Shakespeare's voice against the historical record, the typical sentiments and opinions of his day. Find how he is of his time in this way, as well as other ways in which he is ahead of it.

Philosophy and Ideas

Othello is a play about passions far more than it is a play about ideas; the heart and not the head is Shakespeare's primary setting for this text. Othello's great weakness, as he understands it, is precisely that he does not think enough. (How might this be considered one more of the stereotypical traits of Shakespeare's tragic heros?) Iago, however, thinks quickly and spontaneously, but it might be difficult to identify any overarching or grand philosophy animating his thoughts. Indeed, many have argued that Iago's significant intelligence is ungoverned by any cohesive intellect. Nonetheless, there is still scope for writing an essay about the philosophical content of the play. Iago's very rejection of a guiding philosophy creates a philosophical problem for a writer considering the nature of evil in this play. Othello's self-division could also be viewed as a philosophical problem of consciousness that is as much internal as it is social. These essays might encourage you to take on philosophical questions hand-in-hand with an analysis of the play's social conditions. However, *Othello* also asks philosophical questions that escape social context and approach the universal.

Sample Topic

The relationship between appearances and reality: What does the play say about the relationship between perceptions and actualities, what we see and feel compared with what actually is? To what degree can the characters of *Othello* (and, by implication, the rest of us too) trust their senses?

To write an essay of this kind, you must be willing to look at many different aspects of the play. This philosophical theme manifests itself so frequently and in so many different contexts that you should certainly give it thought. As you read and prepare to write, identify moments where appearance and reality are at odds. Look for ironic details such as the frequent labeling of Iago as "honest" or for moments when speech and language appear to be persuasive and clear but are merely lies. Perhaps more important and more troubling is the way in which Othello's demand for "ocular proof" results in Iago's staging the convincing but utterly false scene of Cassio's "confession." It might be inevitable that we cannot always trust other people when they talk, but what is Shakespeare attempting to say by showing how Othello's most reliable of senses, his sight, is as vulnerable to deception as his ears? Follow closely, too, the passage of the the handkerchief, perhaps the clearest and most famous symbol of how truth is so difficult to find in *Othello*. Look for and comment on ways in which the meaning of this piece of fabric shifts several times throughout the play. Finally, and perhaps most difficult of all, you might want to consider how this theme is connected to the play's consideration of race. The strongest case for a racially sympathetic *Othello* might rest in the play's obsession with inaccurate and mistaken perceptions, cautioning against the failure to look beneath the surface and see what truly matters.

Form and Genre

For a very long time *Othello* was maligned by many critics. They perceived a number of dramatic failures that supposedly compromised the play's success. Questions of Shakespeare's workmanship in *Othello* have largely been supplanted (or explained) by the kinds of critical interests we have already discussed, but they nonetheless offer good material for students interested in the mechanics of the play. As you write, however, be sure to look for connections between form and content. In other words, are Shakespeare's seeming mistakes really mistakes at all? Do they in fact help illuminate the themes treated in the play?

Sample Topics

1. **The failures of characterization in *Othello*:** To what extent are Shakespeare's characters in *Othello* plausible? Are their motives and actions naturalistic or psychologically real enough to be credible?

   An essay of this type might address two of the most common charges against Shakespeare's development of character in *Othello:* first, that Iago's murderous scheme is not explained or adequately justified by any compensating motive (see the "Character" section on Iago above for suggestions on how to approach this question), and second, that Othello is too gullible to earn the audience's respect, too lightweight compared with Shakespeare's great tragic heroes. Perhaps you agree with one or both of these statements, in which case your essay will be an attempt to support these familiar claims. In the case of Othello, you will focus on what appears to some to be a frustrating lack of healthy suspicion or awareness of those around him. It might be more interesting, however, to challenge one or both of these objections. Again, to take Othello as an example, it might be that his apparently inexplicable naivete is actually nothing less than justifiable self-doubt born from an acute awareness of his vulnerable position in Venetian society.

2. **The quality of Othello's tragedy:** What is the tragic catharsis of *Othello*? Does its tragic movement compare well to Shakespeare's other great tragedies?

Tragedies were expected to contain a certain number of characteristics, including a clear cathartic value likened to a purging of fearful emotions. To put this simply, tragedy was expected to be grand, with great men falling against obstacles of universal magnitude. Such an awesome spectacle cleansed the common audience member by instructing him or her at the expense of the tragic character. In short, the criticism often leveled at *Othello* over the last 400 years has been that it is not serious or grand enough, that Othello, his decisions, and his circumstances are too poorly contrived and explained for the play to function as a tragedy should. Your essay would proceed from this charge, defending it or challenging it as you wish. The latter approach might begin by identifying a substantial cathartic effect at work in the play, showing how *Othello* is more than a mere domestic drama driven by foolish decisions and a lady's handkerchief. Where is the significant dramatic power located in the text? In what way have critics misinterpreted or undervalued the tragic elements of the play? You might develop a number of ideas from this chapter to help you make your case, but also consider the possibility that this tradition of devaluing the play is a product of the same kind of social prejudices visible in the action of the play itself. After all, until as recently as the mid-20th century, a good deal of criticism on this play had a distinctly racist flavor (see, for example, M. R. Ridley's notorious discussion of the play in his introduction to the Arden Shakespeare edition of *Othello* in the 1950s).

Compare and Contrast Essays:

Othello lends itself more easily to certain kinds of compare and contrast essays than others. It may be a little difficult to find elements of character, action, or structure within the play that invite comparison or contrast. Nonetheless, set about looking for pairs in *Othello* and you will find them. For example, you could compare the only two women in the play, Desdemona and Emilia. In this essay, you would want to pay close attention to the conversations they have with each other, especially the remarkable exchange about adultery shortly before their deaths. Shakespeare seems to be presenting two different models of womanhood, but be careful not to jump quickly to judgment against Emilia. After all, her speech might be read as the only moment of female empowerment in the play. Try to characterize the two models of feminine conduct that these women represent, but try to see ways in which Shakespeare might intend them to be complementary as well as oppositional.

Some of the most energetic student essays, however, will look outside the play for reference points. One play that encourages comparison of this kind is *The Tempest*, another of Shakespeare's works dramatizing the encounter between white Europeans and a foreign other. Although the settings may differ, look for ways in which the Europeans' treatment of Ariel, Caliban, and the island itself overlaps with the Venetians' treatment of Othello.

Sample Topics

1. **Comparing Shylock in *The Merchant of Venice* to Othello:** To what extent do these marginalized figures resemble each other? Does Shakespeare make similar or different points about otherness through these characters?

   An essay such as this might focus on moments in which sympathy is created for each of these outsiders. Look at Shylock's well-known speech in act 3, scene 1, lines 45–61, but also at other moments that bring Shylock and the audience together. These might include Jessica's desertion of Shylock (and her sale of his treasured engagement ring for a monkey), as well as the complex emotional makeup of the trial scene. Both Shylock and Othello eloquently express themselves and articulate their place in society, so look for moments in both plays when this occurs. Are their fates in any way similar, brought about by related social dynamics?

2. **Contrast Shakespeare's *Othello* to Tim Blake Nelson's film adaptation *O* (2001):** What changes occur in the process of updating *Othello* by 400 years?

Contrasting a Shakespeare play to a film adaptation can make for a good essay, but in this case the possibilities are especially varied because this 2001 film takes more liberties with the text than a traditional adaptation might. Indeed, the film entirely abandons Shakespeare's language in the process of modernizing the story, though it remains thematically true to the spirit of the text. Watch the film closely for shifts, omissions, or additions to the narrative of the play. Consider the way in which race functions differently in the movie. The relationship between Odin (Mekhi Phifer) and Desi (Julia Stiles) is now less outwardly controversial than Othello and Desdemona's, but look for moments when race inevitably influences this modern tragedy. For example, does it still seem that Desi is drawn to Odin at least in part because of his difference? Watch for moments where the lovers discuss race with an openness and candor unavailable on Shakespeare's stage. Think, too, about shifts in the motivations of Hugo (the Iago character in the movie, played by Josh Hartnett) that help make his behavior more comprehensible, in particular, his use of steroids and the addition of a troubled relationship with his father, Duke, who appears to love Odin more than his own son.

Bibliography and Online Resources for *Othello*

Cowhig, Ruth. "Blacks in English Renaissance Literature and the Role of Shakespeare's Othello." *The Black Presence in English Literature.* Ed. David Dabydeen. Manchester, England: Manchester UP, 1985. 1–26.

Hall, Kim. *Things of Darkness: Economies of Race and Gender in Early Modern England.* Ithaca, N.Y.: Cornell UP, 1995.

Hendricks, Margo, and Patricia Parker, eds. *Women, "Race," and Writing in the Early Modern Period.* London and New York: Routledge, 1994.

Loomba, Ania, and Martin Orkin, eds. *Postcolonial Shakespeares.*London and New York: Routledge, 1998.

"Othello. Home Page. Internet Shakespeare Editions." Retrieved 16 Mar. 2007. <http://ise.uvic.ca/Library/plays/Oth.html>.

Vitkus, Daniel. "Turning Turk in *Othello:* The Conversion and Damnation of the Moor." *Shakespeare Quarterly* 48, no. 2 (Summer 1997): 145–76.

KING LEAR

READING TO WRITE

KING LEAR makes large demands of the reader in at least three ways. First, it is a very long play. This may sound like a shallow point, but it affects how we read and write about the work. Indeed, the play is so immense that it may be useful to keep a log as you read, writing a short summary of each scene. If you jot down important episodes, ideas, and speeches in one place, navigating the play in your prewriting and writing stages will become easier (and a detailed essay plan or outline will be even more essential here than ever). Try to keep the log relatively brief; otherwise, it will itself become a daunting text. Next, as numerous critics have observed, the play is emotionally demanding for readers and audiences, requiring them to follow increasingly painful events (see the "Form and Genre" section below). Finally, the play is intellectually demanding, pressing us to see and perceive despite the play's recurring bouts of blindness, even to find something in the play's obsession with "nothing." All of this amounts to a significant challenge for both the reader and the essay writer, but there is enormous satisfaction at the end. The following passage from the play, Edmund's soliloquy at the beginning of act 1, scene 2, illuminates some important themes and issues in the text.

> Thou, nature, art my goddess; to thy law
> My services are bound. Wherefore should I
> Stand in the plague of custom, and permit
> The curiosity of nations to deprive me,

For that I am some twelve or fourteen moon-shines
Lag of a brother? Why bastard? wherefore base?
When my dimensions are as well compact,
My mind as generous, and my shape as true,
As honest madam's issue? Why brand they us
With base? with baseness? bastardy? base, base?
Who, in the lusty stealth of nature, take
More composition and fierce quality
Than doth, within a dull, stale, tired bed,
Go to the creating a whole tribe of fops,
Got 'tween asleep and wake? Well, then,
Legitimate Edgar, I must have your land:
Our father's love is to the bastard Edmund
As to the legitimate: fine word,—legitimate!
Well, my legitimate, if this letter speed,
And my invention thrive, Edmund the base
Shall top the legitimate. I grow; I prosper:
Now, gods, stand up for bastards! (1.2.1–22)

Edmund's speech begins with a rejection of law in favor of nature. He understands the latter to mean a chaotic, disordered free-for-all in which human custom is trumped by a kind of Darwinian survival of the fittest or smartest. However, this interpretation forms just one strand of the play's thinking on the theme of nature, and an essay writer could take Edmund's anarchic vision as the starting point for a much broader essay. If human laws and customs represent the unnatural for Edmund, while brutal self-reliance is for him the sole character of the natural world, does the play agree? If not, what does nature mean in *King Lear*? Look for the way in which human customs and natural laws seem to overlap in the play. For example, the devotion of children to their parents, tender and respectful treatment of the aged, and the integrity of a nation are all human laws so entrenched in our lives that they appear to be part of nature. Look for ways in which these and other natural laws are abused and broken. Assess signs that nature is angry at these breaches of faith; for example, Gloucester's superstitious foreboding (1.2.101) and the great storm at the center of the play (see "Themes" below). Finally, the fates of the characters might be used to discuss the role of nature in the play's tragedy. In his final line of the passage above, Edmund exclaims, "Now, gods, stand up for bastards!" But do they do so in the play? How exactly do the gods and nature behave toward the characters? Does nature triumph? At what cost? Perhaps the most chilling conclusion to reach is that Edmund's assessment of nature and the play's assessment of nature are in many ways alike. You might finally argue that the play also believes that nature is chaotic, random, and brutal, that nature itself is a human construct that masks the disordered universe of *King Lear.*

The passage might also lead you toward an essay based on character analysis. Indeed, Edmund is a remarkable creation who deserves intensive study. For writers attempting such an essay, act 1, scene 2 is an important scene. It contains not only the passage cited above but several others that provide insight into Edmund's motivations and malign independence (1.2.109–25; 1.2.102–8). Think carefully about the social limitations placed on Edmund as an illegitimate child, but, more important, reflect on his philosophical challenges to those limitations. Ask what makes Edmund an attractive or at least seductive character not only to Goneril and Regan but to the audience as well. Finally, no paper on Edmund would be complete without consideration of his perplexing behavior at the play's close (5.3). Assess not only his commitment to the speedy execution of Lear and Cordelia but the curious conversion of his final lines (242–46). Formulate an explanation for his desire to "do some good," and consider what he means when he says to do so would be "Despite of mine own nature." Does Edmund, the memorable villain of the piece, finally have his own tragedy to suffer as well?

TOPICS AND STRATEGIES

Every essay requires a focus; you cannot write about everything in the play at once. The section on how to write an essay shows you a number of ways to turn a focus into a thesis, observations into arguments. However, the starting point is nearly always finding an initial focus and making first observations. What follows is a discussion of *King Lear* geared toward helping you make the most of the budding ideas you will have as you read the play. By no means should you feel limited to these topics, however.

Themes

King Lear takes for its themes some of the most important issues of human existence; indeed, it might even be argued that it is transcendent, stretching beyond the limits of this world and the common mind. Certainly the play's greatness (and it is routinely talked of as Shakespeare's finest, most powerful work) is located in the text's ideas and themes rather than in its story. Indeed, its plot has prompted much criticism over the centuries, and it is difficult to see how the story alone could make an enduring work of literature. Yet somehow the glaringly silly mistakes of an old man, potentially implausible and contemptible, are the starting point for one of the most celebrated works of art in Western civilization; the themes of the piece quickly soar far above the narrative starting point, and writers must be willing to follow. This is no small commitment.

Many of the themes considered in this chapter immediately betray their philosophical, transcendent substance: vision, nature, nothingness. There are, however, some more worldly themes offered by the play. For example, if you are interested in gender, you could certainly engage the play successfully from a feminist stance. You might take as your starting point the oft-noted absence of a wife for Lear, contemplating why Shakespeare might omit the figure of a wife and mother and what effect it has on the domestic dynamics of the play. The figures of Goneril and Regan would clearly offer you much material, as would Lear's misogynist declarations throughout the middle section of the play. And, of course, for contrast, there is Cordelia. But what is gained by this contrast? What does the play seem to say about female authority (think about the treatment of fathers and husbands)? If Cordelia is to be seen as the play's idealized vision of woman, assess exactly what that vision entails.

This material or political approach to the play, examining the text's conscious and unconscious revelations about Shakespeare's treatment of gender, is a vital part of reappraising *Lear.* However, many students are drawn to the challenges of *Lear's* universal aspirations, its timeless study of human folly and suffering.

1. **Vision:** What are the limits of human vision in *King Lear*? Is it possible to truly see? What would true sight reveal?

Such an essay might start with the idea that there are two types of blindness and two types of sight in the play: literal sight and blindness (what we see or cannot see with our eyes) and the superior vision of true perception, the mind's eye. Catalog and interpret examples of both literal and symbolic blindness in *Lear.* For example, assess how Lear's blindly misguided actions in act 1, scene 1 (the disowning of Cordelia, the banishment of Kent, and the division of his kingdom) mirror the literal (and symbolic) blindness of Gloucester. Catalog other parts of the text where sight is mentioned, using such examples both as evidence of the play's preoccupation with sight and as part of your own formulation of what sight means in *Lear.* Particularly important scenes include act 3, scene 7 (where Gloucester's eyes are plucked out to Cornwall's magnificently grisly cry of "out, vile jelly!") and the powerful act 4, scene 6 in which Edgar leads his blind father to an imaginary cliff (analyze the way so much that is not real is seen in this episode). Consider the idea that it is possible to have literal vision while seeing nothing at all (Lear in act 1, scene 1; Gloucester's pitiful acknowledgment in act 4, scene 1 that he "stumbled when I saw"). Equally, contemplate the way in which the play suggests that sight and true vision can be achieved even when a person is literally blind (Gloucester) or maddened (Lear). What is it that Lear and Gloucester finally come to see? While you can certainly begin answering this question by noting that the fathers finally see which of their children can be trusted and which cannot, the more powerful insights will address what the two aging men see, or realize, about themselves and their behavior.

2. **The storm:** What symbolic power does the storm of act 3 possess?

Storms are important symbols in Shakespearean drama (if you are interested in a comparative approach to the theme of the storm, other examples can be found in *Twelfth Night, Othello,*

The Winter's Tale, and *The Tempest*), but nowhere does Shakespeare imbue a storm with more meaning and complexity than in *King Lear.* In short, Shakespeare tends to associate the power of the storm with a moment of change or transition. But in *Lear* the storm is not merely a catalyst but rather the centerpiece of the drama, a presence as strong and memorable as any of the characters. Perhaps the most accessible way to approach this essay would be to examine the storm's effects primarily on Lear, but a broader approach could be taken as well. An essay of the former type might begin by assessing Lear's character before the storm and end with an evaluation of Lear after the storm. The bulk of the essay, however, should probably be devoted to a close reading of the storm scenes (3.2, 3.4, and 3.6) and the steady transformation of Lear taking place during his encounter with the storm. The best essays will chart a progression rather than a sudden enlightenment, seeing in each of the three scenes a different stage in Lear's transformation. One model, for example, might focus on Lear's anger in act 3, scene 2 as the violence of the storm mirrors his rage; then move into act 3, scene 4, looking for evidence of newly acquired insights on Lear's part; and conclude with his final, overwhelming collapse of act 3, scene 6 into a tempest of madness and pain.

Character

Lear contains some of Shakespeare's most complex and memorable characters. The thematic ambitions of the play demand characters who develop and change, bend and twist in the ferocious storm of the play's tragedy. Literally, even the most minor characters in the play are capable of offering enormous material for an essay. For example, as Cornwall gouges out Gloucester's eye, one of Cornwall's servants tries to intervene and stop his master (3.7.73–85). The servant has only nine lines, fails to stop Cornwall, and indeed is killed by Regan, but only after fatally wounding his lord. There is something enigmatic about this fellow who is so unimportant in the grand scheme, tries to do a good deed, harbors dreams of justice and heroism, but dies almost as quickly as he arrived on the scene. There is something all too human and genuinely tragic about him. And while it might be a bit much to attempt an entire essay on this ill-fated but well-intentioned figure, he could become a meaningful part of wider essays. For example, a paper on servant characters in the play would allow a blend of character study and thematic analysis. Two other characters who would certainly belong in such an essay are the chivalric Kent and the toadying Oswald. Using these three characters, such an essay might explore the servant's place in the social or natural order. You might liken it to the parent-child relationship also explored in the play; thus, the servant becomes another example of a person born into a natural place who must come to terms with the limits of that existence and determine how to live best within those confines. This is precisely what Edmund cannot do, for example, and what Kent appears utterly devoted to. Assess how a servant should serve his master according to the thematic structure of the play, and look for telling similarities and differences between the apparently divergent Kent and Oswald. Once you have defined how the play understands good service, you can explore the paradoxes and complexity of this concept. For example, the man who tries to stop Cornwall from ripping out an old man's eyes does so by reminding his master of the lifetime of faithful service he has given to Cornwall and by framing this intervention as part of that service. Yet to Cornwall and Regan he is an impudent peasant, a bad servant who deserves no more thanks than to be stabbed in the back.

1. **King Lear:** What has Lear's tragedy taught him?

> A character study of Lear is a large task, but by no means unmanageable. Indeed, in some ways, the more there is to say on a subject the easier it is to write an essay on it. You certainly will not run out of things to say in a five- or 10-page paper on this topic. However, there are several important strategy points to be made. First, while the basic technique of a character study is to trace the progression of a character from point A to point B, this is rarely a straight line. Perhaps nowhere is this truer than Lear; the play takes him to enormous depths of anguish and suffering, anger and blindness, before his sight is restored. Lear's progress is imperfect and filled with lapses; be prepared to trace a winding path as you follow Lear's passage

from the start of the play to the close. Nor is it clear what Lear achieves, what his newly found vision perceives. This is for you to decide, and this assessment would make an excellent thesis statement with which to start the paper. The body of the essay would then track and interpret the steps in Lear's journey.

It is arguably much easier to know where Lear starts than to understand where he ends. Such an essay should surely begin with a detailed examination of act 1, scene 1, identifying the nature of what Kent calls Lear's "hideous rashness" (1.1.151). Try to understand the king's apparently inexplicable behavior, characterizing the possible psychological motivations behind it. You might follow these same faults as they appear in the buildup to the storm scenes. See, for example, Lear's insistence on keeping a large retinue of men and Goneril and Regan's calculated efforts to strip him of his train. Then a careful consideration of the storm scenes is required, recognizing again that the storm does not cause an instant epiphany for Lear but a gradual weathering of self (see "Themes" above). The essay might follow an analysis of the storm scenes with an explication of Lear immediately after the storm as his madness slowly transitions into vision, or, as Edgar puts it, Lear develops "reason in madness" (4.6.169). Close read act 4, scene 6 and act 4, scene 7, looking in the former for growing wisdom and in the latter for Lear's redemption through Cordelia. It is possible to argue that Lear's education is complete by the end of act 4, scene 7 and that the remainder of the play intensifies his suffering and destroys him. You may or may not agree with this position, but a careful consideration of his death scene in act 5, scene 3 will probably be a good idea regardless. There is a lot of material to work with, so give yourself ample time to write and a put together a detailed plan before starting the essay. This will help you avoid spending too long, for example, on Lear before the storm and running out of time, energy, and pages before the final gusts of the storm have blown. Indeed, you might give significantly more weight to the storm scenes and the scenes immediately after. It is your understanding of these scenes of Lear's complicated transformation that are central to your essay.

2. **The Fool:** Why does the Fool disappear in the second half of the play?

Such an essay understands the Fool more as a function than a character and seeks to understand why he is no longer needed after the storm scenes. The writer might begin by evaluating the Fool's contribution to the play in the earlier scenes. Clearly, he is an example of a traditional type called the "wise fool," a figure whose position as a clown grants him the freedom to speak truths that would be punishable from the lips of other characters (see Kent's banishment, for example). What truths does the Fool reveal to Lear? Examine the corrective reproaches offered by the Fool in act 1, scene 4 and subsequent scenes. To account for the Fool's disappearance, it might be useful to say that perhaps Lear no longer needs the clown's blunt chastisements. But why, do you think? What is it that Lear now understands that he did not before? You might also see the Fool as a childlike figure and assess the treatment he receives in the storm scenes from Lear. This angle adds to the idea of the Fool teaching Lear traits and insights he must gain in order to find redemption later in the play. In this light, you might want to tackle and explain the puzzling blur between Cordelia and the Fool in act 5, scene 3. As Lear clutches the body of his daughter he exclaims, "My poor fool is hanged." While *fool* is a term of endearment not out of place here, given the audience's awareness of the character called the Fool and his sudden absence, the line resonates with a strange double meaning. A difficult but praiseworthy final step for this essay, then, might be to assign the Fool a place in the resolution of this tragedy, explaining why he reappears in this perplexingly ghostly manner.

3. **Edgar:** Edgar is often described as being a collection of characters rather than a single, unified person. Is this correct? If so, what importance does each of his characters have in the play?

Such an essay might begin by establishing Edgar's function in the play before act 2, scene 3. Central to this might be the contrast of Edgar with Edmund. Close read the brief episode of act 2, scene 3, which culminates with Edgar's "I nothing am." An enigmatic statement like this is a gift to the essay writer because it opens up numerous interpretive possibilities. The statement could be connected to the theme of nothing, a motif so prominent in the play starting with Lear and Cordelia's early quibble over the word (1.1.86–90). Alternatively, you could interpret the statement in terms of Edgar's mutability, his ceaseless changing and transforming from this point on.

Certainly Edgar's most memorable disguise is Poor Tom, the deranged and homeless beggar who haunts the open country. Assess the functions of Tom, perhaps connecting him with the Fool. What truth emerges from Tom's apparently fearful babble? What purpose does Tom serve in the slow transformation of Lear and Gloucester? Consider the symbolic importance of other disguises adopted by Edgar, the kindly peasant who finds Gloucester at the bottom of the imaginary cliff and the nameless knight who triumphs over Edmund.

Related to the issue of disguise is the idea of ambiguity in Edgar's character (if there is enough continuity through the sequence of disguises to call Edgar a cohesive character, of course). Critics have pointed to at least two causes for concern here, and in writing an essay on Edgar you would do well to treat both. First, some have suggested that Edgar unnecessarily prolongs his father's anguish by not revealing himself earlier. An important counterpoint here is that Edgar has a reason to delay the revelation of his identity, that Gloucester requires more anguish in order to find his redemption. Second, scholars have also taken Edgar to task for his belief that a kind of justice runs through the play, vindicating and explaining the play's great heap of suffering with his final claim that the "gods are just" (5.3.171). Consider whether this is a heartless and rather ugly statement given his father's plight, or whether it is perhaps the view of the play as articulated through Edgar.

Form and Genre

King Lear's emotional strain is one area of difficulty that faces the audience and reader. That emotional stress comes from the overwhelming force of the play's tragic movement. In the 18th century, audiences preferred to watch an adaptation of *Lear* that ended happily, the original tragic resolution being deemed simply unwatchable. To avoid or turn away from Lear's tragedy, however, is not an option available when you are writing an essay on the play; instead, you must harness for the essay the brutal energy of the text's vision. For many critics, *Lear* is Shakespeare's most compelling and perfect engagement with the tragic form. A. C. Bradley, for example, an early 20th-century scholar who wrote extensively on Shakespeare's tragedies, argued that *Lear* is "the most terrible picture that Shakespeare painted of the world. In no other of his tragedies does humanity appear more pitiably infirm or more hopelessly bad." You might attempt a paper that looks for good and for hope in *Lear,* but the task of identifying and characterizing the nature of the tragedy is philosophically simpler and allows you to draw material from the entire play. What is at the heart of the picture Shakespeare paints of the world in *Lear*? You might agree with Bradley that it is the infirmity and immorality of mankind, but this is simply a place to start rather than a place to finish. In what ways does the play highlight our frailties and weaknesses? Does the play offer an explanation for the wickedness that corrupts us?

> **Tragedy:** What is the significance of the recurring *nothing* motif? What might the idea of nothing contribute to the play's tragic vision?

> A good beginning for such an essay might be to identify and close read several passages that seem to articulate powerfully the spirit of tragedy animating *King Lear.* Among the various passages that do exactly this are Gloucester's terrifying observation that the gods are like naughty children and humans like the flies these children "kill for their sport" (4.1.37–38), or Lear's no less chilling "stage of fools" speech (4.6.176–81). Having characterized the nature of the tragedy, the essay could continue by connecting these dark visions with the motif of

nothing so prominent in the play. Look for utterances of the word *nothing* (see the discussion of Edgar in the "Character" section above for one example), but do not simply catalog these instances. Instead, try to spot philosophical patterns developing with each example. Connect the idea of nothing with the tragic movement of the play. One way to do this might be to focus on connecting *nothing* with the idea of disorder, of chaos. Here *nothing* becomes a watchword for the kind of unruly and chaotic world that allows old men to be abandoned and betrayed by their children and Poor Tom to be abandoned by the comforts and good fortune that others enjoy. You might play with the word further to find other ways in which it articulates what the play has to say about the world. But is *nothing* the dominant force in the play, or can it be challenged? For example, you might feel obliged to treat a number of issues: the goodness and devotion of characters such as Cordelia and Kent; Edgar's claim that the "gods are just," suggesting, of course, a very large something, rather than nothing, giving order to the play's action; the redemptions that Gloucester and Lear experience, regardless of their exceptional price; the deaths of all the principal villains, and even Edmund's ambiguous turnaround. When writing about comedy or tragedy, you must always consider the final scene of the play, as this is where the shape of the drama is completed. You might consider the neatness of Albany's closing declaration (5.3.294–303), Kent's haunting promise that sounds unhappily like a suicide note (5.3.320–21), and, of course, Lear's final lines over Cordelia's body (5.3.304–306). If there is a something in the world of the play, what is it? If there is nothing but nothing in *Lear,* what other names does the text assign to nothing? How do we come to know a force that is inherently an absence or a lack?

Bibliography for *King Lear*

Bloom, Harold, ed. *Modern Critical Interpretations: King Lear.* New York: Chelsea House, 1987.
Bradley, A. C. *Shakespearean Tragedy: Lectures on Hamlet, Othello, King Lear, Macbeth.* Basingstoke, England: Macmillan, 1904.

Danson, Lawrence, ed. *On King Lear.* Princeton, N.J.: Princeton UP, 1981.

Foakes, R. A. *Hamlet versus Lear.* Cambridge: Cambridge UP, 1993.

Goldberg, Jonathan. "Perspectives: Dover Cliff and the Conditions of Representation." *Shakespeare and Deconstruction.* Ed. Douglas Atkins and David Bergeron. New York: Peter Lang, 1988. 245–67.

Khan, Coppelia. "The Absent Mother in King Lear." *Rewriting the Renaissance: The Discourses of Sexual Difference in Early Modern Europe.* Chicago: U of Chicago P, 1986. 33–50.

Taylor, Gary, and Michael Warren, eds. *The Division of the Kingdoms: Shakespeare's Two Versions of King Lear.* Oxford: Clarendon P, 1986.

MACBETH

READING TO WRITE

MACBETH PROVIDES ample choices for essay topics. There are several psychologically complex and vivid characters, a variety of thematic concerns, and prominent marks of Shakespeare's engagement with Jacobean politics. Despite this abundance, the play is often noted for its economy: It is a very efficient piece of drama that does not waste a scene. As a result, you can find significance and meaning almost anywhere you look in *Macbeth;* nearly all points of the text are connected to every other point in narrative, symbolic, and thematic terms. Close reading is especially important here because so many speeches are dense with good material for essays but also because spotting patterns within the rapid and consequential action will help prevent your essay from becoming a hodgepodge of disjointed observations or from missing out on important parallels.

Lady Macbeth's soliloquy, spoken during act 1, scene 5 as she anticipates the arrival of Duncan, shows how character, theme, and tone can be so tightly compacted in *Macbeth.*

> . . . Come, you spirits
> That tend on mortal thoughts, unsex me here,
> And fill me, from the crown to the toe, top-full
> Of direst cruelty! Make thick my blood,
> Stop up th' access and passage to remorse,
> That no compunctious visitings of nature
> Shake my fell purpose, nor keep peace between
> Th' effect and it! Come to my woman's breasts
> And take my milk for gall, you murd'ring ministers,

Wherever in your sightless substances
You wait on nature's mischief! Come, thick night,
And pall thee in the dunnest smoke of hell,
That my keen knife see not the wound it makes,
Nor heaven peep through the blanket of the dark,
To cry "Hold, hold!" (1.5.41–54)

The first three words of this passage make an important thematic statement, as well as forging a key connection between characters. In invoking these spirits, Lady Macbeth solidifies the already clear presence of the
supernatural in this play, showing how the reach of the mysterious and
occult is far from limited to the isolated heaths, and she symbolically but
unmistakably connects herself with the witches. The role of the supernatural is discussed in the "Themes" section below, but consider how you might
develop into an essay the second observation, that Lady Macbeth is linked
to the witches through her incantation (an alternative approach to such an
essay can be found in the "Compare and Contrast" section of this chapter).
Having made this connection, you might begin the essay by establishing
the characteristics of the witches and, more important, what they cause
to happen in the play. This might be usefully followed with a similar section treating Lady Macbeth, followed by a third, longer portion discussing
the overlap between Macbeth's wife and the witches. Look for similarities of function within the play. Both appear to drive Macbeth forward
initially, molding his thoughts and deeds, though both eventually become
superfluous to his multiplying acts of violence. However, there will be few
moments that make the connection as directly as Lady Macbeth's speech
quoted above, so you will need to establish the link through careful use of
the play's thematic content.

For example, two such connections grow out of the second line of the
quotation. In Lady Macbeth's demand that the spirits "unsex" her, there
is a parallel to the witches' androgyny, but Lady Macbeth also desires to
be unnatural and monstrous, a status that connects her with the cruelty of the witches and allies her with the darkest forces operating in the
play—broadly, with the unnatural in opposition to what the play appears
to deem natural. To oppose nature, whether the laws of the organic world
or the divinely ordained (and thus natural) order of society, is to be evil
in the world of *Macbeth*.

This power is nowhere seen more clearly than in the repeated allusions to child killing, hinted at here in Lady Macbeth's desired transformation of her breast milk into venomous gall. This is a fine example of how Shakespeare peppers the play with patterns for the reader to find and contemplate. Read carefully through the text for references to child killing or the Macbeths' childlessness, and you will find numerous appearances of this disturbing theme. However, this is just one element of a much bigger thematic movement, and you might try to identify as many strands of the unnatural in the play as you can find. Such a list will be of enormous help in writing about many aspects of the play, as it will encourage you to read the play as a web of interconnected motifs and ideas. However, when you write, avoid merely making a list that shows Shakespeare's concern with the tensions between the natural and the unnatural; instead, try to characterize that tension. For example, you might draw a connection between the murder of children in the play (actual and symbolic) with the disruption Macbeth temporarily causes in the natural order of royal descent.

See, too, how yet another theme emerges from the passage following these ghoulish demands of Lady Macbeth, striking a clearly different note. The references to her acts being hidden, from heaven and even from the knife she murders with, anticipate the enormous role to be played in *Macbeth* by the power of guilt. Try to make links between such seeds of emotion and fear planted in the first part of the play and their fruit grimly growing later in the text. Also note that the tone of this passage suggests that even with these nascent anxieties, Lady Macbeth is still very much in control here. You could use this confidence and surety as the starting point for an essay considering the relationship between Lady Macbeth and Macbeth, exploring in particular the balance of power between the two and how that power is maintained. Obviously, moments in which this married couple is alone together will be the key. Ask yourself, moreover, at which point this relationship shifts and how the balance of power alters with it.

TOPICS AND STRATEGIES

Every essay requires a focus; you cannot write about everything in the play at once. The section on how to write an essay shows you a number of ways to turn a focus into a thesis, observations into arguments. However, the starting point is nearly always finding an initial focus and making first observations. What follows is a discussion of *Macbeth* geared toward helping you make the most of the budding ideas you will have as you read the play. By no means should you feel limited to these topics, however.

Themes

Thematic approaches to *Macbeth* are as plentiful as they are rich. One soliloquy can open many doors as you seek a topic. This creates an even higher than usual need for self-control and the firm establishment of boundaries in your essay plan. For example, the theme of the natural versus the unnatural overlaps with many others in the play, such as gender roles or witchcraft, for example. Both gender roles and witchcraft could by themselves be the subjects of excellent essays, of course, so the problem might be in allotting these subthemes enough space to explore the main theme of the natural versus the unnatural thoroughly without your paper unintentionally becoming an essay about gender roles or witches (the witches in particular have a tendency to take over an essay). A key here is to acknowledge in your work any elements of *Macbeth* that you will only briefly touch on or will pass by entirely. If you are assigned or decide to write a short paper on gender in the play, you may feel that, given a limited page count and a desire for depth of analysis more than breadth, your essay should focus on the shifting gender roles of Macbeth and Lady Macbeth. An acknowledgment that the witches are an important part of the play's discourse on gender but are beyond the scope of the current essay shows the reader that you are aware of the connection and have not missed something important. Instructors often mark with one eye on what the student has not written about, so it is always important to know the parameters of your essay and to make sure your reader is aware of them also. This is particularly helpful when you are writing about a dense but concise work like *Macbeth*.

Sample Topics

1. **Gender:** Gender concerns of many kinds seem ever present in *Macbeth*, but how exactly do these issues become integral to the tragedy?

   An essay such as this might start by establishing how gender functions at the beginning of the play and then tracing a series of subtle shifts that by the end of *Macbeth* have produced an entirely different gender dynamic. One subtle point to consider early on might be Macbeth's manliness before the play begins. All you have to go on here is the captain's report to Duncan in act 1, scene 2. What kind of man does the captain describe? Compare this to Lady Macbeth's anxieties about Macbeth, sometimes expressed in private or as taunts thrown directly to her husband. How is gender an important component of Lady Macbeth's attempts to impel Macbeth to murder Duncan? Most important, perhaps, try to assess how each character compares to the commonplace ideal of man or woman. Look for moments when each character comments on the gender role of the other, such as Macbeth's remark that his wife can only bear male children because she has nothing of woman in her. Finally, from this first part of the play, you might try to describe how Lady Macbeth constructs her gender identity and what that identity is.

Consider carefully, then, how the gender roles change by the end of the play. How has Macbeth's gendering changed? What has happened to Lady Macbeth to change her role in the play? Describe the gender role that each of the pair assumes by the fifth act, but be sure to also account for these changes.

2. **The natural versus the unnatural:** What are some examples of unnatural behavior in the play? What does the text propose as a natural state of affairs? How might you describe the status of this conflict between natural ideals and unnatural powers at various moments in *Macbeth*?

Many critics have observed that Shakespeare begins his play with a world in chaos; the movement of the play's action from this starting point is the gradual and costly process of nature's return to preeminence. Although you are certainly not obliged to agree, accepting this basic shape gives good structure to an essay while still allowing you enormous intellectual and interpretive freedom. How is the world of the opening acts under the shadow of unnatural forces? How has natural order been restored at the close? You might think about the debate on many different levels: moral, social, political. Of course, the play's supernatural elements are also interwoven tightly by Shakespeare into this idea. In the play's vision, there is no distinction between a wife who controls her husband, an aristocrat who murders his king, and the baleful and bearded witches who conjure mischief. All of these acts are opposed to the natural order as many in Shakespeare's audience would have understood it, and you might draw parallels between the various elements as you write. Look for other manifestations of the unnatural as the plot unravels.

Ask yourself what solutions the play offers for each unnatural problem—these solutions are not kind or easily obtained. Think about the political order after Macbeth's death, for example, to explore one way in which natural order has been restored.

Character

The psychological terrain of this play is dominated by only two characters. Lady Macbeth and Macbeth offer complex reflection on future actions in the beginning of the play, and their emotional and intellectual responses to those actions once taken are profoundly harrowing. Even more advantageous to you as a writer, these complex characters also grow and change markedly during the play. This combination of psychological complexity and discernible transformation means that essays on the two main characters might benefit from the formulaic but reliable character study approach of identifying what a character is like at the beginning and then what they are like at the end, drawing to the reader's attention in detail the various factors that bring that change about.

There are, of course, other characters in the play worthy of consideration. (For a discussion of the witches in more detail, see the "History and Context" section below.) Malcom is a character who, given his important role at the end of the play, might merit an essay. However, selecting a relatively minor character for a detailed study presents challenges as well as the rewards of an original topic and a clear, tight focus. Malcom's scenes are few, but pay special attention to his curious and perhaps unsettling exchange with Macduff in act 4, scene 3. What do you make of the way Malcom tests Macduff, as well as his response to Macduff's sorrow at the loss of his family? Overall, try to assess Malcom's role as the natural curative to Macbeth's unnatural blight of Scotland. Look for troubling moments or words that might conceivably complicate the sense of hope accompanying Malcom's ascendancy.

Sample Topics

1. **Macbeth:** How does Macbeth's character change during the play? How does he respond to his crimes?

An essay such as this might explore Macbeth's reluctance to assassinate Duncan at the beginning of the play, as well as identifying what tactics Lady Macbeth employs to coax him toward the murder. It may appear an obvious difference, but Shakespeare seems to emphasize the relationship between Macbeth's bloody and uncompromising performance on the battlefield and his reticence to kill his king. Exploring these differences a little may give you a better sense of Macbeth as well as his society. Look closely at his immediate response to the murder, and guide your reader through the shifting psychological decline that thus sets in. Consider the role of guilt but also the much more complicated feelings of hopelessness and fear that follow. Finally, how does this dangerous mix of emotions and thoughts further deform Macbeth into a serial killer? Consider the fatal tension in Macbeth's psyche between internal and external voices throughout the play; to what extent are his greed and then arrogance the products of his own innate character or the council and prophecies of others?

2. **Lady Macbeth:** If Lady Macbeth initially appears to be the stronger or more ambitious of the couple, how do you account for her decline into a state of debilitating emotional weakness by the end of the play?

In many ways, this essay might share the same basic shape as an essay on Macbeth: an exploration of the character in the buildup to the key dramatic moment of Duncan's murder, and then a careful consideration of the spiraling psychological degeneration that follows. Assess what motivates Lady Macbeth in the early acts and what measures she takes to prepare herself for the event. Look carefully at her decisive and domineering behavior in the immediate wake of the murder, comparing this to her descent into a deep-rooted and destructive guilt in the following acts. It is notable that the immensely strong figure introduced at the start of the play is reduced to such a weak figure who simply vanishes offstage in a reported suicide. How do you account for this? What changes have occurred in Macbeth's character that essentially sideline Lady Macbeth? Think, too, about the role her death may have in the play's restoration of natural order.

3. **Macduff:** How do you understand the play's nominal hero? How does he fit into the complex thematic puzzle of the play?

Such an essay might pay close attention to two key areas; first, think about the problem that gathers around Macduff's character when his family is murdered. He has essentially left them undefended and alone, vulnerable to an attack that he could have anticipated and perhaps prevented. Certainly, before she is killed, Lady Macduff expresses harsh words about her "traitor" husband. Compare this attack on Macduff's domestic honor to Ross's defense of Macduff's political honor and his flight to England. How do you think Shakespeare wants his audience to interpret this action? Second, reflect on the important connection between Macduff and Macbeth; the play appears to offer Macduff as the "anti-Macbeth," but how does he fulfill this role not just in narrative terms but symbolically too? Think, for example, about how Macduff might fit into the play's debates about the relationship between men and women as well as the natural and the unnatural. The death of his family and the infamous circumstances of his birth might be good places to begin making these thematic interpretations.

History and Context

The only version of *Macbeth* that has survived appears to have been written for a court performance in front of James I. Moreover, Shakespeare certainly did his homework in preparing a play that would appeal to (and flatter) the new king; the text is filled with references and themes that would have drawn the royal audience into the entertainment before them. As a result, in writing on *Macbeth* you can follow Shakespeare's lead, doing your own homework to uncover these plentiful and telling historical traces. Historically focused essays on *Macbeth* can take a number of directions, but keep in mind Shakespeare's intended audience as you research and write.

James was a controversial figure in a number of ways. When he came to the throne, many in England were relieved to see the uncertainties of the late Elizabethan era safely buried with the queen. Where Elizabeth was unmarried and childless, James, already king of Scotland, brought with him a wife and children. The honeymoon between king and country, however, if it existed at all, did not last long. The problems and concerns of James's reign palpably shape English drama of the early 17th century and are unmistakably discernible in *Macbeth*. Tensions between the Scottish king, along with his Scottish favorites who traveled south with him, and the existing English court are perhaps wished away in the alliance of England and Scotland forged at the end of *Macbeth*. Moreover, James saw himself as a scholar, writing tracts on subjects as varied as royal power and witchcraft; it is no coincidence that these kingly interests become important thematic concerns of the play. A good text to begin with when researching the connections between James's court and Shakespeare's work is Alvin Kernan's *Shakespeare, the King's Playwright: Theater in the Stuart Court, 1603–1613.*

Sample Topics

1. **Witchcraft:** What function does Shakespeare give the witches in *Macbeth*? How do they become pivotal elements of the tragedy rather than merely atmospheric and peripheral figures?

   Such an essay might begin by describing Shakespeare's use of witchcraft mythology, then proceeding to argue how this representation of the witches complements other thematic concerns in the play. There are two key sources for the student of witchcraft in Shakespeare's world: the enormously influential medieval text *Malleus maleficarum* ("The Hammer of Witches") and the early 17th-century writings of Reginald Scot. Both of these, along with a useful modern introduction to the history of witchcraft, can be conveniently found in *Witch-*

craft in Europe: 1100–1700, edited by Alan Kors and Edward Peters. Scot's writings embody the skeptical and enlightened view of witchcraft dawning in Shakespeare's lifetime, but it is the stereotypical witch of the *Malleus* that Shakespeare explicitly and somewhat sensationally uses. Using your research and understanding of the play as drama, consider the various reasons why Shakespeare—an otherwise enlightened man who elsewhere treats his marginalized figures with at least some trace of sympathy—might employ stereotypes so blatantly in crafting his witches. You might identify a symbolic meaning for the sisters, discussing how they are more than a cheap, theatrical thrill. For example, you will not have to get too far into the text of the *Malleus* to recognize that it harbors a deep mistrust of women, theorizing in detail why women are weak and vulnerable to the temptations of the devil. Think about how this merging of demonology and anxiety over female power is also important in *Macbeth.* More generally, describe how these medieval witches contribute to Shakespeare's broader vision of evil in *Macbeth.*

2. **The divine right of sovereigns:** What does *Macbeth* say about the politics of monarchy, a subject close to James's heart in both theoretical and practical terms?

The thesis for this essay might be relatively straightforward, but the difficulty will lie in compiling and structuring your evidence. A popular reading of the play asserts that *Macbeth* endorses James's writings on the divine authority of monarchs, identifying Macbeth's murder of Duncan and challenge to the natural political order with other manifestations of frightening disorder in the play. As critics often point out, Shakespeare alters the historic record, erasing from his play Macbeth's successful 10-year reign before his real-life tragedy unfolded. Why did Shakespeare make this change? What point does it help him make about royal power and challenges to it? Think, too, about the allusions to Banquo's bloodline leading down the centuries to James I. While this has obvious sycophantic charm for the play's intended audience, consider how it fits into the more serious discussion of kingship and destiny.

Form and Genre

Although Shakespeare took his source material for *Macbeth* from *Holinshed's Chronicles,* a history of England, Scotland, and Ireland by Raphael Holinshed, the same place he finds the material for his English history plays, the text is not considered a history play. There is no mistaking this play as anything but a tragedy of the darkest kind. Indeed, Macbeth's terrifying description of life as "a tale / Told by an idiot, full of sound and fury / Signifying nothing," is perhaps the most concise and powerful articulation of the tragic world in Shakespeare's works, or anywhere else in literature for that matter. The raw, brutal power of this line might lead you to consider the structural, generic makeup of the play that engenders such sentiments. As you read *Macbeth,* look for other phrases and speeches describing the spiritual or moral value of the world in which its characters live. The chief spokesperson for this tragic vision is, of course, Macbeth, so pay close attention to his ever-decreasing estimation of the world after Duncan's death. Identify what forces are at work against the characters of the play, attempting to see both external and internal factors at play in the tragedies of each individual.

Sample Topic

Tragedy: How would you describe Shakespeare's tragic vision in *Macbeth*? How does the play consider the function of fate in Macbeth's life, and how does this debate form a core part of the tragedy?

This is a difficult paper to write because it potentially involves organizing a lot of dense and complex lines of discussion behind a single, clearly stated thesis. Such an essay might begin by asking what forces drive Macbeth toward his tragedy. One of the key functions of the witches, for example, is to raise the question of how much control Macbeth holds over his fate. Read the opening scenes of the play closely, trying to assess the extent to which Macbeth's actions are governed by his own volition. Look carefully at the relationship between the predictions the witches make to Macbeth and his preexisting desires and ambition. At this point, you might also include a discussion of Lady Macbeth's seductive promptings, her influence over him. This analysis might lead you to ask if the outcome of Macbeth's life as the play presents it could have been different. Consider whether the overlap of supernatural and psychological elements creates an insurmountable enemy set against him. You might also return to the idea of the natural versus the unnatural so prominent in the play, asking whether the mere existence of a natural order relieves the overwhelming sense of darkness in the play and challenges Macbeth's fatalistic assertion that life "signif[ies] nothing." In other words, are there sources of hope and inspiration in the play, a sense that there actually is something behind the play's looming nothing? Think about the repetition of the word *done*, and the notion that Macbeth can never find peace of mind once his plot is begun. Nothing is ever done in this play, so consider what factors conspire to prevent Macbeth from resolving the events of his own life. Macbeth's uncontrollable and insidious plotting, the absence of a truly done deed, should act as a caution if you are looking for fixed meanings in this play. However, by reaching for an understanding of why Macbeth commits murder, how he and his wife cope with the moral and emotional implications of their crimes, and how the world of the play craftily ensures his tragic fate, you will be well placed to suggest what Shakespeare is using tragedy in *Macbeth* to say about human behavior and human evil.

Compare and Contrast Essays

Puzzling through the many dualisms and parallels in *Macbeth* is a major part of the play's critical heritage. There are so many mirrorings within the play's narrative and symbolic structure, so many characters and actions with distorted equivalents elsewhere in *Macbeth*. These pairings can be unexpected or can have unexpected consequences. David Scott Kasten, for example, has written provocatively on how Macduff's killing of Macbeth mirrors Macbeth's murder of Duncan. This final murder, Kasten argues, might have been as troubling as Duncan's assassination for proponents of absolute royal power (including James, who argued that even a tyrant king should not be killed).

Another pairing for an essay might be Lady Macbeth and Lady Macduff. Although the latter appears only briefly, a good deal is revealed about her views on the value of domestic versus political life. She seems to be the counterweight to the fiendish Lady Macbeth, a portrait of an idealized model of femininity that contrasts with the aberrant wife of Macbeth. Such an essay would gather evidence for this contrast but explore also the more complex problem of why the play kills both the natural and unnatural examples of womanhood in the play. The play also clearly establishes a relationship between Macbeth and Banquo. Assess what Banquo and Macbeth have in common before the former is killed, focusing perhaps on each man's reaction to the witches' prophesy. Then the essay might explore how the relationship changes after Banquo's death, as Banquo lingers on as a psychological or ghostly presence in Macbeth's conscience and banquet hall.

Macbeth is a play structured by change and progression toward a tragic resolution. While this is true of many plays, of course, transformation really is the key trait of this play's dramatic form. Therefore, many thematic and character essays on *Macbeth* can also be presented as compare and contrast essays: Macbeth at the start versus the end of the play, Lady Macbeth at the start versus the end of the play, the status of the natural order at the beginning of the play versus the end, and so forth.

Sample Topics

1. **Comparing Lady Macbeth with the witches:** What is the relationship between these female figures? How do they fulfill similar roles in the play?

This approach, simply put, might argue that Lady Macbeth can reasonably be termed the fourth witch of the play. While her territory may be distinct from the heathbound witches, she is nonetheless tied surely to the trio. Note, however, that because this is such a commonplace of *Macbeth* criticism, reading against this idea may make for a distinctive essay. Such a paper might need to take as its starting point the observation of broad similarity but then proceed to argue for distinctions between Lady Macbeth and the witches. This could take the subtle form of finding differences of motivation and approach. How is the way Lady Macbeth works on Macbeth, the strategies she uses to beguile him into murder, different from those of the witches? A good hook here might be the identification of two types of seductive magic in the play, one supernatural and one earthly but unnatural.

2. **Contrasting the play to Roman Polanski's film adaptation** *Macbeth* **(1971):** What strategies does Polanski use in his adaptation of Shakespeare's text?

Roman Polanski's version of *Macbeth* is probably the most commonly viewed film of the play in schools and colleges. As in any essay treating an adaptation of Shakespeare's text, look for visible and interesting directorial choices, intriguing casting decisions, and prominent omissions from and additions to the text of drama. The important move is to characterize the sum of these changes in a thesis before exploring them in detail throughout the body of the essay. Your thesis might follow a simple formula: "Roman Polanski's adaptation produces a *Macbeth* that argues. . ." In other words, try to imagine that the director has a thesis about the play just as you do as a reader. In Polanski's film, think about his casting of young and attractive actors in the roles of Macbeth and Lady Macbeth. What aspect of their relationship is made more prominent by emphasizing the beauty of Lady Macbeth in particular? You might also consider the look of the film, gloomy and violent. Think, too, about the representation of the witches, as well as the possible gender implications of a coven of witches in one scene rather than a mere three weird sisters. Finally, reflect on the ominous (and historically accurate) ending of the film.

Bibliography and Online Resources for *Macbeth*

Adelman, Janet. *Suffocating Mothers: Fantasies of Maternal Origin in Shakespeare's Plays.* New York: Routledge, 1992.

Calderwood, James L. *If It Were Done: Macbeth and Tragic Action.* Amherst: U of Massachusetts P, 1986.

Kasten, David Scott. *Shakespeare after Theory.* New York: Routledge, 1999.

Khan, Coppelia. *Man's Estate: Masculine Identity in Shakespeare.* Berkeley: U of California P, 1981.

Norbrook, David. "*Macbeth* and the Politics of Historiography." *Politics of Discourse: The Literature and History of Seventeenth Century England.* Ed. Kevin Sharpe and Stephen Zwicker. Berkeley: U of California P, 1987. 78–116.

"Macbeth Index." Retrieved 16 Mar. 2007. <http://homepages.rootsweb.com/~maggieoh/Macbeth/index.html>.

THE TEMPEST

READING TO WRITE

*T*HE *TEMPEST* offers a mix of "traditional" and "contemporary" approaches for essay writing. Indeed, few of Shakespeare's plays have kept such a consistently high profile among critics. The work's appeal was traditionally founded in its legendary status as Shakespeare's farewell to the theater, a text in which the author not only signals a parting of ways from the stage but feelingly examines the art form he practiced for 20 years. However, since the theoretical turn of literary studies during the second half of the 20th century, the play has remained as popular and attractive to critics for largely different reasons. Where the aesthetic and biographical elements of the text proved irresistible to earlier scholars, contemporary critics have more often been drawn to the worldly and sociological possibilities of *The Tempest.* Notably, many modern writers have approached the play from a postcolonial perspective, identifying in the text a rich treatment of colonial politics. This shift in emphasis coincides with the transformation of many states around the world from colonial subjects to independent nations.

Of course, none of this means that you have to limit yourself to either the more traditional or the newer approach to the play. Certainly, as early 21st-century readers, we will find some things in *The Tempest* that would not have been visible to or would have been seen differently by its original audience, but we can also share a number of pleasures with that original audience. For many readers, then, these new interests have not replaced the elements of the text that fascinated previous generations; they have simply developed organically alongside them. A number of approaches to the play encourage this harmony of traditional and contemporary approaches. Character studies, for example, of Prospero, Caliban, and others, along with essays on the various political concerns of *The Tempest*, would allow you to participate in both fresh and well-established conversations.

The coexistence of contemporary concerns and traditional interests of commentators is evident in the following celebrated passage from *The Tempest*. After staging a masque to celebrate the union of Ferdinand and Miranda, Prospero suddenly curtails the festivities as he recalls Caliban's plot on his life. Clearly taken aback by Prospero's unprecedented distress, Miranda and Ferdinand appear to be surprised, perhaps even frightened. Prospero responds:

> You do look, my son, in a moved sort,
> As if you were dismayed. Be cheerful, sir.
> Our revels now are ended. These our actors,
> As I foretold you, were all spirits, and
> Are melted into air, into thin air;
> And like the baseless fabric of this vision
> The cloud-capped towers, the gorgeous palaces,
> The solemn temples, the great globe itself,
> Yea, all which it inherit, shall dissolve;
> And, like this insubstantial pageant faded,
> Leave not a rack behind. We are such stuff
> As dreams are made on, and our little life
> Is rounded with a sleep. Sir, I am vexed. (4.1.146–58)

The first two lines of this passage show Prospero catching himself, aware of how his intense reaction has troubled the young couple. What is unanswered here, however, and the subject of much critical speculation, is precisely why Prospero has been so animated by a plot that seems to pose such a minor threat. Close readings can sometimes milk what is absent from the text as productively as what is there, and this moment is a fine example of this. Two related essay topics emerge here. First, this strange overreaction might prompt you to think about Prospero's character, what motivates him and haunts him. Second, it highlights the power and centrality of the relationship between Prospero and Caliban, embodiments of the encounter between colonialist and native. Clearly, it is not the fear of being murdered that has Prospero so troubled—Caliban and his drunken cohort hardly pose a threat on that score—so we must assume that Prospero is stung by a sudden and intense awareness of Caliban as a malfunctioning component of his project. Defining the nature of this relationship, with its painful, tragic mix of animosity and commonality, might be the central task of an essay.

This passage is rounded by the troubling presence of Caliban, vexing Prospero in the opening and closing lines. But in between is perhaps the most recognizable speech of the play. Again, at least two closely related essay topics might be generated by these lines. First, Prospero meditates on the ending of the masque. This is a reminder of Prospero's role as artist, traditionally understood as an allegorical representation of Shakespeare's own career as dramatist. The themes of art and authorship naturally grow out of this passage, generating a wider consideration of Prospero as author throughout the play. Instead of pen and paper, Prospero creates through magic—though his books provide a symbolic nexus for magic and letters—and you can study the conception and execution of his project from the opening tempest to his closing renunciation of his art. Intimately connected with this is the idea that art and life are joined by artifice or illusion; we as creations briefly perform our parts and then exit from the cosmic stage. Working closely with the play's mix of fantasy and reality, lush visions of pleasure commingled with the foreshadowing of inevitable tragedy (Prospero ends the play by saying that, despite his immaculate victory, every third thought will be now of his grave), will allow you to articulate an interpretation of Shakespeare's aesthetic vision of life.

TOPICS AND STRATEGIES

Every essay requires a focus; you cannot write about everything in the play at once. The section on how to write an essay shows you a number of ways to turn a focus into a thesis, observations into arguments. However, the starting point is nearly always finding an initial focus and making first observations. What follows is a discussion of *The Tempest* geared toward helping you make the most of the budding ideas you will have as you read the play. By no means should you feel limited to these topics, however.

Themes

Because of the play's magic and fantasy, some first-time readers might be surprised by how much of the real world is located on this magical island of fantasy. *The Tempest* is an unexpectedly political play, relocating the struggles and sufferings of the quotidian world to this most extraordinary setting. Stephen Orgel, for example, has shown in detail the political maneuvering of Prospero in securing not only the return of his dukedom but also, through Miranda's marriage to Ferdinand, a permanent security against any future claim to the title by Antonio. Two major thematic approaches to the text, one aesthetic and one political, are possible. However, these themes are connected by the organizing principles—and it is for each writer to decide what those may be—of Prospero's intricate and ambiguous project.

Sample Topics

1. **Usurpation and rebellion:** What examples are there of overthrows or attempted overthrows of leaders in *The Tempest*? How do these examples become part of a wider analysis of social and political tension in the play? Can you finally assign a political position or philosophy for the play?

Such an essay might begin by identifying the various usurpation attempts dramatized or alluded to in the play. Antonio's overthrowing of Prospero is an obvious example, but note how Antonio imports his political opportunism to the island as he urges Sebastian to kill Alonso. Do not overlook lesser examples of social and political tensions, such as the disagreement between the Boatswain and the nobles in the play's first scene. To help contextualize all of this, look for important symmetry and parallels among these incidents. For example, Prospero has had his dukedom usurped, but he has also seized Caliban's island. Caliban's rebellion seems to be juxtaposed to Antonio and Sebastian's plot. With so much emphasis on usurpation, it will not be enough merely to catalog the incidents and announce its importance. Use the system of parallels to see if a political commentary on the play emerges. For example, is Prospero portrayed as a usurper himself? What are the consequences of challenging or overthrowing the existing political order in *The Tempest*? Look to see who is punished and who is not, using such analysis to arrive at a tentative claim on the play's politics.

2. **Art and magic:** How powerful is Prospero's magic? If magic here is a metaphor for creative energy, including art, what does Shakespeare use this trope to say about himself, his stage, and his world?

It is a commonplace of Renaissance drama to suggest a relationship between life and the stage, people going about their lives and actors performing their parts. Shakespeare employs this conceit throughout his career, but in *The Tempest* it is a central idea, operating on a number of levels. Such an essay might begin by examining the symbolic connection between art and magic, explaining why Shakespeare might have been drawn to the metaphor. You might focus this around a detailed consideration of the famous identification of Prospero with Shakespeare, discussing the relationship between the former's project and the latter's play. Perhaps identify ways in which Prospero's magic, while extremely powerful, has its limits. Is there anything beyond his control or out of his reach in *The Tempest*? It might be useful, finally, to consider why Prospero feels the need to abandon his art. As Prospero naturally will be an important part of this essay, the discussion of him in the "Character" section below will also be useful.

Character

Shakespeare seems not to have invested much in the marginal characters of *The Tempest*. For example, while the ideas of Gonzalo or the machinations of Antonio are interesting, they emanate from relatively thin characters. Even the comparatively central figures of Miranda and Ferdinand are more or less sketches. While Miranda does offer some promise for the writer, such an essay might discuss what Miranda does not say and do as much as what she does. In this way, for example, Ann Thompson has used the absence of women in the play, along with the comparatively inert or negative portrayals of those we do see or hear of (Miranda as well as the distant presences of Sycorax and Claribel, Alonso's daughter), to construct a feminist interpretation of the play based on male control and fear of female sexuality. A character study of Miranda, then, might particularly benefit from a close analysis of Prospero's treatment of her. However, if the supporting cast at times appears undeveloped, this paucity is compensated for by a pair of characters who offer much to the writer, both as individual character studies and as a complex political system of two.

Sample Topics

1. **Prospero:** Although Prospero is traditionally viewed as the benevolent embodiment of Shakespeare, what elements of his character might lead you to question this warm assessment? What are Prospero's flaws, and how do they color your estimation of his project?

   Such an essay has a lot of ground to cover. Prospero is central to almost everything that happens in *The Tempest,* apparently controlling the fates of all other characters. In a well-known essay, Stephen Greenblatt even referred to Prospero's authoritarian style as "martial law." But what are Prospero's motives, and do you admire his magic or call into question his methods? Identifying elements of his character will help you better understand and interpret Prospero's actions. For example, you might comment on Prospero's sudden changes of mood, as well as moments in which he appears to be acting as unkindly to those he loves as to his enemies. Think, for example, about his stringent, controlling relationship with Miranda and his treatment of Ferdinand. Most character studies will benefit from charting progress in a character, but this is especially difficult to do with Prospero. As he gives up his magic, discarding his occult books, he signals that he has grown and learned from the process of the play—a play devised by himself. Ask what the implications of this are (were there moments when his authority ebbed, forcing Prospero to adapt and change?), as well as attempting to identify what exactly Prospero has learned. Some critics have suggested that Prospero's celebrated rejection of magic is simply the result of his victory, having brought his play to a close exactly as he wished. You might ask if there are alternative moments of epiphany, perhaps, aside from his denouncement of magic. A clear alternative can be found in his claim of ownership (is that what it is, though?) of

Caliban at the play's close. This certainly leads to perhaps the most contentious area of Prospero's project: his treatment of Caliban, Ariel, and the island over which he has assumed control. This is discussed at more length in the "History and Context" section below, but a character study of Prospero should not ignore the complex psychological and political elements of Prospero's relationship with the island's indigenous inhabitants, especially Caliban.

2. **Caliban:** Does the play encourage the audience to see Caliban through the eyes of Prospero and Miranda, as a "devil" and a "slave," or to arrive at a more nuanced, even sympathetic view?

In some ways, this question is a direct challenge to the tradition of seeing Prospero as Shakespeare, or an omnipotent dramatist figure. If the play asks the audience to question or disagree with Prospero over Caliban, Prospero begins to lose his authorial control—there is a powerful countercurrent working against him. Describe Caliban as you see him in the play, but recognize that he is a complicated creation. For example, alongside his unforgivable attempted rape of Miranda, consider Caliban's eloquent protests against his own ill treatment, as well as his knowledge and understanding of the island (indeed, he even has a rationale for his attempted rape, one that frames his crime less as an act of sexual violence than one of political calculation—he will create a race of Calibans, presumably to restore the balance of the island). Look for moments where Caliban evidently undercuts the image of a brute, animalistic creature and rhetorically challenges Prospero's legitimacy. A careful reading of act 1, scene 2 and act 4, scene 1 will be particularly helpful here. A character essay treating Caliban might lead to the same enigmatic moment as a character study of Prospero: "This thing of darkness I / Acknowledge mine" (5.1.278). An interpretation of Caliban's role in the play requires you to take a stand on this line, assessing its meaning for both Prospero and Caliban, two figures united by this phrase and whatever relationship it defines.

History and Context

Was Europe's encounter with the New World merely an exciting spark for Shakespeare's fancy, provider of some imagery and ideas, or did he craft *The Tempest* to be a careful engagement with the politics of exploration in the Americas? Critics do not agree over Shakespeare's intentions in this regard, so a number of historical approaches to the play have been taken over the last several decades. Terence Hawkes, for example, has suggested that the most relevant relationship in *The Tempest* is not the master and slave of the colonial setting but the aristocrat and peasant of Shakespeare's England. Alternatively, Jerry Brotton claims that while the most pressing political concerns of the play are indeed grounded in foreign soil, critics have been too strenuous in asserting the play's New World focus. Instead, Brotton argues, the play's clear geographical setting is the Mediterranean, its political concerns more with the Old World than the New, while attempts to make this a play explicitly about the New World are the result of scholars' desire to transform *The Tempest* into an American story. Despite this objection, the weight of historical approaches to the play have grown out of abundant evidence that Shakespeare, at least in part, had the distant lands of a newly discovered continent in mind as he wrote.

After all, Shakespeare's primary source for *The Tempest* is a document of the New World, William Strachey's pamphlet *A True Reportory of the Wrack and Redemption of Sir Thomas Gates.* This account of the wreck of an Englishman's ship off the coast of Bermuda appears to have given Shakespeare the inspiration for *The Tempest,* though his additions to the basic premise suggest that Shakespeare wanted to explore the political and philosophical implications of discovering new lands far from home. For a start, he adds the figure of Caliban to his narrative, a presence with no equivalent in his source text.

For many writers, the tension between Prospero and Caliban has become emblematic of the play's engagement with colonialism. Some historians have argued that the responses of settlers frequently passed from enchantment with native peoples through disenchantment—all too often a brutal stage—to paternalism. Certainly, this model seems to describe accurately Prospero's encounter with Caliban, if you believe that his final claim of ownership is more a claim of responsibility.

Sample Topics

1. **Colonial encounters:** Is *The Tempest* a text that supports the ideology of colonialism, or does it challenge and subvert it?

Such an essay would ask a clear but difficult question: Does this play applaud the colonial project or critique it? Critics have been evenly divided on this point, so you will be in good company whichever way you lean. If you believe the play forms a broad endorsement of Prospero's seizure of the island (or at least does not question it), you might make much of efforts within the play to demonize Caliban. For example, his lineage—son of a witch—suggests a moral ugliness, while frequent descriptive details point to monstrous physical deformity. You might further find evidence of Prospero's positioning in the play as a force for moral good, a restorer of balance and harmony, as well as the holder of enormous creative energy. If you can amply demonstrate these points, you should be well on your way to showing how the play's endorsement of Prospero's broader project includes advocacy of his colonization of the island.

If you wish to make the counterpoint, you might structure your essay by reversing the strategies in the preceding paragraph. To make a case for this play's opposition to the colonial project, you will flag moments that might question Prospero's status as benevolent creator artist (see the "Character" section above). Such an essay might then proceed to show how Caliban makes persuasive claims to the ownership of the island, as well as highlighting ways in which the play sympathizes with him in his servitude and (perhaps most compellingly of all) suggests a parallel between Antonio's toppling of Prospero in Milan and Prospero's usurpation of Caliban's island.

2. **Utopias:** Does this play offer multiple versions of the colonial project? Rather than merely side with or against Prospero's right to control the island, does *The Tempest* become a debate on the possibilities of colonialism? If so, what role does the vision of a utopian state have in this debate?

The discovery of the New World had enormous philosophical as well as economic and political consequences. Europeans were forced to confront different and unknown models of human society; while this could have triggered introspection and the interrogation of European norms, almost universally Europeans used their own standards to judge and relegate New World peoples.

One thinker who opposed this trend was the remarkable Michel de Montaigne. In his *Essays,* Montaigne questions countless assumptions of European thinking. Famously, for example, in his essay "On Cannibals," and again in "On Coaches," Montaigne argues that Europeans should not be so quick to see themselves as superior, revealing how they exceeded the New World peoples in cruelty and brutality.

Montaigne, then, has at least two connections with *The Tempest* that might come together in a single essay on utopian ideals in this play. First, Shakespeare lifts some of Montaigne's ideas, almost word for word, from "On Cannibals." The speaker of them in *The Tempest* is Gonzalo in act 2, scene 1, lines 147–56. Here Gonzalo fantasizes over the possibility that the island might become a utopia, a perfect society. Study carefully Gonzalo's vision, identifying the qualities of his utopia, but also note the pointed and cynical responses of Antonio and Sebastian. The latter pair attempt to dismantle Gonzalo's vision with an almost point-by-point challenge; pay close attention to the logic at work on each side of the argument. This speech might become the starting point for a broader consideration of utopian ideals. Where else might the theme of utopias be implicitly treated in *The Tempest*? Does the play say something about what an ideal state might be like or what ideal leadership would entail?

These questions might lead you to the second point of contact between Montaigne and *The Tempest.* Shakespeare's borrowing from Montaigne reveals that the former was clearly aware of Montaigne's defense of indigenous peoples. It seems clear, then, that for Shakespeare the role of Caliban is signal to the play's political debate. Indeed, Prospero and Caliban initially cooperated to form perhaps the closest thing to a utopia in *The Tempest.* Identify what this state looked like and how and why it changed, and finally ask, perhaps, what the political prospects are at the end of the play. Does the play reject, along with Antonio and Sebastian, Gonzalo's vision of a possible utopia? If not, use the evidence contained in the play to describe what the criteria for such a state might be.

Form and Genre

From the perspective of genre, *The Tempest* is unique among the plays discussed in this book. While it is a comedy, it is a specific type of comedy called romance. Some confusion might develop here because of today's understanding of a romance as nothing more than a love story. When the term *romance* is used to describe a Shakespeare play, it means something different: A romance here features impossible events, fanciful settings, and, typically, magic. Sometimes the dramatic action of the play will span many years, as it does in another of Shakespeare's romances, *The Winter's Tale.*

Shakespeare turned to romances late in his career, writing four of them as his final solo contributions to the stage. *The Tempest* is traditionally recognized to be the last of these four late romances, and it does provide a decorous ending to his career. Perhaps he was drawn to the freedom and imaginative possibilities of the genre, or perhaps, as an aging man nearing retirement, he was attracted to the wistful qualities of romance. Whatever the reasons for Shakespeare's turn to this genre, consideration of the role of romance here creates opportunities for essay writing.

Sample Topic

Romance: What mood and shape does the romance genre give *The Tempest*? If some of Shakespeare's comedies resist full comic closure, what about the resolution of this play, Shakespeare's most celebrated romance? Do you agree with critics who label *The Tempest* a tragicomedy, a hybrid of comic and tragic elements?

If you have read some of Shakespeare's comedies, you might be familiar with the idea of incomplete comic resolution;

Shakespeare often makes all the right moves for a comic conclusion, yet somehow he manages to leave the play unexpectedly and uncomfortably open-ended (see the "Form and Genre" sections of the chapters on *As You Like It* and *The Merchant of Venice*, for example). Does he use romance similarly in *The Tempest*?

You might start by asking an important generic question: How do the magical and impossible qualities of romance promise enormous comic potential, the capacity to resolve a play happily? Think about Prospero's magic, defining its usage in the play. Certainly it brings about the results he wants, but are these results comic, that is, happy? Consider carefully the resolution of the play, looking especially for loose ends. For example, you might discuss Antonio's response to his brother at the close of the play or Prospero's ambiguous claim on Caliban. Think, in particular, about whether the fulfillment of Prospero's wishes is really enough to make for a happy, comic ending. What role, if any, does tragedy have in this play? Look for traces of the tragic behind and between comic moments. Pain and death, for example, even if narrowly avoided in the latter case, introduce a tragic presence. Consider also the final standing of the characters, whether all share in the comic spirit of resolution, restoration, and forgiveness.

Compare and Contrast Essays

The Tempest offers exciting and even quirky compare and contrast options. For a start, there are a large number of film versions of (or films inspired by) *The Tempest,* ranging from the faithful to the bizarre. Peter Greenaway's *Prospero's Books* (1991) is a surreal and difficult take on the play but a titillating prospect for the student who enjoys working with highly abstract material. Much more fun is *The Forbidden Planet* (1956), a science-fiction classic that transports *The Tempest* into futuristic outer space. The bare bones of the plot and the characters are more or less faithful to the play, but most interesting is the way the themes of the play are adapted to the 20th century. A useful crux for a compare and contrast essay might be to see the invisible creature of the film, the "monster of the id," as an internalized Caliban. The movie thus makes Caliban and Prospero two parts of a whole, taking to a new, literal level Prospero's "this thing of darkness" line. Think about how Caliban becomes the repressed rage and violence of the Prospero figure, Dr. Morbeus, linking this to the psychically close relationship of Caliban and Prospero in *The Tempest.* Meanwhile, if you wish to work with a second text but not stray so far from Shakespeare's canon, some clearly relevant plays might be *The Merchant of Venice* and *Othello.* The hinge of such essays might be the issue of sympathy, perhaps comparing or contrasting Shakespeare's treatment of his outsider figures, Caliban, Shylock and Othello.

Within the play itself, there are a number of possibilities for compare and contrast. A postcolonial essay could be structured as a compare and contrast by studying Prospero's claims to the island compared with Caliban's. Comparative character studies also offer possibilities.

Sample Topics

1. **Comparing Prospero and Sycorax:** What connections does the play establish between these two magical figures?

    The most interesting slant on this topic might be the search for unexpected similarities. While it is easy to say that the two characters represent good and bad magic, look for ways in which Prospero resembles Sycorax, Caliban's mother. Not much information is provided about Sycorax, but there is enough to prompt the comparison. The trick here will not be to suggest that Sycorax is "good," but to qualify Prospero's presence in some of the ways listed above in the "Character" section. For example, compare Prospero's treatment of Caliban to Sycorax's treatment of Ariel. Think, too, about the connection not only of magic but also of ownership of the island. Sycorax, as Caliban mentions, was the original matriarch of the island, just as Prospero is the usurping patriarch.

2. **Contrasting Ariel and Caliban:** How does Shakespeare use these two island natives differently? In what ways (and why) do Prospero's relationships with the two differ?

You might begin by establishing the nature of each character. Caliban is discussed in the "Characters" section above, but there is also much to be said about Ariel. Think, for example, about the character's past, imprisoned by Sycorax and released by Prospero. The nexus of such an essay might be the issue of servitude. Both characters serve Prospero, but the way they serve is very different. What emerges, perhaps, are two models of how natives might respond to a colonial encounter, one meekly and hopeful of eventual equilibrium and one begrudgingly, on the lookout for ways to reclaim authority and land. Equally, study Prospero's treatment of the pair; his sometimes harsh dealings with Ariel, for example, suggest a likeness between the ethereal sprite and the hulking Caliban that belies their physical differences. Consider also how Prospero, despite his power, needs both, whether it be to fetch and carry wood or to execute details of the plot to regain his dukedom.

Bibliography and Online Resources for *The Tempest*

Barker, Francis, and Peter Hulme. "Nymphs and Reapers Heavily Vanish: The Discursive Con-Texts of *The Tempest*." Alternative Shakespeares. Ed. John Drakakis. New York: Methuen, 1985. 191–205.

Brotton, Jerry. "'This Tunis, sir, was Carthage': Contesting Colonialism in *The Tempest*." *Post-colonial Shakespeares*. Ed. Ania Loomba and Martin Orkin. New York: Routledge, 1998. 23–43.

Greenblatt, Stephen. *Shakespearean Negotiations: The Circulation of Social Energy in Renaissance England*. Berkeley: U of California P, 1988.

Mirza, Munira. "*The Tempest*: The Globe, London." Culture Wars. Posted 26 May 2005. Retrieved 16 Mar. 2007. <http://www.culturewars.org.uk/2005-01/globe.htm>.

Orgel, Stephen. "Prospero's Wife." *Representations* 8 (1984): 1–13.

Thompson, Ann. "'Miranda, Where's Your Sister?': Reading Shakespeare's *The Tempest*." Feminist Criticism: Theory and Practice. Ed. Susan Sellers. Toronto: U of Toronto P, 1991. 45–57.

INDEX